AF566760

Data Mining and Warehousing

Data Mining and Warehousing

Dr. Pooja Sharma

SHREE PUBLISHERS & DISTRIBUTORS
NEW DELHI-110 002

Edition : 2013

Published by :

SHREE PUBLISHERS & DISTRIBUTORS

22/4735 Prakash Deep Building,
Ansari Road, Darya Ganj,
New Delhi–110 002

ISBN : 978–81–8329–518–5

Printed by :

Anvi Composers

New Delhi–110 063

Preface

Data Mining is the process of analyzing large amount of data in search of previously undiscovered business patterns. Data Warehousing is a relational/multidimensional database that is designed for Query and Analysis rather than Transaction Processing.

Data Mining deals with discovering hidden data and unexpected patterns and rules in large databases. It can bring significant gains to organizations, for example, through better-targeted marketing and enhanced internal performance.

The present work is purely a research compilation based on authoritative publications/readings/excerpts/notes/reviews/researches authored by eminent information scientists and IT professionals.

Assistance has been sought from Websites through Internet.

The author, humbly, acknowledges the contributions of all those eminent information scientists and IT experts alongwith their respective publishers and Websites in preparation of this book.

Dr. Pooja Sharma

Contents

1

Introduction

DATA MINING

Generally, data mining (sometimes called data or knowledge discovery) is the process of analysing data from different perspectives and summarizing it into useful information - information that can be used to increase revenue, cuts costs, or both. Data mining software is one of a number of analytical tools for analysing data. It allows users to analyse data from many different dimensions or angles, categorize it, and summarize the relationships identified. Technically, data mining is the process of finding correlations or patterns among dozens of fields in large relational databases.

OVERVIEW

Data mining, *the extraction of hidden predictive information from large databases,* is a powerful new technology with great potential to help companies focus on the most important information in their data warehouses. Data mining tools predict future trends and behaviours, allowing businesses to make proactive, knowledge-driven decisions. The automated, prospective analyses offered by data mining move beyond the analyses of past events provided by retrospective tools typical of decision support systems. Data mining tools can answer business questions that traditionally were too time consuming to resolve. They scour databases for hidden patterns, finding predictive information that experts may miss because it lies outside their expectations.

Most companies already collect and refine massive quantities of data. Data mining techniques can be implemented rapidly on existing software and hardware platforms to enhance the value of existing information resources, and can be integrated with new products and systems as they are brought on-line. When implemented on high performance client/server or parallel processing computers, data mining tools can analyse massive databases to deliver answers to questions such as, "Which clients are most likely to respond to my next promotional mailing, and why?"

This white chapter provides an introduction to the basic technologies of data mining. Examples of profitable applications illustrate its relevance to today's business environment as well as a basic description of how data warehouse architectures can evolve to deliver the value of data mining to end users.

THE FOUNDATIONS OF DATA MINING

Data mining techniques are the result of a long process of research and product development. This evolution began when business data was first stored on computers, continued with improvements in data access, and more recently, generated technologies that allow users to navigate through their data in real time. Data mining takes this evolutionary process beyond retrospective data access and navigation to prospective and proactive information delivery. Data mining is ready for application in the business community because it is supported by three technologies that are now sufficiently mature:

- Massive data collection
- Powerful multiprocessor computers
- Data mining algorithms.

Table : Steps in the Evolution of Data Mining.

Evolutionary Step	Business Question	Enabling Technologies	Product Providers	Characteristics
Data Collection (1960s)	"What was my total revenue in the last five years?"	Computers, tapes, disks	IBM, CDC	Retrospective, static data delivery
Data Access (1980s)	"What were unit sales in New England last March?"	Relational databases (RDBMS), Structured Query Language (SQL), ODBC	Oracle, Sybase, Informix, IBM, Microsoft	Retrospective, dynamic data delivery at record level
Data Warehousing & Decision Support (1990s)	"What were unit sales in New England last March? Drill down to Boston."	On-line analytic processing (OLAP), multidimensional databases, data warehouses	Pilot, Comshare, Arbor, Cognos, Microstrategy	Retrospective, dynamic data delivery at multiple levels
Data Mining (Emerging Today)	"What's likely to happen to Boston unit sales next month? Why?"	Advanced algorithms, multiprocessor computers, massive databases	Pilot, Lockheed, IBM, SGI, numerous startups (nascent industry)	Prospective, proactive information delivery

Commercial databases are growing at unprecedented rates. A recent META Group survey of data warehouse projects found that 19% of respondents are beyond the 50 gigabyte level, while 59% expect to be there by second quarter of 1996. In some industries, such as retail, these numbers can be much larger. The accompanying need for improved computational engines can now be met in a cost-effective manner with parallel multiprocessor computer technology. Data mining algorithms embody techniques that have existed for at least 10 years, but have only recently been implemented as mature, reliable, understandable tools that consistently outperform older statistical methods.

In the evolution from business data to business information, each new step has built upon the previous one. For example, dynamic data access is critical for drill-through in data navigation applications, and the ability to store large databases is critical to data mining. From the user's point of view, the four steps were revolutionary because they allowed new business questions to be answered accurately and quickly.

The core components of data mining technology have been under development for decades, in research areas such as statistics, artificial intelligence, and machine learning. Today, the maturity of these techniques, coupled with high-performance relational database engines and broad data integration efforts, make these technologies practical for current data warehouse environments.

THE SCOPE OF DATA MINING

Data mining derives its name from the similarities between searching for valuable business information in a large database — for example, finding linked products in gigabytes of store scanner data — and mining a mountain for a vein of valuable ore. Both processes require either sifting through an immense amount of material, or intelligently probing it to find exactly where the value resides. Given databases of sufficient size and quality, data mining technology can generate new business opportunities by providing these capabilities:

- Automated prediction of trends and behaviours. Data mining automates the process of finding predictive information in large databases. Questions that traditionally required extensive hands-on analysis can now be answered directly from the data — quickly. A typical example of a predictive problem is targeted marketing. Data mining uses data on past promotional mailings to identify the targets most likely to maximize return on investment in future mailings. Other predictive problems include forecasting bankruptcy and other forms of default, and identifying segments of a population likely to respond similarly to given events.
- Automated discovery of previously unknown patterns. Data mining tools sweep through databases and identify previously hidden patterns in one step. An example of pattern discovery is the analysis of retail sales data to identify seemingly unrelated products that are often purchased together. Other pattern discovery problems include detecting fraudulent credit card transactions and identifying anomalous data that could represent data entry keying errors.

Data mining techniques can yield the benefits of automation on existing software and hardware platforms, and can be implemented on new systems as existing platforms are upgraded and new products developed. When data minirtools are implemented on high performance parallel processing systems, they can analyse massive databases in minutes.

Faster processing means that users can automatically experiment with more models to understand complex data. High speed makes it practical for users to analyse huge quantities of data. Larger databases, in turn, yield improved predictions.

Databases can be larger in both depth and breadth:

- More columns. Analysts must often limit the number of variables they examine when doing hands-on analysis due to time constraints. Yet variables that are discarded because they seem unimportant may carry information about unknown patterns. High performance data mining allows users to explore the full depth of a database, without preselecting a subset of variables.
- More rows. Larger samples yield lower estimation errors and variance, and allow users to make inferences about small but important segments of a population.

A recent Gartner Group Advanced Technology Research Note listed data mining and artificial intelligence at the top of the five key technology areas that "will clearly have a major impact across a wide range of industries within the next 3 to 5 years." Gartner also listed parallel architectures and data mining as two of the top 10 new technologies in which companies will invest during the next 5 years.

According to a recent Gartner HPC Research Note, "With the rapid advance in data capture, transmission and storage, large-systems users will increasingly need to implement new and innovative ways to mine the after-market value of their vast stores of detail data, employing MPP [massively parallel processing] systems to create new sources of business advantage (0.9 probability)."

The most commonly used techniques in data mining are:

- Artificial neural networks: Non-linear predictive models that learn through training and resemble biological neural networks in structure.
- Decision trees: Tree-shaped structures that represent sets of decisions. These decisions generate rules for the classification of a dataset. Specific decision tree methods include Classification and Regression Trees (CART) and Chi Square Automatic Interaction Detection (CHAID).
- Genetic algorithms: Optimization techniques that use processes such as genetic combination, mutation, and natural selection in a design based on the concepts of evolution.
- Nearest neighbour method: A technique that classifies each record in a dataset based on a combination of the classes of the k record(s) most similar to it in a historical dataset (where k ^{3} 1). Sometimes called the k-nearest neighbour technique.
- Rule induction: The extraction of useful if-then rules from data based on statistical significance.

Many of these technologies have been in use for more than a decade in specialized analysis tools that work with relatively small volumes of data. These capabilities are now evolving to integrate directly with industry-standard data warehouse and OLAP platforms.

HOW DATA MINING WORKS

How exactly is data mining able to tell you important things that you didn't know or what is going to happen next? The technique that is used to perform these feats in data mining is called modelling. Modelling is simply the act of building a model in one situation where you know the answer and then applying it to another situation that you don't.

For instance, if you were looking for a sunken Spanish galleon on the high seas the first thing you might do is to research the times when Spanish treasure had been found by others in the past. You might note that these ships often tend to be found off the coast of Bermuda and that there are certain characteristics to the ocean currents, and certain routes that have likely been taken by the ship's captains in that era.

You note these similarities and build a model that includes the characteristics that are common to the locations of these sunken treasures. With these models in hand you sail off looking for treasure where your model indicates it most likely might be given a similar situation in the past. Hopefully, if you've got a good model, you find your treasure.

This act of model building is thus something that people have been doing for a long time, certainly before the advent of computers or data mining technology. What happens on computers, however, is not much different than the way people build models.

Computers are loaded up with lots of information about a variety of situations where an answer is known and then the data mining software on the computer must run through that data and distil the characteristics of the data that should go into the model. Once the model is built it can then be used in similar situations where you don't know the answer. For example, say that you are the director of marketing for a telecommunications company and you'd like to acquire some new long distance phone customers. You could just randomly go out and mail coupons to the general population - just as you could randomly sail the seas looking for sunken treasure. In neither case would you achieve the results you desired and of course you have the opportunity to do much better than random - you could use your business experience stored in your database to build a model.

As the marketing director you have access to a lot of information about all of your customers: their age, sex, credit history and long distance calling usage. The good news is that you also have a lot of information about your prospective customers: their age, sex, credit history *etc.* Your problem is that you don't know the long distance calling usage of these prospects (since they are most likely now customers of your competition). You'd like to concentrate on those prospects who have large amounts of long distance usage. You can accomplish this by building a model. The data used for building a model for new customer prospecting in a data warehouse.

Table : Data Mining for Prospecting

	Customers	*Prospects*
General information (*e.g.* demographic data)	Known	Known
Proprietary information (*e.g.* customer transactions)	Known	Target

The goal in prospecting is to make some calculated guesses about the information in the lower right hand quadrant based on the model that we build going from Customer General Information to Customer Proprietary Information. For instance, a simple model for a telecommunications company might be:

'98% of my customers who make more than $60,000/year, spend more than $80/month on long distance calls.'

This model could then be applied to the prospect data to try to tell something about the proprietary information that this telecommunications company does not currently have access to. With this model in hand new customers can be selectively targeted.

Test marketing is an excellent source of data for this kind of modelling. Mining the results of a test market representing a broad but relatively small sample of prospects can provide a foundation for identifying good prospects in the overall market. Another common scenario for building models: predict what is going to happen in the future.

Table : Data Mining for Predictions

	Yesterday	*Today*	*Tomorrow*
Static information and current plans (*e.g.* demographic data, marketing plans)	Known	Known	Known
Dynamic information (*e.g.* customer transactions)	Known	Known	Target

If someone told you that he had a model that could predict customer usage how would you know if he really had a good model? The first thing you might try would be to ask him to apply his model to your customer base - where you already knew the answer.

With data mining, the best way to accomplish this is by setting aside some of your data in a vault to isolate it from the mining process. Once the mining is complete, the results can be tested against the data held in the vault to confirm the model's validity. If the model works, its observations should hold for the vaulted data.

AN ARCHITECTURE FOR DATA MINING

To best apply these advanced techniques, they must be fully integrated with a data warehouse as well as flexible interactive business analysis tools. Many data mining tools currently operate outside of the warehouse, requiring extra steps for extracting, importing, and analysing the data. Furthermore, when new insights require operational implementation, integration with the warehouse simplifies the application of results from data mining.

The resulting analytic data warehouse can be applied to improve business processes throughout the organization, in areas such as promotional campaign management, fraud detection, new product rollout, and so on. An architecture for advanced analysis in a large data warehouse.

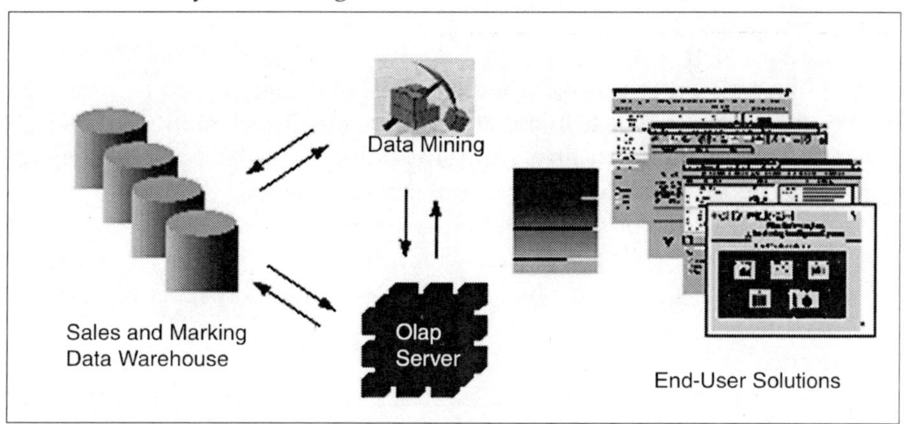

Figure : Integrated Data Mining Architecture

The ideal starting point is a data warehouse containing a combination of internal data tracking all customer contact coupled with external market data about competitor activity. Background information on potential customers also provides an excellent basis for prospecting. This warehouse can be implemented in a variety of relational database systems: Sybase, Oracle, Redbrick, and so on, and should be optimized for flexible and fast data access.

An OLAP (On-Line Analytical Processing) server enables a more sophisticated end-user business model to be applied when navigating the data warehouse. The multidimensional structures allow the user to analyse the data as they want to view their business – summarizing by product line, region, and other key perspectives of their business.

The Data Mining Server must be integrated with the data warehouse and the OLAP server to embed ROI-focused business analysis directly into this infrastructure. An advanced, process-centric metadata template defines the data mining objectives for specific business issues like campaign management, prospecting, and promotion optimization.

Integration with the data warehouse enables operational decisions to be directly implemented and tracked. As the warehouse grows with new decisions and results, the organization can continually mine the best practices and apply them to future decisions. This design represents a fundamental shift from conventional decision support systems. Rather than simply delivering data to the end user through query and reporting software, the Advanced Analysis Server applies users' business models directly to the warehouse and returns a proactive analysis of the most relevant information. These results enhance the metadata in the OLAP Server by providing a dynamic metadata layer that represents a distilled view of the data. Reporting, visualization, and other analysis tools can then be applied to plan future actions and confirm the impact of those plans.

PROFITABLE APPLICATIONS

A wide range of companies have deployed successful applications of data mining. While early adopters of this technology have tended to be in information-intensive industries such as financial services and direct mail marketing, the technology is applicable to any company looking to leverage a large data warehouse to better manage their customer relationships.

Two critical factors for success with data mining are: a large, well-integrated data warehouse and a well-defined understanding of the business process within which data mining is to be applied (such as customer prospecting, retention, campaign management, and so on).

Some successful application areas include:

- A pharmaceutical company can analyse its recent sales force activity and their results to improve targeting of high-value physicians and determine which marketing activities will have the greatest impact in the next few months. The data needs to include competitor market activity as well as information about the local health care systems. The results can be distributed to the sales force via a wide-area network that enables the representatives to review the recommendations from the perspective of the key attributes in the decision process. The ongoing, dynamic analysis of the data warehouse allows best practices from throughout the organization to be applied in specific sales situations.
- A credit card company can leverage its vast warehouse of customer transaction data to identify customers most likely to be interested in a new credit product. Using a small test mailing, the attributes of customers with an affinity for the product can be identified. Recent projects have indicated more than a 20-fold decrease in costs for targeted mailing campaigns over conventional approaches.
- A diversified transportation company with a large direct sales force can apply data mining to identify the best prospects for its services. Using data mining to analyse its own customer experience, this company can build a unique segmentation identifying the attributes of high-value prospects. Applying this segmentation to a general business database such as those provided by Dun & Bradstreet can yield a prioritized list of prospects by region.

- A large consumer package goods company can apply data mining to improve its sales process to retailers. Data from consumer panels, shipments, and competitor activity can be applied to understand the reasons for brand and store switching. Through this analysis, the manufacturer can select promotional strategies that best reach their target customer segments.

Each of these examples has a clear common ground. They leverage the knowledge about customers implicit in a data warehouse to reduce costs and improve the value of customer relationships. These organizations can now focus their efforts on the most important (profitable) customers and prospects, and design targeted marketing strategies to best reach them.

2

Data

Data are values of qualitative or quantitative variables, belonging to a set of items. Data in computing (or data processing) are often represented by a combination of items organized in rows and multiple variables organized in columns. Data are typically the results of measurements and can be visualised using graphs or images. Data as an abstract concept can be viewed as the lowest level of abstraction from which information and then knowledge are derived. *Raw data, i.e.*, unprocessed data, refers to a collection of numbers, characters and is a relative term; data processing commonly occurs by stages, and the "processed data" from one stage may be considered the "raw data" of the next. Field data refers to raw data collected in an uncontrolled in situ environment. Experimental data refers to data generated within the context of a scientific investigation by observation and recording. The word *data* is the plural of *datum*, neuter past participle of the Latin *dare*, "to give", hence "something given". In discussions of problems in geometry, mathematics, engineering, and so on, the terms *givens* and *data* are used interchangeably. Such usage is the origin of *data* as a concept in computer science or data processing: data are numbers, words, images, *etc.*, accepted as they stand.

TYPES OF DATA

There are four types of data that may be gathered in social research, each one adding more to the next. Thus ordinal data is also nominal, and so on.

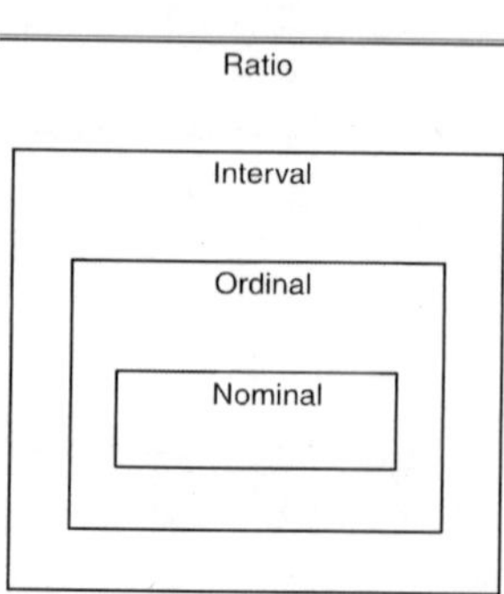

NOMINAL

The name 'Nominal' comes from the Latin *nomen*, meaning 'name' and nominal data are items which are differentiated by a simple naming system. The only thing a nominal scale does is to say that items being measured have something in common, although this may not be described.

Nominal items may have numbers assigned to them. This may appear ordinal but is not — these are used to simplify capture and referencing. Nominal items are usually *categorical*, in that they belong to a definable category, such as 'employees'.

Example

The number pinned on a sports person.
A set of countries.

ORDINAL

Items on an ordinal scale are set into some kind of *order* by their position on the scale. This may indicate such as temporal position, superiority, *etc.*

The order of items is often defined by assigning numbers to them to show their relative position. Letters or other sequential symbols may also be used as appropriate.

Ordinal items are usually categorical, in that they belong to a definable category, such as '1956 marathon runners'.

You cannot do arithmetic with ordinal numbers — they show sequence only.

Example

The first, third and fifth person in a race.
Pay bands in an organization, as denoted by A, B, C and D.

INTERVAL

Interval data (also sometimes called *integer*) is measured along a scale in which each position is equidistant from one another. This allows for the distance between two pairs to be equivalent in some way.

This is often used in psychological experiments that measure attributes along an arbitrary scale between two extremes.

Interval data cannot be multiplied or divided.

Example

My level of happiness, rated from 1 to 10.
Temperature, in degrees Fahrenheit.

RATIO

In a ratio scale, numbers can be compared as multiples of one another. Thus one person can be twice as tall as another person. Important also, the number zero has meaning. Thus the difference between a person of 35 and a person 38 is the same as the difference between people who are 12 and 15. A person can also have an age of zero. Ratio data can be multiplied and divided because not only is the difference between 1 and 2 the same as between 3 and 4, but also that 4 is twice as much as 2.

Interval and ratio data measure quantities and hence are *quantitative*. Because they can be measured on a scale, they are also called *scale data*.

Example

A person's weight.
The number of pizzas I can eat before fainting.

PARAMETRIC VS. NON-PARAMETRIC

Interval and ratio data are *parametric*, and are used with parametric tools in which distributions are predictable (and often Normal).

Nominal and ordinal data are *non-parametric*, and do not assume any particular distribution. They are used with non-parametric tools such as the Histogram.

Continuous and Discrete

Continuous measures are measured along a continuous scale which can be divided into fractions, such as temperature. Continuous variables allow for infinitely fine sub-division, which means if you can measure sufficiently accurately, you can compare two items and determine the difference.

Discrete variables are measured across a set of fixed values, such as age in years (not microseconds). These are commonly used on arbitrary scales, such as scoring your level of happiness, although such scales can also be continuous.

THE CHOICE OF THE BEST ATTRIBUTES SELECTION MEASURE IN DECISION TREE INDUCTION

Data Mining is a relatively young area of research that builds on the older disciplines of statistics, databases, artificial intelligence, machine learning and data visualization. The main ideas behind Data Mining are often completely opposite to main-stream statistics. Data Mining is commonly defined as the computer-assisted search for interesting patterns and relations in large databases. The process must be automatic or semiautomatic. The data is always present in substantial quantities.

Data Mining is synonymous with Knowledge Discovery in Databases. The emergence of Data Mining is often explained by the ever increasing size of databases together with the availability of computing power and algorithms to analyse them. Data Mining is usually considered to be a form of secondary data analysis. This means that it is often performed on data collected and stored for a different purpose than analysis.

Decision Trees are one of the most popular Data Mining models. Decision Trees are able to provide a set of rules which improves the user's understanding. Decision Trees represent variables and variable values as trees, branches and leaves from which Decision Rules must be transformed. A Decision Tree classifier builds a model by recursively dividing the training set into partitions so that all or most of the records in a partition have the same class label.

Most Decision Tree classifiers perform classification in two phases: tree-induction (growing or building) and tree-pruning. In the tree-induction phase the algorithm starts with the whole data set at the root node. The data set is partitioned according to a splitting criterion into subsets. This procedure is repeated recursively for each subset until each subset contains only members belonging to the same class or is sufficiently small. In the tree-pruning phase the full grown tree is cut back to prevent over-fitting and to improve the accuracy of the tree. During the induction phase the attribute selection measure (splitting criterion) is determined by choosing the

Attribute (A) that will best separate the remaining samples of the nodes partition into individual classes. This attribute becomes the decision attribute at the node.

Using this attribute a splitting criterion for partitioning the data is defined, which is either of the form A < v (v 2 dom(A)) for numeric attributes for categorical attributes. For selecting the best split point several measures were proposed (*e.g.* ID3 and C4.5 select the split that minimizes the information entropy of the partitions, while SLIQ and SPRINT use the gini index). Once an attribute is associated with a node, it needs not be considered in the node's children.

The most time-consuming part of Decision Tree induction is obviously the choice of the best attribute selection measure. For each active node the subset of data fulfilling the conjunction of the splitting conditions of the node and its predecessors has to be constructed and for each remaining attribute the possible splits have to be evaluated.

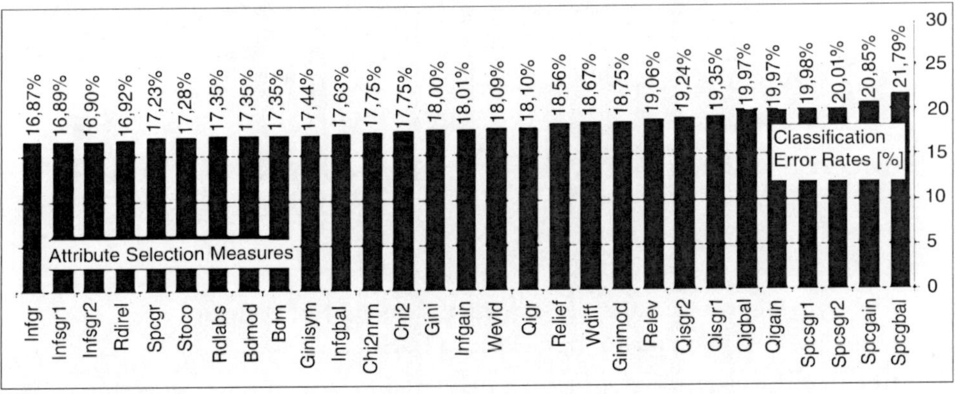

Figure : Classification Error Rates on the Test Data for Unpruned Decision Trees.

Decision Tree Induction: Decision Trees induced at this step on the 32, 561 training records of the Adult Database with all the 29 attribute selection measures, have been executed on the 16,281 test samples of the same database. The most important performance for the classification of the different Decision Trees, the classification accuracy on the test data, data completely unknown at the training of Decision Trees, has been noticed. This performance is expressed by classification error rate on the test data and is represent. The performances are sorted in the ascending order of the classification error rates values on the test data. It can be noticed that the highest performance for the error rate on the test data is obtained by the *infgr* measure.

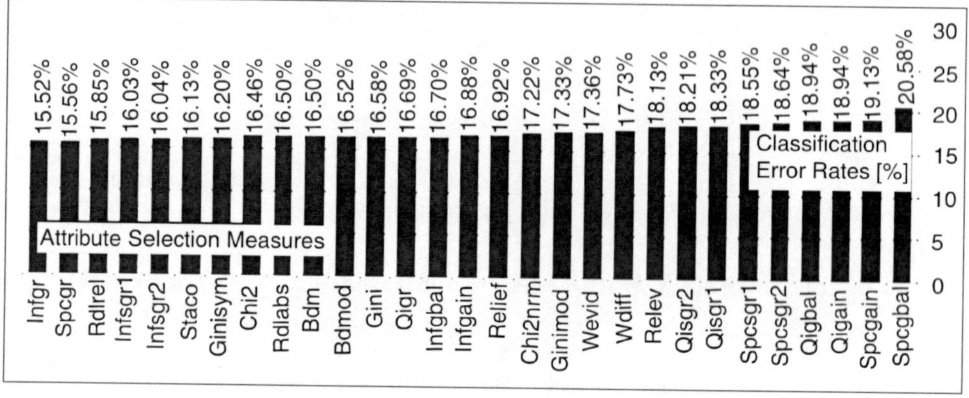

Figure : Classification Error Rates on the Test Data for Pessimistic Pruned Decision Trees.

Decision Tree pruning with pessimistic pruning method. Decision Trees induced at the previous step was pruned by using the pessimistic pruning method.

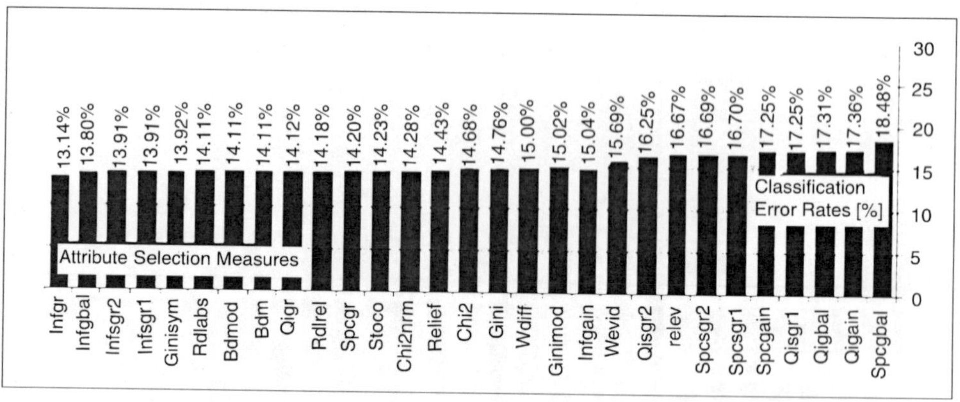

Figure : Classification Error Rates on the Test Data for Confidence Level Pruned Decision Trees.

After that, Decision Trees pruned at this step was executed on the 16,281 test data of the Adult Database. The most important performance for the classification of the different Decision Trees, the accuracy of classification on the test data, which are completely unknown at the Decision Trees training, is represent. The performances are sorted in ascending order by values of the classification error rates. We can notice that the best performance at the classification error rate is obtained by the same *infgr* measure. For pruned Decision Trees with pessimistic pruning method the accuracy of the classification error rate is better than for unpruned Decision Trees.

Decision Tree pruning with confidence level pruning. Decision Trees induced at first step was pruned using confidence level pruning. Pruned Decision Trees at this step, with confidence level pruning method, was executed on the 16, 281 test samples of the Adult Database. The accuracy of the classification on the test data is expressed in the classification error rate and is represent.

The performances are sorted in the ascending order of the values of the classification error rates on the test data. We can notice that the best performance of the classification error rate on the test data is obtained by the same *infgr* measure.

The accuracy of the classification is better than for the unpruned Decision Trees and for the Decision Trees pruned with pessimistic pruning method.

FEATURE SELECTION

In machine learning and statistics, feature selection, also known as variable selection, feature reduction, attribute selection or variable subset selection, is the technique of selecting a subset of relevant features for building robust learning models. Feature selection is a particularly important step in analysing the data from many experimental techniques in biology, such as DNA microarrays, because they often entail a large number of measured variables (features) but a very low number of samples. By removing most irrelevant and redundant features from the data, feature selection helps improve the performance of learning models by:

- Alleviating the effect of the curse of dimensionality.
- Enhancing generalization capability.
- Speeding up learning process.
- Improving model interpretability.

Feature selection also helps people to acquire better understanding about their data by telling them which are the important features and how they are related with each other.

Simple feature selection algorithms are ad hoc, but there are also more methodical approaches. From a theoretical perspective, it can be shown that optimal feature selection for supervised learning problems requires an exhaustive search of all possible subsets of features of the chosen cardinality. If large numbers of features are available, this is impractical. For practical supervised learning algorithms, the search is for a satisfactory set of features instead of an optimal set.

Feature selection algorithms typically fall into two categories: feature ranking and subset selection. Feature ranking ranks the features by a metric and eliminates all features that do not achieve an adequate score. Subset selection searches the set of possible features for the optimal subset.

In statistics, the most popular form of feature selection is stepwise regression. It is a greedy algorithm that adds the best feature (or deletes the worst feature) at each round. The main control issue is deciding when to stop the algorithm. In machine learning, this is typically done by cross-validation. In statistics, some criteria are optimized. This leads to the inherent problem of nesting. More robust methods have been explored, such as branch and bound and piecewise linear network.

SUBSET SELECTION

Subset selection evaluates a subset of features as a group for suitability. Subset selection algorithms can be broken into Wrappers, Filters and Embedded. Wrappers use a search algorithm to search through the space of possible features and evaluate each subset by running a model on the subset. Wrappers can be computationally expensive and have a risk of over fitting to the model. Filters are similar to Wrappers in the search approach, but instead of evaluating against a model, a simpler filter is evaluated. Embedded techniques are embedded in and specific to a model.

Many popular search approaches use greedy hill climbing, which iteratively evaluates a candidate subset of features, then modifies the subset and evaluates if the new subset is an improvement over the old. Evaluation of the subsets requires a scoring metric that grades a subset of features. Exhaustive search is generally impractical, so at some implementor (or operator) defined stopping point, the subset of features with the highest score discovered up to that point is selected as the satisfactory feature subset. The stopping criterion varies by algorithm; possible criteria include: a subset score exceeds a threshold, a program's maximum allowed run time has been surpassed, *etc.*

Alternative search-based techniques are based on targeted projection pursuit which finds low-dimensional projections of the data that score highly: the features that have the largest projections in the lower dimensional space are then selected.

Search approaches include:

- Exhaustive
- Best first
- Simulated annealing
- Genetic algorithm
- Greedy forward selection
- Greedy backward elimination
- Targeted projection pursuit
- Scatter Search
- Variable Neighbourhood Search.

Two popular filter metrics for classification problems are correlation and mutual information, although neither are true metrics or 'distance measures' in the mathematical sense, since they fail to obey the triangle inequality and thus do not compute any actual 'distance' – they should rather be regarded as 'scores'. These scores are computed between a candidate feature (or set of features) and the desired output category. There are, however, true metrics that are a simple function of the mutual information.

Other available filter metrics include:

- Class separability :
  (a) Error probability
  (b) Inter-class distance
  (c) Probabilistic distance
  (d) Entropy
- Consistency-based feature selection
- Correlation-based feature selection.

OPTIMALITY CRITERIA

There are a variety of optimality criteria that can be used for controlling feature selection. The oldest are Mallows' Cp statistic and Akaike information criterion (AIC). These add variables if the *t*-statistic is bigger than $\sqrt{2}$.

Other criteria are Bayesian information criterion (BIC) which uses $\sqrt{\log n}$, minimum description length (MDL) which asymptotically uses $\sqrt{\log n}$, Bonnferroni/RIC which use $\sqrt{2\log p}$, maximum dependency feature selection, and a variety of new criteria that are motivated by false discovery rate (FDR) which use something close to $\sqrt{2\log \frac{p}{q}}$.

Minimum-redundancy-maximum-relevance (mRMR) Feature Selection

Peng *et al.* proposed an mRMR feature-selection method that can use either mutual information, correlation, distance/similarity scores to select features. For example, with mutual information, relevant features and redundant features are considered simultaneously. The relevance of a feature set S for the class c is defined by the average value of all mutual information values between the individual feature f_i and the class as follows:

$$D(S,c) = \frac{1}{|S|}\sum_{f_i \in S} I(f_i;c).$$

The redundancy of all features in the set S is the average value of all mutual information values between the feature f_i and the feature f_j :

$$R(S) = \frac{1}{|S|^2} \sum_{f_i, f_j \in S} I(f_i; f_j)$$

The mRMR criterion is a combination of two measures given above and is defined as follows:

$$mRMR = \max_S \left[\frac{1}{|S|} \sum_{f_i \in S} I(f_i; c) - \frac{1}{|S|^2} \sum_{f_i, f_j \in S} I(f_i; f_j) \right].$$

Suppose that there are n full-set features. Let x_i be the set membership indicator function for feature f_i, so that $x_i = 1$ indicates presence and $x_i = 0$ indicates absence of the feature f_i in the globally optimal feature set. Let $c_i = I(f_i; c)$ and $a_{ij} = I(f_i, f_j)$. The above may then be written as an optimization problem:

$$mRMR = \max_{x \in \{0,1\}^n} \left[\frac{\sum_{i=1}^{n} c_i x_i}{\sum_{i=1}^{n} x_i} - \frac{\sum_{i,j=1}^{n} a_{ij} x_i x_j}{(\sum_{i=1}^{n} x_i)^2} \right].$$

It may be shown that mRMR feature selection is an approximation of the theoretically optimal maximum-dependency feature selection that maximizes the mutual information between the joint distribution of the selected features and the classification variable. However, since mRMR turned a combinatorial problem as a series of much smaller scale problems, each of which only involves two variables, the estimation of joint probabilities is much more robust. In certain situations the algorithm can underestimate the usefulness of features as it has no way to measure interactions between features. This can lead to poor performance when the features are individually useless, but are useful when combined (a pathological case is found when the class is a parity function of the features). Overall the algorithm is more efficient (in terms of the amount of data required) than the theoretically optimal max-dependency selection, yet produces a low redundancy feature set.

It can be seen that mRMR is also related to the correlation based feature. It may also be seen a special case of some generic feature selectors.

CORRELATION FEATURE SELECTION

The Correlation Feature Selection (CFS) measure evaluates subsets of features on the basis of the following hypothesis: "Good feature subsets contain features highly correlated with the classification, yet uncorrelated to each other". The following equation gives the merit of a feature subset S consisting of k features:

$$Merit_{S_k} = \frac{k\overline{r_{cf}}}{\sqrt{k + k(k-1)\overline{r_{ff}}}}.$$

Here, $\overline{r_{cf}}$ is the average value of all feature-classification correlations, and $\overline{r_{ff}}$ is the average value of all feature-feature correlations. The *CFS* criterion is defined as follows:

$$CFS = \max_{S_k}\left[\frac{r_{cf_1}+r_{cf_2}+\cdots+r_{cf_k}}{\sqrt{k+2(r_{f_1f_2}+\cdots+r_{f_if_j}+\cdots+r_{f_kf_1})}}\right].$$

The r_{cf_i} and $r_{f_if_j}$ variables are referred to as correlations, but are not necessarily Pearson's correlation coefficient or Spearman's ρ. Dr. Mark Hall's dissertation uses neither of these, but uses three different measures of relatedness, minimum description length (MDL), symmetrical uncertainty, and relief.

Let x_i be the set membership indicator function for feature f_i; then the above can be rewritten as an optimization problem:

$$CFS = \max_{x\in\{0,1\}^n}\left[\frac{(\sum_{i=1}^{n} a_i x_i)^2}{\sum_{i=1}^{n} x_i + \sum_{i\neq j} 2b_{ij}x_ix_j}\right].$$

The combinatorial problems above are, in fact, mixed 0-1 linear programming problems that can be solved by using branch-and-bound algorithms.

General L1-norm Support Vector Machine for Feature Selection

It has been shown in that the traditional L1-norm SVM proposed by Bradley and Mangasarian in can be generalized to a general L1-norm SVM (GL1-SVM).

Moreover, it has been proved that solving the new proposed optimization problem (GL1-SVM) gives smaller error penalty and enlarges the margin between two support vector hyper-planes, thus possibly gives better generalization capability of SVM than solving the traditional L1-norm SVM.

GL1-SVM may also be seen a special case of some generic feature selectors.

Regularized Trees

The features from a decision tree or a tree ensemble are shown to be redundant. A recent method called regularized tree can be used for feature subset selection. Regularized trees penalize using a variable similar to the variables selected at previous tree nodes for splitting the current node. Regularized trees only need build one tree model (or one tree ensemble model) and thus are computationally efficient.

Regularized trees naturally handle numerical and categorical features, interactions and nonlinearities. They are invariant to attribute scales (units) and insensitive to outliers, and thus, require little data preprocessing such as normalization. Regularized random forest (RRF) is one type of regularized trees. The guided RRF is an enhanced RRF which is guided by the importance scores from an ordinary random forest.

CHALLENGES OF DISCRETE AND ATTRIBUTE DATA MEASUREMENT

Measurement is more important than ever. How measurement systems are evaluated is influenced by the types of data gathered. More than ever, companies today realise the importance of measurement – everything from measuring performance to measuring gap closure – in order to achieve goals. Measurement is the process of estimating the ratio of the magnitude of a quantity to a unit of the same type. A measurement is the result of such a process, normally expressed as the multiple of a real number and a unit, where the real number is the ratio. For example, nine meters is an estimate of an object's length relative to a unit of length, one meter.

Organizations measure for two primary reasons:

- To make a decision
- As the basis for process improvement.

The act of measuring an object normally involves using a measuring instrument under "controlled" conditions. In today's industries, the convenience of controlled conditions is seldom found. To measure accurately, measuring instruments must be carefully constructed and calibrated. Another variable of measurement systems is the human factor – the person taking the measurement when the measurement process is not automated.

All measurements have some degree of uncertainty associated with them, usually expressed as a standard error of measurement. Thus, while a measurement is usually given as a number followed by a unit, every measurement has three components – the estimate, error bounds and a probability that the actual magnitude lies within the error bounds of the estimate. For example, a measurement of a plank might result in a measurement of 9 meters plus or minus 0.01 meters, with a probability of 0.95.

ACKNOWLEDGE, ACCEPT, THEN DEAL WITH MEASUREMENT CAPABILITIES

Organizations need to understand how good their decisions are relative to chance, and how good their decisions are relative to the true variation of what is being measured. Measurement of many quantities is very difficult and prone to large error. This difficulty is due to both uncertainty and to limited time available in which to measure.

Examples of things that are difficult to measure in some respects and for some purposes include social-related items such as:

- A person's knowledge

- A person's feelings, emotions or beliefs
- A person's senses
- A customer's satisfaction.

Gaining an accurate measurement can be difficult even for more physical types of data. To ensure accuracy, organizations often make repeated measurements. However, even repeated measurements will vary due to factors affecting the quantity, such as time of day, resource availability and measurement method. A company must effectively evaluate its measurement systems, especially when dealing with discrete data.

DISCRETE DATA: IMPROVING/EVALUATING MEASUREMENT SYSTEMS

There are several ways to evaluate measurement systems, and approaches are influenced by the types of data gathered, for example, continuous or discrete data. While a Gage R&R evaluates measurement systems for continuous data, attribute data can be analysed using an attribute measurement system analysis (MSA) to deal with discrete data.

Another form of MSA can be determined through reliability coefficients. Examples include kappa analysis and intraclass correlation. The high-level distinctions between the kappa analysis and intraclass correlation.

MSA for Continuous and Discrete Data

The MSA can be generated to deal with discrete or continuous data. For continuous data, process output data is measured and re-measured to compare measurement variation to overall process variation.

TYPES OF DATA SETS

A data set (or dataset) is a collection of data, usually presented in tabular form. Each column represents a particular variable. Each row corresponds to a given member of the data set in question. It lists values for each of the variables, such as height and weight of an object. Each value is known as a datum. The data set may comprise data for one or more members, corresponding to the number of rows.

Nontabular data sets can take the form of marked up strings of characters, such as an XML file.

Properties

A data set has several characteristics which define its structure and properties. These include the number and types of the attributes or variables and the various statistical measures which may be applied to them such as standard deviation and kurtosis. In the simplest case, there is only one variable, and then the data set; consists of a single column of values, often represented as a list. In spite of the name, such a univariate data set is not a set in the usual mathematical sense, since a given value may occur multiple times. Normally the order does not matter, and then the collection of values may be considered to be a multi-set rather than an (ordered) list.

The values may be numbers, such as real numbers or integers, for example representing a person's height in centimetres, but may also be nominal data (*i.e.*, not consisting of numerical values), for example representing a person's ethnicity. More generally, values may be of any of the kinds described as a level of measurement. For each variable, the values will normally all be of the same kind. However, there may also be "missing values", which need to be indicated in some way.

In statistics, data sets usually come from actual observations obtained by sampling a statistical population, and each row corresponds to the observations on one element of that population. Data sets may further be generated by algorithms for the purpose of testing certain kinds of software. Some modern statistical analysis software such as PSPP still presents their data in the classical data set fashion.

DATA QUALITY

Data quality is a perception or an assessment of data's fitness to serve its purpose in a given context.

Aspects of data quality include:

- Accuracy
- Completeness
- Update status
- Relevance
- Consistency across data sources
- Reliability
- Appropriate presentation
- Accessibility.

Within an organization, acceptable data quality is crucial to operational and transactional processes and to the reliability of business analytics (BA)/business intelligence (BI) reporting. Data quality is affected by the way data is entered, stored and managed. Data quality assurance (DQA) is the process of verifying the reliability and effectiveness of data. Maintaining data quality requires going through the data periodically and scrubbing it. Typically this involves updating it, standardizing it, and de-duplicating records to create a single view of the data, even if it is stored in multiple disparate systems. There are many vendor applications on the market to make this job easier.

MEASUREMENT AND DATA COLLECTION ISSUES

As the World Wide Web has become more prominent as a mode of communication, it has opened up new possibilities for research data collection.

This section identifies measurement issues that occur with Internet data collection that are relevant to qualitative and quantitative research approaches as they occurred in a triangulated Internet study of perimenopausal women with migraine headaches. Issues associated with quantitative data collection over the Internet include: (a) selecting and designing Internet data collection protocols that adequa-tely address study aims while also taking advantage of the Internet, (b) ensuring the reliability and validity of Internet data collected, (c) adapting quantitative paper-and-pencil data collection protocols for the Internet, (e) making Internet data collection practical for respondents and researchers, and (f) Ensuring the quality of quantitative data collected.

Qualitative data collection over the Internet needs to remain true to the philosophical stance of the qualitative approach selected. Researcher expertise in qualitative data collection must be combined with expertise in computer technology and information services if data are to be of ultimate quality. The advantages and limitations of collecting qualitative data in real time or at a later time are explored, as well as approaches to enhance qualitative data collection over the Internet. It was concluded that like any research approach or method, Internet data collection requires considerable creativity, expertise, and planning to take advantage of the technology for the collection of reliable and valid research data. The establishment of the Internet, and specifically the World Wide Web, as a common mode of communication during the past 2 decades has greatly enhanced interaction among individuals and groups in all areas of life. Although the business community readily recognized and integrated Internet communication into its daily mode of operating, the nursing and research communities have been more cautious in their use of this communication tool in their activities. The major use of the Internet in nursing has been as a resource locator or for data collection with demographic surveys.

- While researchers have found the Internet to be quite useful for gaining access to information by searching the World Wide Web, they have been more reluctant to use it to conduct one of its core activities-collection of research data from respondents. Undoubtedly, Internet data collection can have an important role in research. Data collected over the Internet are likely to be less affected by social desirability and inhibition than that collected via paper-and-pencil methods.
- Although the World Wide Web can offer researchers global access, fast interaction with subjects, and automation,
- The facility and adeptness with which data are collected will depend upon the type of data collected (*i.e.* qualitative vs. quantitative), the computer skills of the respondent, and the computer hardware and software available.

The primary goal of measurement of any phenomenon is that the data collected are consistent, accurate, and as precise as possible. It is crucial to adequately address these goals no matter whether qualitative or quantitative data are obtained. However, when data are collected via the Internet these aims can be uniquely addressed and challenged regardless of the type of data obtained. This chapter will address measurement issues related to both qualitative and quantitative research approaches, as they occurred in a triangulated Internet study of perimenopausal women with migraine headaches.

MINING FREQUENT PATTERNS, ASSOCIATIONS AND CORRELATIONS

MARKET BASKET ANALYSIS

Market basket analysis may be performed on the retail data of customer transactions at a store that can be then used to plan marketing or advertising strategies, or in the design of a new catalogue. Market basket analysis can also help retailers plan which items to put on sale at reduced prices. If customers tend to purchase computers and printers together, then having a sale on printers may encourage the sale of printers as well as computers.

Frequent Itemsets, Closed Itemsets, and Association Rules

$$\text{support}\left(A \Rightarrow B\right) = P\left(A \cup B\right)$$

$$\text{confidence}\left(A \Rightarrow B\right) = P\left(B \mid A\right).$$

$$\text{confidence}\left(A \Rightarrow B\right) = P\left(B \mid A\right) = \frac{\text{support}(A \cup B)}{\text{support }(A)} = \frac{\text{support\_count}(A \cup B)}{\text{support\_count }(A)}$$

Association rule mining can be viewed as a two-step process:

- Find all frequent itemsets: By definition, each of these itemsets will occur at least as frequently as a predetermined minimum support count, min sup.
- Generate strong association rules from the frequent itemsets: By definition, these rules must satisfy minimum support and minimum confidence.

Frequent Pattern Mining can be based on:

- The completeness of patterns to be mined
- The levels of abstraction involved in the rule set
- The number of data dimensions involved in the rule:
- The types of values handled in the rule
- The kinds of rules to be mined:
- The kinds of patterns to be mined.

EFFICIENT AND SCALABLE FREQUENT ITEMSET MINING METHODS

The Apriori Algorithm-Frequent Itemsets mining using Candidate Generation

Apriori property: All nonempty subsets of a frequent itemset must also be frequent. Join and prune actions:

- The join step
- The Prune step.

Generating Association Rules from Frequent Itemsets

Once the frequent itemsets from transactions in a database D have been found, it is straightforward to generate strong association rules from them (where strong association rules satisfy both minimum support and minimum confidence).

Example: Generating association rules. Let's try an example based on the transactional data for DMT. Suppose the data contain the frequent itemset l = {I1, I2, I5}. What are the association rules that can be generated from l? The nonempty subsets of l are {I1, I2}, {I1, I5}, {I2, I5}, {I1}, {I2}, and {I5}. The resulting association rules, each listed with its confidence:

I1 $\wedge$ I2 =>15, confidence = 2/4 = 50%
I1 $\wedge$ I5 => I2, confidence = 2/2 = 100%
I2 $\wedge$ I5 => I1, confidence = 2/2 = 100%
I1 => I2 $\wedge$ I5, confidence = 2/6 = 33%
I2 => I1 $\wedge$ I5, confidence = 2/7 = 29%
I5 = I1 $\wedge$ I2, confidence = 2/2 = 100%

Methods to improve the efficiency of Apriori algorithm: Hash-based technique (hashing itemsets into corresponding buckets): A hash-based technique can be used to reduce the size of the candidate k-itemsets, Ck, for k > 1.

Transaction reduction (reducing the number of transactions scanned in future iterations): A transaction that does not contain any frequent k-itemsets cannot contain any frequent (k + 1)-itemsets.

Partitioning (partitioning the data to find candidate itemsets): A partitioning technique can be used that requires just two database scans to mine the frequent itemsets. It has two phases.

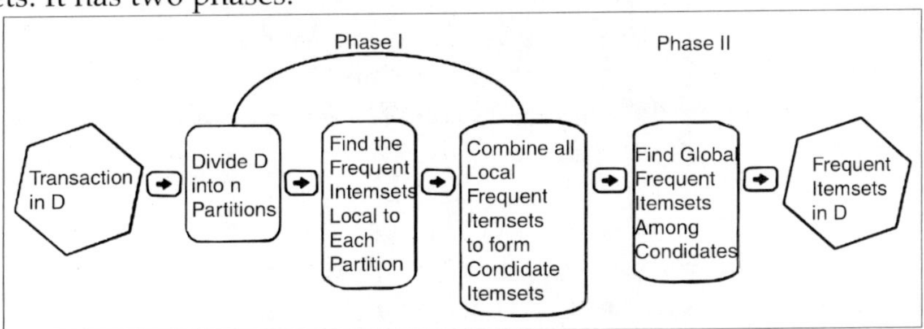

Sampling (mining on a subset of the given data): The basic idea of the sampling approach is to pick a random sample S of the given data D, and then search for frequent itemsets in S instead of D. In this way, we trade off some degree of accuracy against efficiency

Dynamic itemset counting (adding candidate itemsets at different points during a scan): A dynamic itemset counting technique was proposed in which the database is partitioned into blocks marked by start points.

Mining Frequent Itemsets without Candidate Generation

In many cases the Apriori candidate generate-and-test method significantly reduces the size of candidate sets, leading to good performance gain.

However, it can suffer from two nontrivial costs:

- It may need to generate a huge number of candidate sets
- It may need to repeatedly scan the database and check a large set of candidates by pattern matching.

Mining Frequent Itemsets Using Vertical Data Format

Algorithm: FP growth. Mine frequent itemsets using an FP-tree by pattern fragment growth.

```
Input:
D, a transaction database; min sup, the minimum support
count threshold.
Output: The complete set of frequent patterns.
Method:
1. The FP-tree is constructed in the following steps:
(a) Scan the transaction database D once. Collect F, the set
of frequent items, and their support counts. Sort F in support
count descending order as L, the list of frequent items.
(b) Create the root of an FP-tree, and label it as "null."
For each transaction Trans in D do the following. Select and
sort the frequent items in Trans according to the order of
L. Let the sorted frequent item list in Trans be [p|P],
where p is the first element and P is the remaining list.
Call insert tree([pP], T), which is performed as follows.
If T has a child N such that N.item-name = p.item-name, then
increment N's count by 1; else create a new node N, and let
its count be 1, its parent link be linked to T, and its
node-link to the nodes with the same item-name via the node
link structure. If P is nonempty, call insert tree(P, N)
recursively.
2. The FP-tree is mined by calling FP growth(FP tree, null),
which is implemented as follows. Procedure FP growth(Tree, α)
(1) if Tree contains a single path P then
(2) for each combination (denoted as β) of the nodes in the
path P
(3) generate pattern β α with support count = minimum support
count o f nodes in β;
(4) else for each ai in the header of Tree {
(5) generate pattern β = ai ∪ α with support count = ai
.support count;
```

```
(6) construct β's conditional pattern base and then β's
conditional FP tree Tree β ;
(7) if Treeβ = 0 then
(8) call FP growth (Tree, beta);
}
```

MINING CLOSED FREQUENT ITEMSETS

Pruning strategies include the following: Item merging: If every transaction containing a frequent itemset X also contains an itemset Y but not any proper superset of Y, then $X \cup Y$ forms a frequent closed itemset and there is no need to search for any itemset containing X but no Y. Sub-itemset pruning: If a frequent itemset X is a proper subset of an already found frequent closed itemset Y and support count(X) = support count(Y), then X and all of X's descendants in the set enumeration tree cannot be frequent closed itemsets and thus can be pruned.

Item skipping: In the depth-first mining of closed itemsets, at each level, there will be a prefix itemset X associated with a header table and a projected database. If a local frequent item p has the same support in several header tables at different levels, we can safely prune p from the header tables at higher levels.

Mining Multilevel Association Rules

Suppose we are given the task-relevant set of transactional data for sales in an DMT store, showing the items purchased for each transaction. The concept hierarchy for the items.

A concept hierarchy defines a sequence of mappings from a set of low-level concepts to higher-level, more general concepts. Data can be generalized by replacing low-level concepts within the data by their higher-level concepts, or ancestors, from a concept hierarchy.

Constraint-Based Association Mining

Fora a Constraint-based mining, the constraints can include the following:

Knowledge type constraints: These specify the type of knowledge to be mined, such as association or correlation.

Data constraints: These specify the set of task-relevant data.

Dimension/level constraints: These specify the desired dimensions (or attributes) of the data, or levels of the concept hierarchies, to be used in mining.

Interestingness constraints: These specify thresholds on statistical measures of rule interestingness, such as support, confidence, and correlation.

Rule constraints: These specify the form of rules to be mined. Such constraints may be expressed as metarules (rule templates), as the maximum or minimum number of predicates that can occur in the rule antecedent or consequent, or as relationships among attributes, attribute values, and/or aggregates.

Metarule-Guided Mining of Association Rules

Metarules allow users to specify the syntactic form of rules that they are interested in mining. The rule forms can be used as constraints to help improve the efficiency of the mining process.

Constraint Pushing or Mining Guided by Rule Constraints

Rule constraints specify expected set/subset relationships of the variables in the mined rules, constant initiation of variables, and aggregate functions.

Example: A closer look at mining guided by rule constraints. Suppose that DMT has a sales multidimensional database with the following interrelated relations:

- Sales (customer name, item name, TID)
- Lives in (customer name, region, city)
- Item (item name, group, price)
- Transaction (TID, day, month, year).

Classification and Prediction

The data analysis task is classification, where a model or classifier is constructed to predict categorical labels, such as "safe" or "risky" for the loan application data; "yes" or "no" for the marketing data; or "treatment A," "treatment B," or "treatment C" for the medical data.

Suppose that the marketing manager would like to predict how much a given customer will spend during a sale at DMT. This data analysis task is an example of numeric prediction, where the model constructed predicts a continuous-valued function, or ordered value, as opposed to a categorical label. This model is a predictor.

Issues Regarding Classification and Prediction

Steps in preparing the Data for Classification and Prediction Data cleaning:

- Relevance analysis
- Data transformation and reduction
- Comparing Classification and Prediction Methods
- Accuracy
- speed
- Robustness
- scalability
- Interpretability.

Classification by Decision Tree Induction

Decision tree induction is the learning of decision trees from class-labelled training tuples. A decision tree is a flowchart-like tree structure, where each internal node (nonleaf node) denotes a test on an attribute, each branch represents an outcome of the test, and each leaf node (or terminal node) holds a class label.

Decision Tree Induction

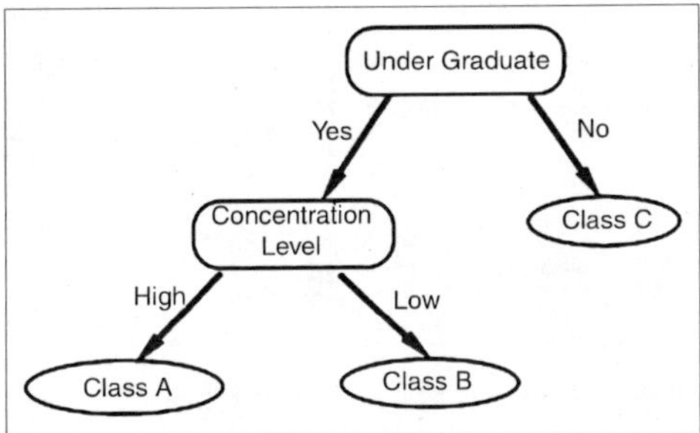

BASIC ALGORITHM FOR GENERATING A DECISION TREE FROM TRAINING TUPLES

```
Algorithm: Generate decision tree. Generate a decision tree
from the training tuples of data
partition D.
Input:
Data partition, D, which is a set of training tuples and
their associated class labels;
attribute list, the set of candidate attributes;
Attribute selection method, a procedure to determine the
splitting criterion that "best" partitions
the data tuples into individual classes. This criterion
consists of a splitting attribute
and, possibly, either a split point or splitting subset.
Output: A decision tree.
Method:
create a node N;
if tuples in D are all of the same class, C then
return N as a leaf node labelled with the class C;
if attribute list is empty then
return N as a leaf node labelled with the majority class in
D;// majority voting
apply Attribute selection method (D, attribute list) to find
the "best" splitting criterion;
label node N with splitting criterion;
if splitting attribute is discrete-valued and
multiway splits allowed then// not restricted to binary trees
attribute list ← attribute list "splitting attribute;//
remove splitting attribute
for each outcome j of splitting criterion
// partition the tuples and grow subtrees for each partition
let D j be the set of data tuples in D satisfying outcome
j;// a partition
```

```
if D j is empty then
attach a leaf labelled with the majority class in D to node N;
else attach the node returned by Generate decision tree
(D j, attribute list) to node N;
endfor
return N;
```

ATTRIBUTE SELECTION MEASURES

An attribute selection measure is a heuristic for selecting the splitting criterion that "best" separates a given data partition, D, of class-labelled training tuples into individual classes.

Tree Pruning

When a decision tree is built, many of the branches will reflect anomalies in the training data due to noise or outliers. Tree pruning methods address this problem of overfitting the data. Scalability and Decision Tree Induction problem: Most often, the training data will not fit in memory! Decision tree construction therefore becomes inefficient due to swapping of the training tuples in and out of main and cache memories., thats why it is necessary to have scalable decision tree.

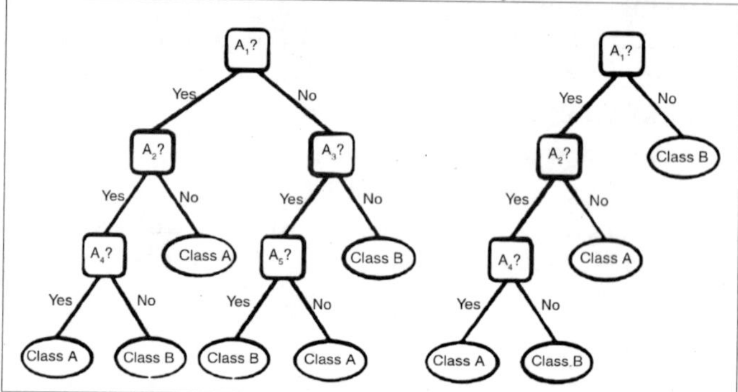

Bayesian Classification

Bayesian classifiers are statistical classifiers. They can predict class membership probabilities, such as the probability that a given tuple belongs to a particular class.

Bayes' Theorem

$$P(H \mid X) = \frac{P(X \mid H)P(H)}{P(X)}.$$

Naïve Bayesian Classification

- Let D be a training set of tuples and their associated class labels. As usual, each tuple is represented by an n-dimensional attribute vector, X = (x1, x2, . .., xn), depicting n measurements made on the tuple from n attributes, respectively, A1, A2,..., An.

- Suppose that there are m classes, C1, C2,..., Cm. Given a tuple, X, the classifier will predict that X belongs to the class having the highest posterior probability, conditioned on X. That is, the naïve Bayesian classifier predicts that tuple X belongs to the class Ci if and only if $P(Ci \mid X) > P(C j \mid X)$ for $1 \leq j \leq m, j = i$.
Thus we maximize P(Ci |X). The class Ci for which P(Ci |X) is maximized is called the maximum posteriori hypothesis. By Bayes' theorem
- As P(X) is constant for all classes, only P(X|Ci)P(Ci) need be maximized. If the class prior probabilities are not known, then it is commonly assumed that the classes are equally likely, that is, P(C1) = P(C2) = · · · = P(Cm), and we would therefore maximize P(X|Ci). Otherwise, we maximize P(X|Ci)P(Ci). Note that the class prior probabilities may be estimated by P(Ci) = |Ci,D |/|D|, where |Ci,D | is the number of training tuples of class Ci in D.
- Given data sets with many attributes, it would be extremely computationally expensive to compute P(X|Ci). In order to reduce computation in evaluating P(X|Ci), the naive assumption of class conditional independence is made. This presumes that the values of the attributes are conditionally independent of one another, given the class label of the tuple (*i.e.*, that there are no dependence relationships among the attributes).
- In order to predict the class label of X, P(X|Ci)P(Ci) is evaluated for each class Ci. The classifier predicts that the class label of tuple X is the class Ci if and only if In other words, the predicted class label is the class Ci for which P(X|Ci)P(Ci) is the maximum.

BAYESIAN BELIEF NETWORKS

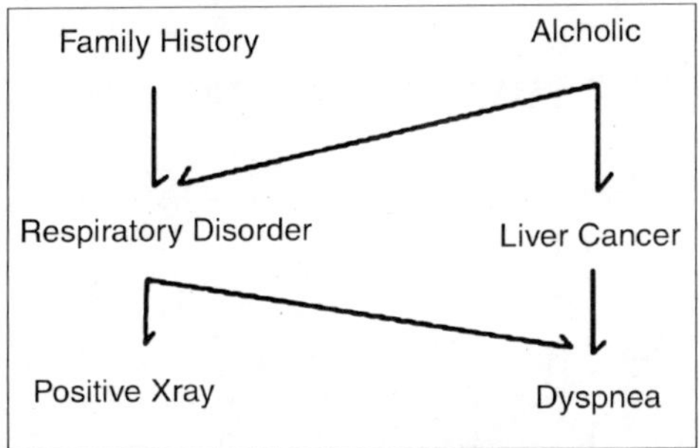

Conditional probability table showing, probability of lung cancer based on family history (FH) and Alcoholic (A)

	FH, A	*FH, ~A*	*~FH, A*	*~FH, ~A*
RD	0.8	0.4	0.6	0.1
~RD	0.2	0.6	0.4	0.9

Training Bayesian Belief Networks

In the learning or training of a belief network, a number of scenarios are possible. The network topology (or "layout" of nodes and arcs) may be given in advance or inferred from the data. The network variables may be observable or hidden in all or some of the training tuples. The case of hidden data is also referred to as missing values or incomplete data.

Rule Induction Using a Sequential Covering Algorithm

Algorithm: Sequential covering. Learn a set of IF-THEN rules for classification.

```
Input:
D, a data set class-labelled tuples;
Att vals, the set of all attributes and their possible values.
Output: A set of IF-THEN rules.
Method:
Rule set = {};// initial set of rules learned is empty
for each class c do
repeat
Rule = Learn One Rule(D, Att vals, c);
remove tuples covered by Rule from D;
until terminating condition;
Rule set = Rule set + Rule;// add new rule to rule set
endfor
return Rule Set;
```

Classification by Backpropagation

Backpropagation is a neural network learning algorithm. The field of neural networks was originally kindled by psychologists and neurobiologists who sought to develop and test computational analogues of neurons.

A MULTILAYER FEED-FORWARD NEURAL NETWORK

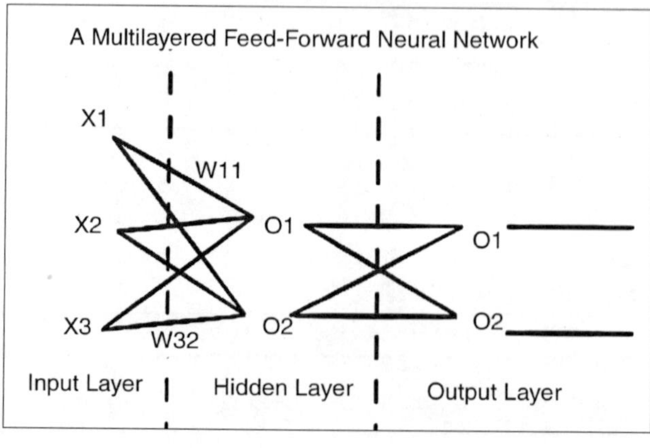

Defining a Network Topology

Before training can begin, the user must decide on the network topology by specifying the number of units in the input layer, the number of hidden layers (if more than one), the number of units in each hidden layer, and the number of units in the output layer.

BACKPROPAGATION ALGORITHM

Backpropagation is a common method of training artificial neural networks so as to minimize the objective function.

Arthur E. Bryson and Yu-Chi Ho described it as a multi-stage dynamic system optimization method in 1969. It wasn't until 1974 and later, when applied in the context of neural networks and through the work of Paul Werbos, David E. Rumelhart, Geoffrey E. Hinton and Ronald J. Williams, that it gained recognition, and it led to a "renaissance" in the field of artificial neural network research.

It is a supervised learning method, and is a generalization of the delta rule. It requires a dataset of the desired output for many inputs, making up the training set.

It is most useful for feed-forward networks (networks that have no feedback, or simply, that have no connections that loop). The term is an abbreviation for "backward propagation of errors". Backpropagation requires that the activation function used by the artificial neurons (or "nodes") be differentiable.

The backpropagation algorithm looks for the minimum of the error function in weight space using the method of gradient descent. The combination of weights which minimizes the error function is considered to be a solution of the learning problem.

Since this method requires computation of the gradient of the error function at each iteration step, we must guarantee the continuity and differentiability of the error function. Obviously we have to use a kind of activation function other than the step function used in perceptrons, because the composite function produced by interconnected perceptrons is discontinuous, and therefore the error function too.

Modes of Learning

There are two modes of learning to choose from: One is on-line (incremental) learning and the other is batch learning. In on-line (incremental) learning, each propagation is followed immediately by a weight update. In batch learning, many propagations occur before weight updating occurs. Batch learning requires more memory capacity, but on-line learning requires more updates.

Algorithm

Actual algorithm for a 3-layer network (only one hidden layer):

```
Initialize the weights in the network (often randomly)
 Do
     For each example e in the training set
        O = neural-net-output(network, e) ; forward pass
        T = teacher output for e
        Calculate error (T - O) at the output units
         Compute delta_wh for all weights from hidden layer
to output layer ; backward pass
          Compute delta_wi for all weights from input layer
to hidden layer ; backward pass continued
          Update the weights in the network
 Until all examples classified correctly or stopping criterion
satisfied
  Return the network
```

As the algorithm's name implies, the errors propagate backwards from the output nodes to the inner nodes. Technically speaking, backpropagation calculates the gradient of the error of the network regarding the network's modifiable weights. This gradient is almost always used in a simple stochastic gradient descent algorithm to find weights that minimize the error. Often the term "backpropagation" is used in a more general sense, to refer to the entire procedure encompassing both the calculation of the gradient and its use in stochastic gradient descent. Backpropagation usually allows quick convergence on satisfactory local minima for error in the kind of networks to which it is suited.

Backpropagation networks are necessarily multilayer perceptrons (usually with one input, one hidden, and one output layer). In order for the hidden layer to serve any useful function, multilayer networks must have non-linear activation functions for the multiple layers: a multilayer network using only linear activation functions is equivalent to some single layer, linear network. Non-linear activation functions that are commonly used include the logistic function, the softmax function, and the gaussian function.

The backpropagation algorithm for calculating a gradient has been rediscovered a number of times, and is a special case of a more general technique called automatic differentiation in the reverse accumulation mode.

It is also closely related to the Gauss–Newton algorithm, and is also part of continuing research in neural backpropagation.

Multithreaded Backpropagation

Backpropagation is an iterative process that can often take a great deal of time to complete. When multicore computers are used multithreaded techniques can greatly decrease the amount of time that backpropagation takes to converge. If batching is being used, it is relatively simple to adapt the backpropagation algorithm to operate in a multithreaded manner. The training data is broken up into equally large batches for each of the threads. Each thread executes the forward and backward propagations. The weight and threshold deltas are summed for each of the threads. At the end of each iteration all threads must pause briefly for the weight and threshold deltas to be summed and applied to the neural network. This process continues for each iteration. This multithreaded approach to backpropagation is used by the Encog Neural Network Framework.

Limitations

- The convergence obtained from backpropagation learning is very slow.
- The convergence in backpropagation learning is not guaranteed.
- The result may generally converge to any local minimum on the error surface, since stochastic gradient descent exists on a surface which is not flat.
- Backpropagation learning requires input scaling or normalization.

Backpropagation learns by iteratively processing a data set of training tuples, comparing the network's prediction for each tuple with the actual known target value.

```
Algorithm: Backpropagation. Neural network learning for
classification or prediction,
Using the backpropagation algorithm.
Input:
D, a data set consisting of the training tuples and their
associated target values;
l, the learning rate;
network, a multilayer feed-forward network.
Output: A trained neural network.
Method:
(1) Initialize all weights and biases in network;
(2) while terminating condition is not satisfied {
(3) for each training tuple X in D {
(4)// Propagate the inputs forward:
(5) for each input layer unit j {
(6) O j = I j ; // output of an input unit is its actual
input value
(7) for each hidden or output layer unit j {
(8) I j = εi wi j Oi + θj ; //compute the net input of unit
j with respect to the previous layer, i
(9) O j = 1-I j ; } // compute the output of each unit j 1+e
(10) // Backpropagate the errors:
(11) for each unit j in the output layer
(12) Err j = O j (1 - O j)(T j - O j); // compute the error
(13) for each unit j in the hidden layers, from the last to
the first hidden layer
(14) Err j = O j (1 - Oj) εk Errk w jk ; // compute the error
```

```
with respect to the
next higher layer, k
(15) for each weight wi j in network {
(16) Δwi j = (l)Err j Oi ; // weight increment
(17) wi j = wi j + Δwi j ; } // weight update
(18) for each bias θ j in network {
(19) Δθ j = (l)Err j ; // bias increment
(20) θ j = θ j + Δθ j ; } // bias update
(21)}}
```

ASSOCIATIVE CLASSIFICATION: CLASSIFICATION BY ASSOCIATION RULE ANALYSIS

Frequent patterns and their corresponding association or correlation rules characterize interesting relationships between attribute conditions and class labels, and thus have been recently used for effective classification. Association rules show strong associations between attribute-value pairs (or items) that occur frequently in a given data set. Association rules are commonly used to analyse the purchasing patterns of customers in a store.

Lazy Learners (or Learning from Your Neighbours)

Eager learners, when given a set of training tuples, will construct a generalization (*i.e.*, classification) model before receiving new (*e.g.*, test) tuples to classify. Lazy approach, in which the learner instead waits until the last minute before doing any model construction in order to classify a given test tuple. That is, when given a training tuple, a lazy learner simply stores it (or does only a little minor processing) and waits until it is given a test tuple. Only when it sees the test tuple does it perform generalization in order to classify the tuple based on its similarity to the stored training tuples.

Examples of lazy learners: k-nearest-neighbour classifiers and case-based reasoning classifiers.

Other Classification Methods Include

Genetic Algorithms Genetic algorithms attempt to incorporate ideas of natural evolution.

Rough Set Approach Rough set theory can be used for classification to discover structural relationships within imprecise or noisy data.

Fuzzy Set Approaches Rule-based systems for classification have the disadvantage that they involve sharp cutoffs for continuous attributes.

Prediction

Linear Regression Straight-line regression analysis involves a response variable, y, and a single predictor variable, x. It is the simplest form of regression, and models y as a linear function of x.

$$W_1 = \frac{\sum_{i=1}^{|D|}(x_i - \bar{x})(y_i - \bar{y})}{\sum_{i=1}^{|D|}(x_i - \bar{x})^2}$$

Nonlinear Regression

Transformation of a polynomial regression model to a linear regression model.

Consider a cubic polynomial relationship given by

$y = w_0 + w_1x_1 + w_2\, x_2 + w_3\, x_3$............ (1)

To convert this equation to linear form, we define new variables:

$x_1 = x$

$x_2 = x_2$

$x_3 = x_3$

Equation (1) can then be converted to linear form by applying the above assignments, resulting in the equation $y = w_0 + w_1x_1 + w_2\, x_2 + w_3\, x_3$, which is easily solved by the method of least squares using software for regression analysis. Note that polynomial regression is a special case of multiple regression. That is, the addition of high-order terms like x_2, x_3, and so on, which are simple functions of the single variable, x, can be considered equivalent to adding new independent variables.

Ensemble Methods—Increasing the Accuracy

Bagging

We first take an intuitive look at how bagging works as a method of increasing accuracy. For ease of explanation, we will assume at first that our model is a classifier.

```
Algorithm: Bagging. The bagging algorithm—create an ensemble
of models (classifiers or predictors) for a learning scheme
where each model gives an equally-weighted prediction.
Input:
D, a set of d training tuples;
k, the number of models in the ensemble;
a learning scheme (e.g., decision tree algorithm,
backpropagation, etc.)
Output: A composite model, M*.
Method:
for i = 1 to k do // create k models:
create bootstrap sample, Di, by sampling D with replacement;
use Di to derive a model, Mi ;
endfor
To use the composite model on a tuple, X:
```

```
if classification then
let each of the k models classify X and return the majority
vote;
if prediction then
let each of the k models predict a value for X and return
the average predicted value;
```

Boosting

In boosting, weights are assigned to each training tuple. A series of k classifiers is iteratively learned. After a classifier Mi is learned, the weights are updated to allow the subsequent classifier, Mi + 1, to "pay more attention" to the training tuples that were misclassified by Mi. The final boosted classifier, M*, combines the votes of each individual classifier, where the weight of each classifier's vote is a function of its accuracy. The boosting algorithm can be extended for the prediction of continuous values.

```
Algorithm: Adaboost. A boosting algorithm—create an ensemble
of classifiers.
Each one
gives
a weighted vote.
Input:
D, a set of d class-labelled training tuples;
k, the number of rounds (one classifier is generated per
round);
a classification learning scheme.
Output: A composite model.
Method:
initialize the weight of each tuple in D to 1/d;
for i = 1 to k do // for each round:
sample D with replacement according to the tuple weights to
obtain Di ;
use training set Di to derive a model, Mi ;
compute error(Mi), the error rate of Mi (Equation 6.66)
if error(Mi) > 0.5 then
reinitialize the weights to 1/d
go back to step 3 and try again;
endif
for each tuple in Di that was correctly classified do
multiply the weight of the tuple by error(Mi)/(1 - error(Mi));
// update weights
normalize the weight of each tuple;
endfor
To use the composite model to classify tuple, X:
```

```
initialize weight of each class to 0;
for i = 1 to k do // for each classifier:
wi = log
1-error(Mi)
;
error(Mi)
// weight of the classifier's vote
c = Mi (X); // get class prediction for X from Mi
add wi to weight for class c
endfor
return the class with the largest weight;
```

DATA PREPROCESSING

Computer data processing is any process that a computer programme does to enter data and summarize, analyse or otherwise convert data into usable information. The process may be automated and run on a computer. It involves recording, analysing, sorting, summarizing, calculating, disseminating and storing data. Because data are most useful when well-presented and actually *informative*, data-processing systems are often referred to as information systems. Nevertheless, the terms are roughly synonymous, performing similar conversions; data-processing systems typically manipulate raw data into information, and likewise information systems typically take raw data as input to produce information as output.

Data processing may or may not be distinguished from data conversion, when the process is merely to convert data to another format, and does not involve any data manipulation.

Today's real-world databases are highly susceptible to noisy, missing, and inconsistent data due to their typically huge size (often several gigabytes or more) and their likely origin from multiple, heterogenous sources. Low-quality data will lead to low-quality mining results. *"How can the data be preprocessed in order to help improve the quality of the data and, consequently, of the mining results? How can the data be preprocessed so as to improve the efficiency and ease of the mining process?"*

There are several data preprocessing techniques. *Data cleaning* can be applied to remove noise and correct inconsistencies in data. *Data integration* merges data from multiple sources into a coherent data store such as a data warehouse. *Data reduction* can reduce data size by, for instance, aggregating, eliminating redundant features, or clustering. *Data transformations* (*e.g.*, normalization) may be applied, where data are scaled to fall within a smaller range like 0.0 to 1.0. This can improve the accuracy and efficiency of mining algorithms involving distance measurements. These techniques are not mutually exclusive; they may work together. For example, data cleaning can involve transformations to correct wrong data, such as by transforming all entries for a *date* field to a common format.

WHY PREPROCESS THE DATA

Data have quality if they satisfy the requirements of the intended use. There are many factors comprising data quality, including *accuracy, completeness, consistency, timeliness, believability*, and *interpretability*.

Imagine that you are a manager at *All Electronics* and have been charged with analysing the company's data with respect to your branch's sales. You immediately set out to perform this task. You carefully inspect the company's database and data warehouse, identifying and selecting the attributes or dimensions (*e.g., item, price*, and *units sold*) to be included in your analysis. Alas! You notice that several of the attributes for various tuples have no recorded value. For your analysis, you would like to include information as to whether each item purchased was advertised as on sale, yet you discover that this information has not been recorded. Furthermore, users of your database system have reported errors, unusual values, and inconsistencies in the data recorded for some transactions. In other words, the data you wish to analyse by data mining techniques are *incomplete* (lacking attribute values or certain attributes of interest, or containing only aggregate data); *inaccurate* or *noisy* (containing errors, or values that deviate from the expected); and *inconsistent* (*e.g.*, containing discrepancies in the department codes used to categorize items).

This scenario illustrates three of the elements defining data quality: accuracy, completeness, and consistency. Inaccurate, incomplete, and inconsistent data are commonplace properties of large real-world databases and data warehouses. There are many possible reasons for inaccurate data (*i.e.*, having incorrect attribute values). The data collection instruments used may be faulty. There may have been human or computer errors occurring at data entry. Users may purposely submit incorrect data values for mandatory fields when they do not wish to submit personal information (*e.g.*, by choosing the default value "January 1" displayed for birthday). This is known as *disguised missing data*. Errors in data transmission can also occur. There may be technology limitations such as limited buffer size for coordinating synchronized data transfer and consumption.

Incorrect data may also result from inconsistencies in naming conventions or data codes, or inconsistent formats for input fields (*e.g., date*). Duplicate tuples also require data cleaning.

Incomplete data can occur for a number of reasons. Attributes of interest may not always be available, such as customer information for sales transaction data. Other data may not be included simply because they were not considered important at the time of entry. Relevant data may not be recorded due to a misunderstanding or because of equipment malfunctions. Data that were inconsistent with other recorded data may have been deleted. Furthermore, the recording of the data history or modifications may have been overlooked. Missing data, particularly for tuples with missing values for some attributes, may need to be inferred.

Recall that data quality depends on the intended use of the data. Two different users may have very different assessments of the quality of a given database. For example, a marketing analyst may need to access the database mentioned before for a list of customer addresses. Some of the addresses are outdated or incorrect, yet overall, 80% of the addresses are accurate. The marketing analyst considers this to be a large customer database for target marketing purposes and is pleased with the database's accuracy, although, as sales manager, you found the data inaccurate.

Timeliness also affects data quality. Suppose that you are overseeing the distribution of monthly sales bonuses to the top sales representatives at *All Electronics*. Several sales representatives, however, fail to submit their sales records on time at the end of the month. There are also a number of corrections and adjustments that flow in after the month's end. For a period of time following each month, the data stored in the database are incomplete. However, once all of the data are received, it is correct. The fact that the month-end data are not updated in a timely fashion has a negative impact on the data quality.

Two other factors affecting data quality are believability and interpretability. Believability reflects how much the data are trusted by users, while interpretability reflects how easy the data are understood. Suppose that a database, at one point, had several errors, all of which have since been corrected. The past errors, however, had caused many problems for sales department users, and so they no longer trust the data. The data also use many accounting codes, which the sales department does not know how to interpret. Even though the database is now accurate, complete, consistent, and timely, sales department users may regard it as of low quality due to poor believability and interpretability.

MAJOR TASKS IN DATA PREPROCESSING

Data cleaning routines work to "clean" the data by filling in missing values, smoothing noisy data, identifying or removing outliers, and resolving inconsistencies. If users believe the data are dirty, they are unlikely to trust the results of any data mining that has been applied. Furthermore, dirty data can cause confusion for the mining procedure, resulting in unreliable output. Although most mining routines have some procedures for dealing with incomplete or noisy data, they are not always robust. Instead, they may concentrate on avoiding over-fitting the data to the function being modelled. Therefore, a useful preprocessing step is to run your data through some data cleaning routines. Getting back to your task at *All Electronics*, suppose that you would like to include data from multiple sources in your analysis. This would involve integrating multiple databases, data cubes, or files (*i.e.*, data integration). Yet some attributes representing a given concept may have different names in different databases, causing inconsistencies and redundancies. For example, the attribute for customer identification may be referred to as *customer id* in one data store and *cust id* in another. Naming inconsistencies may also occur for attribute values. For example, the same first name could be registered as "Bill" in one database, "William" in another, and "B." in a third. Furthermore, you suspect that some attributes may be inferred from others (*e.g.*, annual revenue). Having a large amount of redundant data may slow down or confuse the knowledge discovery process. Clearly, in addition to data cleaning, steps must be taken to help avoid redundancies during data integration. Typically, data cleaning and data integration are performed as a preprocessing step when preparing data for a data warehouse. Additional data cleaning can be performed to detect and remove redundancies that may have resulted from data integration.

You wonder, as you consider your data even further. *"The data set we have selected for analysis is HUGE, which is sure to slow down the mining process. Is there a way we can reduce the size of the data set without jeopardizing the data mining results?"*

Data reduction obtains a reduced representation of the data set that is much smaller in volume, yet produces the same (or almost the same) analytical results. Data reduction strategies include *dimensionality reduction* and *numerosity reduction.*

In dimensionality reduction, data encoding schemes are applied so as to obtain a reduced or "compressed" representation of the original data. Examples include data compression techniques (*e.g.*, *wavelet transforms* and *principal components analysis*), *attribute subset selection* (*e.g.*, removing irrelevant attributes), and *attribute construction* (*e.g.*, where a small set of more useful attributes is derived from the original set).

In numerosity reduction, the data are replaced by alternative, smaller representations using parametric models (*e.g.*, *regression* or *log-linear models*) or nonparametric models (*e.g.*, *histograms, clusters, sampling*, or *data aggregation*).

Getting back to your data, you have decided, say, that you would like to use a distance based mining algorithm for your analysis, such as neural networks, nearest-neighbour classifiers, or clustering. Such methods provide better results if the data to be analysed have been *normalized*, that is, scaled to a smaller range such as [0.0, 1.0]. Your customer data, for example, contain the attributes *age* and *annual salary*. The *annual salary* attribute usually takes much larger values than *age*. Therefore, if the attributes are left unnormalized, the distance measurements taken on *annual salary* will generally outweigh distance measurements taken on *age*. *Discretization* and *concept hierarchy generation* can also be useful, where raw data values for attributes are replaced by ranges or higher conceptual levels. For example, raw values for *age* may be replaced by higher-level concepts, such as *youth, adult*, or *senior*.

Discretization and concept hierarchy generation are powerful tools for data mining in that they allow data mining at multiple abstraction levels. Normalization, data given concept may have different names in different databases, causing inconsistencies and redundancies. For example, the attribute for customer identification may be referred to as *customer id* in one data store and *cust id* in another. Naming inconsistencies may also occur for attribute values. For example, the same first name could be registered as

"Bill" in one database, "William" in another, and "B." in a third. Furthermore, you suspect that some attributes may be inferred from others (*e.g.*, annual revenue). Having a large amount of redundant data may slow down or confuse the knowledge discovery process. Clearly, in addition to data cleaning, steps must be taken to help avoid redundancies during data integration. Typically, data cleaning and data integration are performed as a preprocessing step when preparing data for a data warehouse. Additional data cleaning can be performed to detect and remove redundancies that may have resulted from data integration. Data reduction obtains a reduced representation of the data set that is much smaller in volume, yet produces the same (or almost the same) analytical results. Data reduction strategies include *dimensionality reduction* and *numerosity reduction*. In dimensionality reduction, data encoding schemes are applied so as to obtain a reduced or "compressed" representation of the original data. Examples include data compression techniques (*e.g.*, *wavelet transforms* and *principal components analysis*), *attribute subset selection* (*e.g.*, removing irrelevant attributes), and *attribute construction* (*e.g.*, where a small set of more useful attributes is derived from the original set).

DATA CLEANING

Data cleansing, data cleaning, or data scrubbing is the process of detecting and correcting (or removing) corrupt or inaccurate records from a record set, table, or database. Used mainly in databases, the term refers to identifying incomplete, incorrect, inaccurate, irrelevant, *etc.* parts of the data and then replacing, modifying, or deleting this dirty data. After cleansing, a data set will be consistent with other similar data sets in the system. The inconsistencies detected or removed may have been originally caused by user entry errors, by corruption in transmission or storage, or by different data dictionary definitions of similar entities in different stores. Data cleansing differs from data validation in that validation almost invariably means data is rejected from the system at entry and is performed at entry time, rather than on batches of data. The actual process of data cleansing may involve removing typographical errors or validating and correcting values against a known list of entities. The validation may be strict (such as rejecting any address that does not have a valid postal code) or fuzzy (such as correcting records that partially match existing, known records). Real-world data tend to be incomplete, noisy, and inconsistent. *Data cleaning* (or *data cleansing*) routines attempt to fill in missing values, smooth out noise while identifying outliers, and correct inconsistencies in the data.

The process of data cleansing :

- Data auditing: The data is audited with the use of statistical methods to detect anomalies and contradictions. This eventually gives an indication of the characteristics of the anomalies and their locations.

- Workflow specification: The detection and removal of anomalies is performed by a sequence of operations on the data known as the workflow. It is specified after the process of auditing the data and is crucial in achieving the end product of high-quality data. In order to achieve a proper workflow, the causes of the anomalies and errors in the data have to be closely considered. For instance, if we find that an anomaly is a result of typing errors in data input stages, the layout of the keyboard can help in manifesting possible solutions.
- Workflow execution: In this stage, the workflow is executed after its specification is complete and its correctness is verified. The implementation of the workflow should be efficient, even on large sets of data, which inevitably poses a trade-off because the execution of a data-cleansing operation can be computationally expensive.
- Post-processing and controlling: After executing the cleansing workflow, the results are inspected to verify correctness. Data that could not be corrected during execution of the workflow is manually corrected, if possible. The result is a new cycle in the data-cleansing process where the data is audited again to allow the specification of an additional workflow to further cleanse the data by automatic processing.

Popular methods used :

- Parsing: Parsing in data cleansing is performed for the detection of syntax errors. A parser decides whether a string of data is acceptable within the allowed data specification. This is similar to the way a parser works with grammars and languages.
- Data transformation: Data transformation allows the mapping of the data from its given format into the format expected by the appropriate application. This includes value conversions or translation functions, as well as normalizing numeric values to conform to minimum and maximum values.
- Duplicate elimination: Duplicate detection requires an algorithm for determining whether data contains duplicate representations of the same entity. Usually, data is sorted by a key that would bring duplicate entries closer together for faster identification.
- Statistical methods: By analysing the data using the values of mean, standard deviation, range, or clustering algorithms, it is possible for an expert to find values that are unexpected and thus erroneous. Although the correction of such data is difficult since the true value is not known, it can be resolved by setting the values to an average or other statistical value. Statistical methods can also be used to handle missing values which can be replaced by one or more plausible values, which are usually obtained by extensive data augmentation algorithms.

Missing Values

Imagine that you need to analyse sales and customer data. You note that many tuples have no recorded value for several attributes such as customer *income*. How can you go about filling in the missing values for this attribute? Let's look at the following methods.

Ignore the tuple: This is usually done when the class label is missing (assuming the mining task involves classification). This method is not very effective, unless the tuple contains several attributes with missing values. It is especially poor when the percentage of missing values per attribute varies considerably. By ignoring the tuple, we do not make use of the remaining attributes' values in the tuple. Such data could have been useful to the task at hand.

Fill in the missing value manually: In general, this approach is time consuming and may not be feasible given a large data set with many missing values. Use a global constant to fill in the missing value: Replace all missing attribute values by the same constant such as a label like *"Unknown"* or 1. If missing values are replaced by, say, *"Unknown,"* then the mining programme may mistakenly think that they form an interesting concept, since they all have a value in common—that of *"Unknown."* Hence, although this method is simple, it is not foolproof.

Use a measure of central tendency for the attribute (*e.g.*, the mean or median) to fill in the missing value: For normal (symmetric) data distributions, the mean can be used, while skewed data distribution should employ the median. For example, suppose that the data distribution regarding the income of customers is symmetric and that the mean income is $56,000. Use this value to replace the missing value for *income*.

Use the attribute mean or median for all samples belonging to the same class as the given tuple: For example, if classifying customers according to *credit risk*, we may replace the missing value with the mean *income* value for customers in the same credit risk category as that of the given tuple. If the data distribution for a given class is skewed, the median value is a better choice.

Use the most probable value to fill in the missing value: This may be determined with regression, inference-based tools using a Bayesian formalism, or decision tree induction. For example, using the other customer attributes in your data set, you may construct a decision tree to predict the missing values for *income*. Methods 3 through 6 bias the data—the filled-in value may not be correct. Method 6, however, is a popular strategy. In comparison to the other methods, it uses the most information from the present data to predict missing values. By considering the other attributes' values in its estimation of the missing value for *income*, there is a greater chance that the relationships between *income* and the other attributes are preserved.

It is important to note that, in some cases, a missing value may not imply an error in the data! For example, when applying for a credit card, candidates may be asked to supply their driver's license number. Candidates who do not have a driver's license may naturally leave this field blank. Forms should allow respondents to specify values such as "not applicable." Software routines may also be used to uncover other null values (*e.g.*, "don't know," "?" or "none"). Ideally, each attribute should have one or more rules regarding the *null* condition. The rules may specify whether or not nulls are allowed and/or how such values should be handled or transformed. Fields may also be intentionally left blank if they are to be provided in a later step of the business process. Hence, although we can try our best to clean the data after it is seized, good database and data entry procedure design should help minimize the number of missing values or errors in the first place.

Noisy Data

"What is noise?"

Noise is a random error or variance in a measured variable. Previously, we saw how some basic statistical description techniques (*e.g.*, box plots and scatter plots), and methods of data visualization can be used to identify outliers, which may represent noise. Given a numeric attribute such as, say, *price*, how can we "smooth" out the data to remove the noise? Let's look at the following data smoothing techniques.

Binning: Binning methods smooth a sorted data value by consulting its "neighbourhood," that is, the values around it. The sorted values are distributed into a number of "buckets," or *bins*. Because binning methods consult the neighbourhood of values, they perform *local* smoothing. In this example, the data for *price* are first sorted and then partitioned into *equal-frequency* bins of size 3 (*i.e.*, each bin contains three values). In smoothing by bin means, each value in a bin is replaced by the mean value of the bin. For example, the mean of the values 4, 8, and 15 in Bin 1 is 9. Therefore, each original value in this bin is replaced by the value 9.

Similarly, smoothing by bin medians can be employed, in which each bin value is replaced by the bin median. In smoothing by bin boundaries, the minimum and maximum values in a given bin are identified as the *bin boundaries*. Each bin value is then replaced by the closest boundary value. In general, the larger the width, the greater the effect of the smoothing. Alternatively, bins may be *equal width*, where the interval range of values in each bin is constant. Binning is also used as a discretization technique.

Regression: Data smoothing can also be done by regression, a technique that conforms data values to a function. *Linear regression* involves finding the "best" line to fit two attributes (or variables) so that one attribute can be used to predict the other.

Multiple-linear-regression is an extension of linear regression, where more than two attributes are involved and the data are fit to a multidimensional surface.

Outlier analysis: Outliers may be detected by clustering, for example, where similar values are organized into groups, or "clusters." Intuitively, values that fall outside of the set of clusters may be considered outliers. Many data smoothing methods are also used for data discretization (a form of data transformation) and data reduction. For example, the binning techniques described before reduce the number of distinct values per attribute. This acts as a form of data reduction for logic-based data mining methods, such as decision tree induction, which repeatedly makes value comparisons on sorted data. Concept hierarchies are a form of data discretization that can also be used for data smoothing. A concept hierarchy for *price*, for example, may map real *price* values into *inexpensive, moderately priced,* and *expensive,* thereby reducing the number of data values to be handled by the mining process.

DATA CLEANING AS A PROCESS

Missing values, noise, and inconsistencies contribute to inaccurate data. So far, we have looked at techniques for handling missing data and for smoothing data. *"But data cleaning* is a big job. What about data cleaning as a process? How exactly does one proceed in tackling this task? Are there any tools out there to help?"

The first step in data cleaning as a process is *discrepancy detection*. Discrepancies can be caused by several factors, including poorly designed data entry forms that have many optional fields, human error in data entry, deliberate errors (*e.g.*, respondents not wanting to divulge information about themselves), and data decay (*e.g.*, outdated addresses). Discrepancies may also arise from inconsistent data representations and inconsistent use of codes. Other sources of discrepancies include errors in instrumentation devices that record data and system errors. Errors can also occur when the data are (inadequately) used for purposes other than originally intended. There may also be inconsistencies due to data integration (*e.g.*, where a given attribute can have different names in different databases).

"So, how can we proceed with discrepancy detection?" As a starting point, use any knowledge you may already have regarding properties of the data. Such knowledge or "data about data" is referred to as metadata. This is where we can make use of the knowledge we gained about our data. For example, what are the data type and domain of each attribute? What are the acceptable values for each attribute? The basic statistical data descriptions are useful here to grasp data trends and identify anomalies. For example, find the mean, median, and mode values. Are the data symmetric or skewed? What is the range of values? Do all values fall within the expected range? What is the standard deviation of each attribute? Values that are more than two standard deviations away from the mean for a given attribute may be flagged as potential outliers. Are there any known dependencies between attributes? In this step, you may write your own scripts and/or use some of the tools.

From this, you may find noise, outliers, and unusual values that need investigation. As a data analyst, you should be on the lookout for the inconsistent use of codes and any inconsistent data representations.

Field overloading is another error source that typically results when developers squeeze new attribute definitions into unused (bit) portions of already defined attributes (*e.g.*, an unused bit of an attribute that has a value range that uses only, say, 31 out of 32 bits).

The data should also be examined regarding unique rules, consecutive rules, and null rules. A unique rule says that each value of the given attribute must be different from all other values for that attribute. A consecutive rule says that there can be no missing values between the lowest and highest values for the attribute, and that all values must also be unique (*e.g.*, as in check numbers). A null rule specifies the use of blanks, question marks, special characters, or other strings that may indicate the null condition (*e.g.*, where a value for a given attribute is not available), and how such values should be handled. As mentioned earlier, reasons for missing values may include (1) the person originally asked to provide a value for the attribute refuses and/or finds that the information requested is not applicable (*e.g.*, a *license number* attribute left blank by nondrivers); (2) the data entry person does not know the correct value; or (3) the value is to be provided by a later step of the process. The null rule should specify how to record the null condition, for example, such as to store zero for numeric attributes, a blank for character attributes, or any other conventions that may be in use (*e.g.*, entries like "don't know" or "?" should be transformed to blank).

There are a number of different commercial tools that can aid in the discrepancy detection step. Data scrubbing tools use simple domain knowledge (*e.g.*, knowledge of postal addresses and spell-checking) to detect errors and make corrections in the data. These tools rely on parsing and fuzzy matching techniques when cleaning data from multiple sources. Data auditing tools find discrepancies by analysing the data to discover rules and relationships, and detecting data that violate such conditions. They are variants of data mining tools. For example, they may employ statistical analysis to find correlations, or clustering to identify outliers.

Some data inconsistencies may be corrected manually using external references. For example, errors made at data entry may be corrected by performing a paper trace. Most errors, however, will require *data transformations*. That is, once we find discrepancies, we typically need to define and apply (a series of) transformations to correct them.

Commercial tools can assist in the data transformation step. Data migration tools allow simple transformations to be specified such as to replace the string *"gender"* by *"sex."* ETL (extraction/transformation/loading) tools allow users to specify transforms through a graphical user interface (GUI). These tools typically support only a restricted set of transforms so that, often, we may also choose to write custom scripts for this step of the data cleaning process. The two-step process of discrepancy detection and data transformation (to correct discrepancies) iterates. This process, however, is error-prone and time consuming. Some transformations may introduce more discrepancies. Some *nested discrepancies* may only be detected after others have been fixed. For example, a typo such as "20010" in a year field may only surface once all date values have been converted to a uniform format.

Transformations are often done as a batch process while the user waits without feedback. Only after the transformation is complete can the user go back and check that no new anomalies have been mistakenly created. Typically, numerous iterations are required before the user is satisfied. Any tuples that cannot be automatically handled by a given transformation are typically written to a file without any explanation regarding the reasoning behind their failure. As a result, the entire data cleaning process also suffers from a lack of interactivity.

New approaches to data cleaning emphasize increased interactivity. Potter's Wheel, for example, is a publicly available data cleaning tool that integrates discrepancy detection and transformation. Users gradually build a series of transformations by composing and debugging individual transformations, one step at a time, on a spreadsheet-like interface. The transformations can be specified graphically or by providing examples.

Results are shown immediately on the records that are visible on the screen. The user can choose to undo the transformations, so that transformations that introduced additional errors can be "erased." The tool automatically performs discrepancy checking in the background on the latest transformed view of the data. Users can gradually develop and refine transformations as discrepancies are found, leading to more effective and efficient data cleaning. Another approach to increased interactivity in data cleaning is the development of declarative languages for the specification of data transformation operators. Such work focuses on defining powerful extensions to SQL and algorithms that enable users to express data cleaning specifications efficiently.

DATA INTEGRATION

Data mining often requires data integration—the merging of data from multiple data stores. Careful integration can help reduce and avoid redundancies and inconsistencies in the resulting data set. This can help improve the accuracy and speed of the subsequent data mining process.

The semantic heterogeneity and structure of data pose great challenges in data integration. How can we match schema and objects from different sources? This is the essence of the *entity identification problem.*

Entity Identification Problem

It is likely that your data analysis task will involve *data integration,* which combines data from multiple sources into a coherent data store, as in data warehousing. These sources may include multiple databases, data cubes, or flat files.

There are a number of issues to consider during data integration. *Schema integration* and *object matching* can be tricky. How can equivalent real-world entities from multiple data sources be matched up? This is referred to as the entity identification problem.

For example, how can the data analyst or the computer be sure that *customer id* in one database and *cust number* in another refer to the same attribute? Examples of metadata for each attribute include the name, meaning, data type, and range of values permitted for the attribute, and null rules for handling blank, zero, or null values.

Such metadata can be used to help avoid errors in schema integration. The metadata may also be used to help transform the data (*e.g.*, where data codes for *pay type* in one database may be *"H"* and *"S"* but *1* and *2* in another). Hence, this step also relates to data cleaning, as described earlier. When matching attributes from one database to another during integration, special attention must be paid to the *structure* of the data. This is to ensure that any attribute functional dependencies and referential constraints in the source system match those in the target system. For example, in one system, a *discount* may be applied to the order, whereas in another system it is applied to each individual line item within the order. If this is not caught before integration, items in the target system may be improperly discounted.

Redundancy and Correlation Analysis

Redundancy is another important issue in data integration. An attribute (such as *annual revenue*, for instance) may be redundant if it can be "derived" from another attribute or set of attributes. Inconsistencies in attribute or dimension naming can also cause redundancies in the resulting data set.

Some redundancies can be detected by correlation analysis. Given two attributes, such analysis can measure how strongly one attribute implies the other, based on the available data. For nominal data, we use the X^2 (*chi-square*) test. For numeric attributes, we can use the *correlation coefficient* and *covariance*, both of which access how one attribute's values vary from those of another.

AGGREGATION

Data aggregation is any process in which information is gathered and expressed in a summary form, for purposes such as statistical analysis. A common aggregation purpose is to get more information about particular groups based on specific variables such as age, profession, or income. The information about such groups can then be used for Web site personalization to choose content and advertising likely to appeal to an individual belonging to one or more groups for which data has been collected. For example, a site that sells music CDs might advertise certain CDs based on the age of the user and the data aggregate for their age group. Online analytic processing (OLAP) is a simple type of data aggregation in which the marketer uses an online reporting mechanism to process the information.

Data aggregation can be user-based: personal data aggregation services offer the user a single point for collection of their personal information from other Web sites. The customer uses a single master personal identification number (PIN) to give them access to their various accounts (such as those for financial institutions, airlines, book and music clubs, and so on). Performing this type of data aggregation is sometimes referred to as "screen scraping."

SAMPLING

In the past, many businesses and other organizations were unable or unwilling to store their historical data. Online transaction processing (OLTP) systems, rather than decision support systems, were key to business. A primary reason for not storing historical data was the fact that disk space was comparatively more expensive than it is now. Even if the storage space was available, IT resources often could not be spared to implement and maintain enterprise wide endeavors like decision support systems.

Times have changed. As disk storage has become increasingly affordable, businesses have realised that their data can, in fact, be used as a corporate asset for competitive advantage. For example, customers' previous buying patterns often are good predictors of their future buying patterns. As a result, many businesses now search their data to reveal those historical patterns. To benefit from the assets bound up in their data, organizations have invested numerous resources to develop data warehouses and data marts. The result has been substantial returns on these kinds of investments. However, now that affordable systems exist for storing and organizing large amounts of data, businesses face new challenges. For example, how can hardware and software systems sift through vast warehouses of data efficiently?

What process leads from data, to information, to competitive advantage? While data storage has become cheaper, CPU, throughput, memory management, and network bandwidth continue to be constraints when it comes to processing large quantities of data. Many IT managers and business analysts are so overwhelmed with the sheer volume, they do not know where to start. Given these massive amounts of data, many ask, "How can we even begin to move from data to information?" The answer is in a data mining process that relies on sampling, visual representations for data exploration, statistical analysis and modelling, and assessment of the results.

Over Sampling and under Sampling in Data Analysis

Over sampling and under sampling in data analysis are techniques used to adjust the class distribution of a data set (*i.e.* the ratio between the different classes/categories represented). Over sampling and under sampling are opposite and roughly equivalent techniques. They both involve using a bias to select more samples from one class than from another.

The usual reason for over sampling is to correct for a bias in the original dataset. One scenario where it is useful is when training a classifier using labelled training data from a biased source, since labelled training data is valuable but often comes from un-representative sources.

For example, suppose we have a sample of 1000 people of which 66% are male (perhaps the sample was collected at a football match). We know the general population is 50% female, and we may wish to adjust our dataset to represent this. Simple *over sampling* will select each female example twice, and this copying will produce a balanced dataset of 1333 samples with 50% female. Simple *under sampling* will drop some of the male samples at random to give a balanced dataset of 667 samples, again with 50% female. There are also more complex over sampling techniques, including the creation of artificial data points.

DIMENSIONALITY REDUCTION

Spectral analysis-based dimensionality reduction algorithms are important and have been popularly applied in data mining and computer vision applications. To date many algorithms have been developed, *e.g.*, principal component analysis, locally linear embedding, Laplacian eigenmaps, and local tangent space alignment. All of these algorithms have been designed intuitively and pragmatically, *i.e.*, on the basis of the experience and knowledge of experts for their own purposes. Therefore, it will be more informative to provide a systematic framework for understanding the common properties and intrinsic difference in different algorithms. In this section, we propose such a framework, named "patch alignment" quo which consists of two stages: part optimization and whole alignment. The framework reveals that (1) algorithms are intrinsically different in the patch optimization stage and (2) all algorithms share an almost identical whole alignment stage. As an application of this framework, we develop a new dimensionality reduction algorithm, termed discriminative locality alignment (DLA), by imposing discriminative information in the part optimization stage. DLA can (1) attack the distribution nonlinearity of measurements; (2) preserve the discriminative ability; and (3) avoid the small-sample-size problem. Thorough empirical studies demonstrate the effectiveness of DLA compared with representative dimensionality reduction algorithms.

Feature Subset Selection

In machine learning, the problem of supervised classification is concerned with using labelled examples to induce a model that classifies objects into a finite set of known classes. The examples are described by a vector of numeric or nominal features. Some of these features may be irrelevant or redundant. Avoiding irrelevant or redundant features is important because they may have a negative effect on the accuracy of the classifier. In addition, by using fewer features we may reduce the cost of acquiring the data and improve the comprehensibility of the classification model.

MEASURES OF SIMILARITY AND DISSIMILARITY

Information retrieval, similarities/dissimilarities, finding and implementing the correct measure are at the heart of data mining. The oldest approach to solving this problem was to have people work with people using meta data (libraries). This functioned for millennia. Roughly one century ago the Boolean searching machines entered but with one large problem. People do not think in Boolean terms which require structured data thus data mining slowly emerged where priorities and unstructured data could be managed.

Are they alike (similarity)? Are they different (dissimilarity)?

To what degree are they similar or dissimilar (numerical measure)? How are they alike/different and how is this to be expressed (attributes)? Measuring similarities/dissimilarities is fundamental to data mining; almost everything else is based on measuring distance. Euclidean Distance: is the distance between two points (p, q) in any dimension of space and is the most common use of distance. When data is dense or continuous, this is the best proximity measure.

$$d(p,q)) = \sqrt{\sum_{k=1}^{n}(p_k - y_k)^2}$$

```
def sim_distance(prefs, person1, person2):
   # Get the list of shared_items
    si = {}
    for item in prefs[person1]:
        if item in prefs[person2]:
            si[item] = 1
    # If they have no ratings in common, return 0
    if len(si)==0: return 0
    # Add up the squares of all the differences
      sum_of_squares = sum([pow(prefs[person1][item]-
prefs[person2][item],2)
           for item in si])
 #         for item in prefs[person1] if item in
prefs[person2]])
 # Euclidean distance, note this one is smaller the closer
they are together
 # return sqrt(sum_of_squares)
 # To give us a higher value when two points are close add
one and take inverse
    return 1/(1+sqrt(sum_of_squares))
```

Pearson correlation Coefficient: measures the strength and the direction of the linear relationship between two variables. The value is always between

[-1; 1] where 1 is strong positive relation, 0 is no relation and -1 is a strong negative correlation. It is the most widely used correlation coefficient and works very well when all is linear but not with curvilinear.

$$p - \frac{\text{cov}(x, y)}{\sigma_x, \sigma_y}$$

```
# Returns the Pearson correlation coefficient for p1 and p2
def sim_pearson(prefs, p1, p2):
     # Get the list of mutually rated items
     si={}
     for item in prefs[p1]:
          if item in prefs[p2]: si[item]=1

    # I'm making a change here, makes no sense to first add
up all calculations
    # and then check if sum is zero or not, better check and
then add. CK
     # if they have no ratings in common, return 0
     if len(si)==0: return 0

     # Sum calculations
       n=len(si)

     # Add all the preferences
     sum1=sum([prefs[p1][it] for it in si])
     sum2=sum([prefs[p2][it] for it in si])

     # Sums of the squares
     sum1Sq=sum([pow(prefs[p1][it],2) for it in si])
     sum2Sq=sum([pow(prefs[p2][it],2) for it in si])

     # Sum of the products
      pSum=sum([prefs[p1][it]*prefs[p2][it] for it in si])

     # Calculate r (Pearson score)
     num=pSum-(sum1*sum2/n)
    den=sqrt((sum1Sq-pow(sum1,2)/n)*(sum2Sq-pow(sum2,2)/n))
     if den==0: return 0

     r=num/den

     return r
```

Cosine Similarity: is often used when comparing two documents against each other. It measures the angle between the two vectors. If the value is zero the angle between the two vectors is 90 degrees and they share no terms. If the value is 1 the two vectors are the same except for magnitude. Cosine is used when data is sparse, asymmetric and there is a similarity of lacking characteristics.

$$\cos(x,y) = \frac{x.y}{\|x\| \cdot \|y\|}$$

```
# Returns the Cosine Similarity Score for p1 and p2
def sim_cosine(prefs, p1, p2):
     # Get the list of mutually rated items
     si={}
     for item in prefs[p1]:
       if item in prefs[p2]: si[item]=1

     # if they have no ratings in common, return 0
     if len(si)==0: return 0

     # Calcuate the normalized vector
    num_p = sum([prefs[p1][it]*prefs[p2][it] for it in si])
    norm_p1 = sqrt(sum([pow(prefs[p1][it],2) for it in si]))
    norm_p2 = sqrt(sum([pow(prefs[p2][it],2) for it in si]))

     # Calculate the Cosine Similarity Score.
     s_cos =  cos(num_p / (norm_p1*norm_p2))

     return s_cos
```

Extended Jaccard Coefficient is used to compare documents. It measures the similarity of two sets by comparing the size of the overlap against the size of the two sets. Should the two sets have only binary attributes then it reduces to the Jaccard Coefficient.

As with cosine, this is useful under the same data conditions and is well suited for market-basket data.

$$EJ(x,y) = \frac{x.y}{\|x\|^2 + \|y\|^2 - x.y}$$

```
# Returns the Extended Jaccard Coefficient for p1 and p2
def sim_ext_jaccard(prefs, p1, p2):
     # Get the list of mutually rated items
     si={}
     for item in prefs[p1]:
          if item in prefs[p2]: si[item]=1
     # if they have no ratings in common, return 0
                    if     len(si)==0:     return     0
```

```
    # Calcuate the different parts of the of score
     cross_p  = sum  ([prefs[p1][it]*prefs[p2][it]  for it  in
si])
    norm_p1  =  sum  ([pow(prefs[p1][it],2)  for it in si])
     norm_p2  =  sum  ([pow(prefs[p2][it],2)  for it  in  si])

    # Calculate the Extended Jaccard Coefficient.
    EJ  =  cross_p /(norm_p1 + norm_p2 - cross_p)

    return EJ
```

EXPLORING DATA

You must understand the data in order to make appropriate decisions when you create the mining models. Exploration techniques include calculating the minimum and maximum values, calculating mean and standard deviations, and looking at the distribution of the data. For example, you might determine by reviewing the maximum, minimum, and mean values that the data is not representative of your customers or business processes, and that you therefore must obtain more balanced data or review the assumptions that are the basis for your expectations. Standard deviations and other distribution values can provide useful information about the stability and accuracy of the results. A large standard deviation can indicate that adding more data might help you improve the model. Data that strongly deviates from a standard distribution might be skewed, or might represent an accurate picture of a real-life problem, but make it difficult to fit a model to the data.

By exploring the data in light of your own understanding of the business problem, you can decide if the dataset contains flawed data, and then you can devise a strategy for fixing the problems or gain a deeper understanding of the behaviours that are typical of your business.

You can use tools such as Master Data Services to canvass available sources of data and determine their availability for data mining. You can use tools such as SQL Server Data Quality Services, or the Data Profiler in Integration Services, to analyse the distribution of your data and repair issues such as wrong or missing data.

After you have defined your sources, you combine them in a Data Source view by using the Data Source View Designer in SQL Server Data Tools. This designer also contains some several tools that you can use to explore the data and verify that it will work for creating a model. Note that when you create a model, Analysis Services automatically creates statistical summaries of the data contained in the model, which you can query to use in reports or further analysis.

3

Cluster Analysis: Basic Concepts and Algorithms

CLUSTER ANALYSIS

The process of grouping a set of physical or abstract objects into classes of similar objects is called clustering.

The following are typical requirements of clustering in data mining:

- Scalability
- Ability to deal with different types of attributes
- Discovery of clusters with arbitrary shape
- Minimal requirements for domain knowledge to determine input parameters
- Ability to deal with noisy data
- Incremental clustering and insensitivity to the order of input records:
- High dimensionality
- Constraint-based clustering
- Interpretability and usability.

TYPES OF DATA IN CLUSTER ANALYSIS

Data matrix (or object-by-variable structure): This represents n objects, such as persons, with p variables (also called measurements or attributes), such as age, height, weight, gender, and so on. The structure is in the form of a relational table, or n-by-p matrix (n objects ×p variables)

$$
\begin{matrix}
x11 & x12 \ldots\ldots\ldots\ldots x1n \\
x21 & x22 \ldots\ldots\ldots\ldots x2n \\
. & . \\
. & . \\
. & . \\
. & . \\
xm1 & xm2 \ldots\ldots\ldots\ldots xmn
\end{matrix}
$$

Dissimilarity matrix (or object-by-object structure): This stores a collection of proximities that are available for all pairs of n objects. It is often represented by an n-by-n table:

$$
\begin{matrix}
0 \\
d(2.1)\ 0 \\
d(3,1)\ d(3,2) 0\ . \\
. \quad . \\
. \quad . \\
. \quad . \\
d(m,1) d(m,2) 0
\end{matrix}
$$

Interval-Scaled Variables Interval-scaled variables are continuous measurements of a roughly linear scale. Typical examples include weight and height, latitude.

Binary Variables A binary variable has only two states: 0 or 1.

A categorical variable is a generalization of the binary variable in that it can take on more than two states. For example, map colour is a categorical variable that may have, say, five states: maroon, yellow, orange, pink, and blue.

A discrete ordinal variable resembles a categorical variable, except that the M states of the ordinal value are ordered in a meaningful sequence.

A ratio-scaled variable makes a positive measurement on a nonlinear scale, such as an exponential scale, approximately following the formula

AeBt or Ae–Bt

MAJOR CLUSTERING METHODS

Methods used in clustering are :

- Partitioning method.
- Hierarchical method.
- Data Density based method.
- Grid based method.
- Model Based Method.

Partitioning Methods

A Classical Partitioning Method used is k-Means and k-Medoids The k-Means method is a Centroid-based technique. Typically, the square-error criterion is used and is defined as

$$E = \sum_{i=1}^{i} \sum_{p \in C_i} | p - m_i |^2,$$

The k-means Algorithm for Partitioning

```
Algorithm: k-means. The k-means algorithm for partitioning,
where each cluster's
```

```
centre is represented by the mean value of the objects in
the cluster.
Input:
k: the number of clusters,
D: a data set containing n objects.
Output: A set of k clusters.
Method:
(1) arbitrarily choose k objects from D as the initial cluster
centres;
(2) repeat
(3) (re)assign each object to the cluster to which the object
is the most similar,
based on the mean value of the objects in the cluster;
(4) update the cluster means, i.e., calculate the mean value
of the objects for each cluster;
(5)until no change;
```

Representative Object-Based Technique: The k-Medoids Method

```
   Algorithm: k-medoids. PAM, a k-medoids algorithm for
partitioning based on medoid
or central objects.
Input:
k: the number of clusters,
D: a data set containing n objects.
Output: A set of k clusters.
Method:
(1) arbitrarily choose k objects in D as the initial
representative objects or seeds;
(2) repeat
(3) assign each remaining object to the cluster with the
nearest representative object;
(4) randomly select a nonrepresentative object, orandom ;
(5) compute the total cost, S, of swapping representative
object, oj, with orandom ;
(6) if S < 0 then swap oj with orandom to form the new set
of k representative objects;
(7)until no change;
```

Hierarchical Methods in Clustering

In general, there are two types of hierarchical clustering methods: Agglomerative hierarchical clustering: This bottom-up strategy starts by placing each object in its own cluster and then merges these atomic clusters into larger and larger clusters, until all of the objects are in a single cluster or until certain termination conditions are satisfied. Most hierarchical clustering methods belong to this category. They differ only in their definition of inter-cluster similarity.

Divisive hierarchical clustering: This top-down strategy does the reverse of agglomerative hierarchical clustering by starting with all objects in one cluster. It subdivides the cluster into smaller and smaller pieces, until each object forms a cluster on its own or until it satisfies certain termination conditions, such as a desired number of clusters is obtained or the diameter of each cluster is within a certain threshold.

Density-Based Methods in Clustering

There are three methods :

- DBSCAN: A Density-Based Clustering Method Based on Connected Regions with Sufficiently High Density
- OPTICS: Ordering Points to Identify the Clustering Structure
- DENCLUE: Clustering Based on Density Distribution Functions.

Grid-Based Methods in Clustering

The grid-based clustering approach uses a multiresolution grid data structure. It quantizes the object space into a finite number of cells that form a grid structure on which all of the operations for clustering are performed.

STING: Statistical Information Grid

STING is a grid-based multi-resolution clustering technique in which the spatial area is divided into rectangular cells.

There are usually several levels of such rectangular cells corresponding to different levels of resolution, and these cells form a hierarchical structure: each cell at a high level is partitioned to form a number of cells at the next lower level.

Statistical information regarding the attributes in each grid cell (such as the mean, maximum, and minimum values) is precomputed and stored

WaveCluster: Clustering Using Wavelet Transformation

WaveCluster is a multiresolution clustering algorithm that first summarizes the data by imposing a multidimensional grid structure onto the data space. It then uses a wavelet transformation to transform the original feature space, finding dense regions in the transformed space.

Model-Based Clustering Methods

This can be carried out in different approaches:

- Expectation-Maximization
- Conceptual Clustering
- Neural Network Approach.

Methods of Clustering High-Dimensional Data

CLIQUE: A Dimension-Growth Subspace Clustering Method

CLIQUE (CLustering In QUEst) was the first algorithm proposed for dimension-growth subspace clustering in high-dimensional space.

PROCLUS: A Dimension-Reduction Subspace Clustering Method

PROCLUS (PROjected CLUStering) is a typical dimension-reduction subspace clustering method. That is, instead of starting from single-dimensional spaces, it starts by finding an initial approximation of the clusters in the high-dimensional attribute space. Each dimension is then assigned a weight for each cluster, and the updated weights are used in the next iteration to regenerate the clusters. This leads to the exploration of dense regions in all subspaces of some desired dimensionality and avoids the generation of a large number of overlapped clusters in projected dimensions of lower dimensionality.

Constraint-Based Cluster Analysis

Constraint-based clustering finds clusters that satisfy user-specified preferences or constraints. Depending on the nature of the constraints, constraint-based clustering may adopt rather different approaches. Here are a few categories of constraints.

- Constraints on individual objects
- Constraints on the selection of clustering parameters
- Constraints on distance or similarity functions
- User-specified constraints on the properties of individual clusters
- Semi-supervised clustering based on "partial" supervision.

OUTLIER ANALYSIS

Very often, there exist data objects that do not comply with the general behaviour or model of the data. Such data objects, which are grossly different from or inconsistent with the remaining set of data, are called outliers.

Many data mining algorithms try to minimize the influence of outliers or eliminate them all together. This, however, could result in the loss of important hidden information because one person's noise could be another person's signal. In other words, the outliers may be of particular interest, such as in the case of fraud detection, where outliers may indicate fraudulent activity. Thus, outlier detection and analysis is an interesting data mining task, referred to as outlier mining or outlier analysis.

Statistical Distribution-Based Outlier Detection

There are two basic types of procedures for detecting outliers:

- Block procedures: In this case, either all of the suspect objects are treated as outliers or all of them are accepted as consistent.

- Consecutive (or sequential) procedures: An example of such a procedure is the insideout procedure.

Distance-Based Outlier Detection

Several efficient algorithms for mining distance-based outliers have been developed. These are outlined as follows.

- Index-based algorithm
- Nested-loop algorithm:
- Cell-based algorithm
- Density-Based Local Outlier Detection
- Deviation-Based Outlier Detection with Sequential Exception Technique.

The technique introduces the following key terms.

- Exception set: This is the set of deviations or outliers.
- Dissimilarity function: This function does not require a metric distance between the objects.

$$\frac{1}{n}\sum_{i=1}^{n}\left(x_i - \overline{x}\right)^2,$$

- Cardinality function: This is typically the count of the number of objects in a given set.
- Smoothing factor: This function is computed for each subset in the sequence.

OLAP Data Cube Technique

An OLAP approach to deviation detection uses data cubes to identify regions of anomalies in large multidimensional data.

MINING STREAM, TIME-SERIES, AND SEQUENCE DATA

Methodologies for Stream Data Processing and Stream Data Systems

- Random Sampling Rather than deal with an entire data stream, we can think of sampling the stream at periodic intervals.
- Sliding Windows Instead of sampling the data stream randomly, we can use the sliding window model to analyse stream data
- Histograms The histogram is a synopsis data structure that can be used to approximate the frequency distribution of element values in a data stream.
- Multiresolution Methods A common way to deal with a large amount of data is through the use of data reduction methods, A popular data reduction method is the use of divide-and conquer strategies such as multiresolution data structures

- Sketches Synopses techniques mainly differ by how exactly they trade off accuracy for storage. Sampling techniques and sliding window models focus on a small part of the data, whereas other synopses try to summarize the entire data, often at multiple levels of detail. Some techniques require multiple passes over the data, such as histograms and wavelets, whereas other methods, such as sketches, can operate in a single pass. frequency moments :

$$F_k = \sum_{i=1}^{v} m_i^k,$$

Randomized Algorithms

Randomized algorithms, in the form of random sampling and sketching, are often used to deal with massive, high-dimensional data streams.

Chebyshev's inequality:

$$P(|X-\mu|>k)\leq\frac{\sigma^2}{k^2}$$

DATA STREAM MANAGEMENT SYSTEMS AND STREAM QUERIES

In traditional database systems, data are stored in finite and persistent databases. However, stream data are infinite and impossible to store fully in a database. In a Data Stream Management System (DSMS), there may be multiple data streams. They arrive on-line and are continuous, temporally ordered, and potentially infinite. Once an element from a data stream has been processed, it is discarded or archived, and it cannot be easily retrieved unless it is explicitly stored in memory.

Stream Query Processing

The special properties of stream data introduce new challenges in query processing. In particular, data streams may grow unboundedly, and it is possible that queries may require unbounded memory to produce an exact answer.

Stream OLAP and Stream Data Cubes

Stream data are generated continuously in a dynamic environment, with huge volume, infinite flow, and fast-changing behaviour. It is impossible to store such data streams completely in a data warehouse.

Example

Multidimensional analysis for power supply stream data. A power supply station generates infinite streams of power usage data. Suppose individual user, street address, and second are the attributes at the lowest level of granularity. Given a large number of users, it is only realistic to analyse the fluctuation of power usage at certain high levels, such as by city or street district and by quarter (of an hour), making timely power supply adjustments and handling unusual situations. Conceptually, for multidimensional analysis, we can view such stream data as a virtual data cube, consisting of one or a few measures and a set of dimensions, including one time dimension, and a few other dimensions, such as location, user-category, and so on. However, in practice, it is impossible to materialize such a data cube, because the materialization requires a huge amount of data to be computed and stored. Some efficient methods must be developed for systematic analysis of such data.

The most recent time is registered at the finest granularity; the more distant time is registered at a coarser granularity; and the level of coarseness depends on the application requirements and on how old the time point is (from the current time). Such a time dimension model is called a tilted time frame.

Types of models:

- Natural tilted time frame model,
- Logarithmic tilted time frame model,
- Progressive logarithmic tilted time frame model.

Critical Layers of Stream Data Cube

Two critical cuboids (or layers):

- The first layer, called the minimal interest layer, is the minimally interesting layer that an analyst would like to study
- The second layer, called the observation layer, is the layer at which an analyst (or an automated system) would like to continuously study the data.

Partial Materialization of a Stream Cube

Materializing a cube at only two critical layers leaves much room for how to compute the cuboids in between. These cuboids can be precomputed fully, partially, or not at all (*i.e.*, leave everything to be computed on the fly)

Example for Frequent-Pattern Mining in Data Streams

Approximate frequent items. A router is interested in all items whose frequency is at least 1% (min support) of the entire traffic stream seen so far. It is felt that 1/10 of min support (*i.e.*, $\varepsilon = 0.1\%$) is an acceptable margin of error. This means that all frequent items with a support of at least min support will be output, but that some items with a support of at least (min support $- \varepsilon$) will also be output.

Hoeffding Tree Algorithm

The Hoeffding tree algorithm is a decision tree learning method for stream data classification. It was initially used to track Web clickstreams and construct models to predict which Web hosts and Web sites a user is likely to access. It typically runs in sublinear time and produces a nearly identical decision tree to that of traditional batch learners. It uses Hoeffding trees, which exploit the idea that a small sample can often be enough to choose an optimal splitting attribute. This idea is supported mathematically by the Hoeffding bound (or additive Chernoff bound).

$$\varepsilon = \sqrt{\frac{R^2 \ln(1/\delta)}{2N}}$$

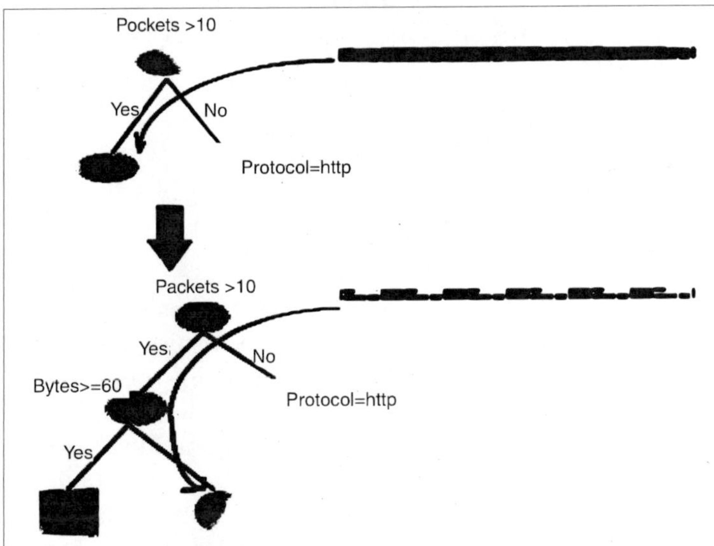

Very Fast Decision Tree (VFDT) and Concept-adapting Very Fast Decision Tree (CVFDT)

The VFDT (Very Fast Decision Tree) algorithm makes several modifications to the Hoeffding tree algorithm to improve both speed and memory utilization. The modifications include breaking near-ties during attribute selection more aggressively, computing the G function after a number of training examples, deactivating the least promising leaves whenever memory is running low, dropping poor splitting attributes, and improving the initialization method. VFDT works well on stream data and also compares extremely well to traditional classifiers in both speed and accuracy To adapt to concept-drifting data streams, the VFDT algorithm was further developed into the

Concept-adapting Very Fast Decision Tree algorithm (CVFDT). CVFDT also uses a sliding window approach; however, it does not construct a new model from scratch each time. Rather, it updates statistics at the nodes by incrementing the counts associated with new examples and decrementing the counts associated with old ones. Therefore, if there is a concept drift, some nodes may no longer pass the Hoeffding bound. When this happens, an alternate subtree will be grown, with the new best splitting attribute at the root. As new examples stream in, the alternate subtree will continue to develop, without yet being used for classification. Once the alternate subtree becomes more accurate than the existing one, the old subtree is replaced.

A Classifier Ensemble Approach to Stream Data Classification

The idea is to train an ensemble or group of classifiers (using, say naïve Bayes) from sequential chunks of the data stream. That is, whenever a new chunk arrives, we build a new classifier from it. The individual classifiers are weighted based on their expected classification accuracy in a time-changing environment. Only the top-k classifiers are kept. The decisions are then based on the weighted votes of the classifiers.

Clustering in Evolving Data Streams

For effective clustering of stream data, several new methodologies have been developed, as follows:

- Compute and store summaries of past data
- Apply a divide-and-conquer strategy
- Incremental clustering of incoming data streams
- Perform microclustering as well as macroclustering analysis
- Explore multiple time granularity for the analysis of cluster evolution
- Divide stream clustering into on-line and off-line processes.

STREAM is a single-pass, constant factor approximation algorithm that was developed for the k-medians problem

CluStream is an algorithm for the clustering of evolving data streams based on userspecified, on-line clustering queries. It divides the clustering process into on-line and offline components. The on-line component computes and stores summary statistics about the data stream using microclusters, and performs incremental on-line computation and maintenance of the microclusters. The off-line component does macroclustering and answers various user questions using the stored summary statistics, which are based on the tilted time frame model.

MINING TIME-SERIES DATA

A time-series database consists of sequences of values or events obtained over repeated measurements of time.

Trend Analysis

A time series involving a variable Y, representing, say, the daily closing price of a share in a stock market, can be viewed as a function of time t, that is, Y = F(t). Such a function can be illustrated as a time-series graph, which describes a point moving with the passage of time.

Similarity Search in Time-Series Analysis

Unlike normal database queries, which find data that match the given query exactly, a similarity search finds data sequences that differ only slightly from the given query sequence.

Mining Sequence Patterns in Transactional Databases

Sequential pattern mining is the mining of frequently occurring ordered events or subsequences as patterns.

An example of a sequential pattern is "Customers who buy a N900 are likely to buy an iTouch notepad within a month."

Scalable Methods for Mining Sequential Patterns

Sequential pattern mining is computationally challenging because such mining may generate and/or test a combinatorially explosive number of intermediate subsequences.

Periodicity Analysis for Time-Related Sequence Data

A full periodic pattern is a pattern where every point in time contributes (precisely or approximately) to the cyclic behaviour of a time-related sequence. For example, all of the days in the year approximately contribute to the month cycle of the year.

A partial periodic pattern specifies the periodic behaviour of a time-related sequence at some but not all of the points in time.

For example, rama have breakfasefrom 7:45 to 8:15 every weekday morning, but her activities at other times do not have much regularity.

Partial periodicity is a looser form of periodicity than full periodicity and occurs more commonly in the real world.

The BLAST Local Alignment Algorithm

BLAST finds regions of local similarity between biosequences. The programme compares nucleotide or protein sequences to sequence databases and calculates the statistical significance of matches.

BLAST can be used to infer functional and evolutionary relationships between sequences as well as to help identify members of gene families.

The Method of Multiple Sequence Alignment

Multiple sequence alignment is usually performed on a set of sequences of amino acids that are believed to have similar structures.

The goal is to find common patterns that are conserved among all the sequences being considered

HIDDEN MARKOV MODEL FOR BIOLOGICAL SEQUENCE ANALYSIS

Markov Chain

A Markov chain is a model that generates sequences in which the probability of a symbol depends only on the previous symbol. An example Markov chain model.

A Markov chain model is defined by (a) a set of states, Q, which emit symbols and (b) a set of transitions between states.

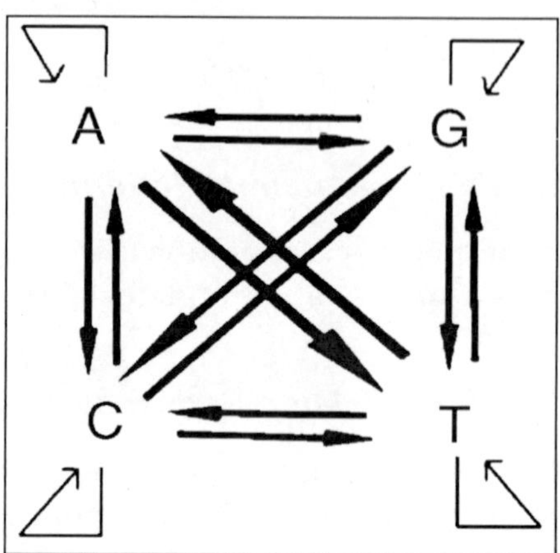

Example: Markov chain. The Markov chain is a probabilistic model for CpG islands. The states are A, C, G, and T. For readability, only some of the transition probabilities are shown.

For example, the transition probability from state G to state T is 0.14, that is, $P(xi = T \mid xi-1 = G) = 0.14$.

Here, the emitted symbols are understood. For example, the symbol C is emitted when transitioning from state C. In speech recognition, the symbols emitted could represent spoken words or phrases.

Tasks using hidden Markov models include:

Evaluation: Given a sequence, x, determine the probability, P(x), of obtaining x in the model.

Decoding: Given a sequence, determine the most probable path through the model that produced the sequence.

Learning: Given a model and a set of training sequences, find the model parameters (*i.e.*, the transition and emission probabilities) that explain the training sequences with relatively high probability. The goal is to find a model that generalizes well to sequences we have not seen before.

GRAPH MINING

Graphs become increasingly important in modelling complicated structures, such as circuits, images, chemical compounds, protein structures, biological networks, social networks, the Web, workflows, and XML documents.

Many graph search algorithms have been developed in chemical informatics, computer vision, video indexing, and text retrieval.

With the increasing demand on the analysis of large amounts of structured data, graph mining has become an active and important theme in data mining.

Methods for Mining Frequent Subgraphs

Apriori-based Approach

```
Algorithm: AprioriGraph. Apriori-based frequent substructure
mining.
Input:
D, a graph data set;
min sup, the minimum support threshold.
Output:
Sk, the frequent substructure set.
Method:
S1 ← frequent single-elements in the data set;
Call AprioriGraph(D, min sup, S1);
procedure AprioriGraph(D, min sup, Sk)
Sk+1 ← x;
for each frequent gi ∈ Sk do
for each frequent gj ∈ Sk do
for each size (k + 1) graph g formed by the merge of gi and
g j do
if g is frequent in D and g ∈ Sk + 1 then
insert g into Sk + 1 ;
if sk + 1 = x then
AprioriGraph(D, min sup, Sk + 1);
return;
```

Apriori-based algorithms for frequent substructure mining include AGM, FSG, and a path-join method. AGM shares similar characteristics with Apriori-based itemset mining. FSG and the path-join method explore edges and connections in an Apriori-based fashion. Each of these methods explores various candidate generation strategies.

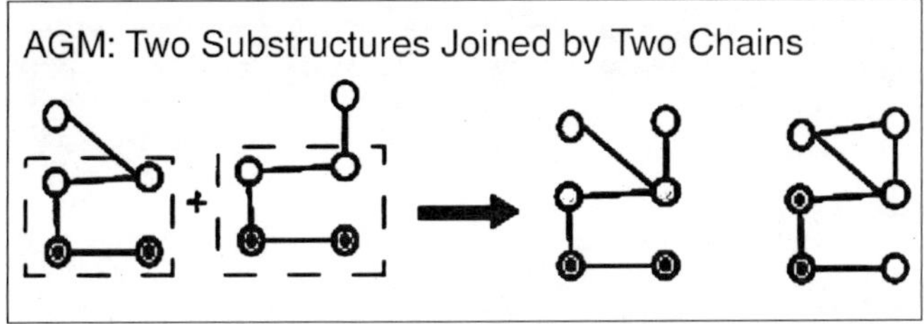

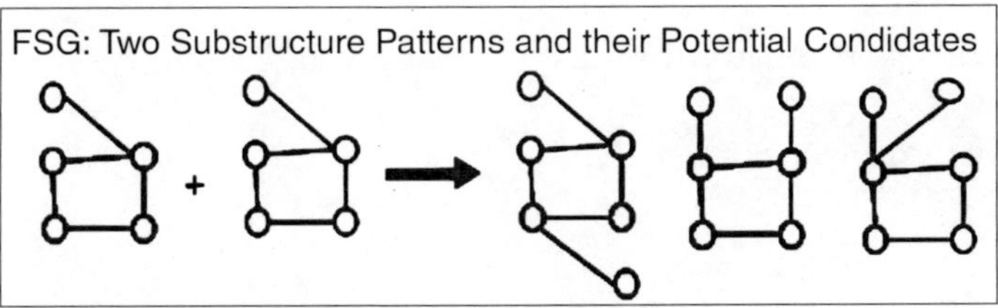

Pattern-Growth Approach

```
Algorithm: PatternGrowthGraph. Simplistic pattern growth-
based frequen
substructure mining.
Input:
g, a frequent graph;
D, a graph data set;
min sup, minimum support threshold.
Output:
The frequent graph set, S.
Method:
S ← x;
Call PatternGrowthGraph(g, D, min sup, S);
procedure PatternGrowthGraph(g, D, min sup, S)
(1) if g ∈ S then return;
(2) else insert g into S;
(3) scan D once, find all the edges e such that g can be
extended to g
(4) for each frequent g
(5) x e;
x e do
PatternGrowthGraph(g
x e, D, min_sup, S);
(6) return;
```

When building a DFS tree, the visiting sequence of vertices forms a linear order. We use subscripts to record this order, where i < j means vi is visited before v j when the depth-first search is performed. A graph G subscripted with a DFS tree T is written as GT. T is called a DFS subscripting of G.

```
gSpan: A pattern-growth algorithm for frequent substructure
mining.
Algorithm: gSpan. Pattern growth-based frequent substructure
mining that reduces
duplicate
graph generation.
Input:
s, a DFS code;
D, a graph data set;
min sup, the minimum support threshold.
Output:
The frequent graph set, S.
Method:
S ← x;
Call gSpan(s, D, min sup, S);
```

```
procedure PatternGrowthGraph(s, D, min sup, S)
(1) if s = d f s(s), then
(2)
return;
(3) insert s into S;
(4) set C to x;
(5) scan D once, find all the edges e such that s can be
right-most extended to s
insert s r e into C and count its frequency; r e;
(6) sort C in DFS lexicographic order;
(7) for each frequent s
(8) gSpan(s r e in C do r e, D, min sup, S);
(9) return;
```

Social Network Analysis

Characteristics of Social Networks:

- Densification power law
- Shrinking diameter
- Heavy-tailed out-degree and in-degree distributions

Link Mining: Tasks and Challenges

Traditional methods of machine learning and data mining, taking, as input, a random sample of homogenous objects from a single relation, may not be appropriate here. The data comprising social networks tend to be heterogeneous, multi-relational, and semi-structured. As a result, a new field of research has emerged called link mining.

Tasks involved in link mining:

- Link-based object classification.
- Object type prediction.
- Link type prediction.
- Predicting link existence
- Link cardinality estimation.
- Object reconciliation.
- Group detection
- Sub-graph detection
- Metadata mining.

Challenges

- Logical versus statistical dependencies
- Feature construction
- Instances versus classes.
- Collective classification and collective consolidation.
- Effective use of labelled and unlabeled data

- Link prediction
- Closed versus open world assumption
- Community mining from multirelational networks.

WHAT IS MULTIRELATIONAL DATA MINING?

Multirelational data mining (MRDM) methods search for patterns that involve multiple tables (relations) from a relational database

ILP Approach to Multirelational Classification

Inductive Logic Programming (ILP) is the most widely used category of approaches to multirelational classification. There are many ILP approaches. In general, they aim to find hypotheses of a certain format that can predict the class labels of target tuples, based on background knowledge (*i.e.*, the information stored in all relations).

The ILP problem is defined as follows: Given background knowledge B, a set of positive examples P, and a set of negative examples N, find a hypothesis H such that:

(1) $\forall t \in P : H \cup B \models t$ (completeness), and

(2) $\forall t\ N : H \cup B \models t$ (consistency), where $\models$ stands for logical implication.

Tuple ID Propagation

Tuple ID propagation is a technique for performing virtual join, which greatly improves efficiency of multirelational classification. Instead of physically joining relations, they are virtually joined by attaching the IDs of target tuples to tuples in nontarget relations.

Multirelational Classification Using Tuple ID Propagation

CrossMine, an approach that uses tuple ID propagation for multirelational classification. To better integrate the information of ID propagation, CrossMine uses complex predicates as elements of rules. A complex predicate, p, contains two parts:

- Prop-path
- Constraint.

CrossMine a Rule-based Classification Across Multiple Relations

```
Algorithm: CrossMine. Rule-based classification across
multiple relations.
Input:
D, a relational database;
Rt a target relation.
Output:
A set of rules for predicting class labels of target tuples.
Method:
```

```
rule set R ! 0;
while (true)
rule r ← empty-rule;
set Rt to active;
repeat
Complex predicate p ←the predicate with highest foil gain;
if foil gain(p) < MIN FOIL GAIN then
break;
else
r ← r + p; // append predicate, increasing rule length by 1
remove all target tuples not satisfying r;
update IDs on every active relation;
if p.constraint is on an inactive relation then
set that relation active;
endif
until (r.length = MAX RULE LENGTH)
if r = empty-rule then break;
R ← R ∪ {r};
remove all positive target tuples satisfying r;
set all relations inactive;
endwhile
return R;
```

MULTIRELATIONAL CLUSTERING WITH USER GUIDANCE

Multirelational clustering is the process of partitioning data objects into a set of clusters based on their similarity, utilizing information in multiple relations. We will introduce CrossClus (Cross-relational Clustering with user guidance), an algorithm for multirelational clustering that explores how to utilize user guidance in clustering and tuple ID propagation to avoid physical joins.

DBSCAN

DBSCAN (density based spatial clustering of applications with noise) is a density based approach to cluster data of arbitrary shape. An example of dbscan.

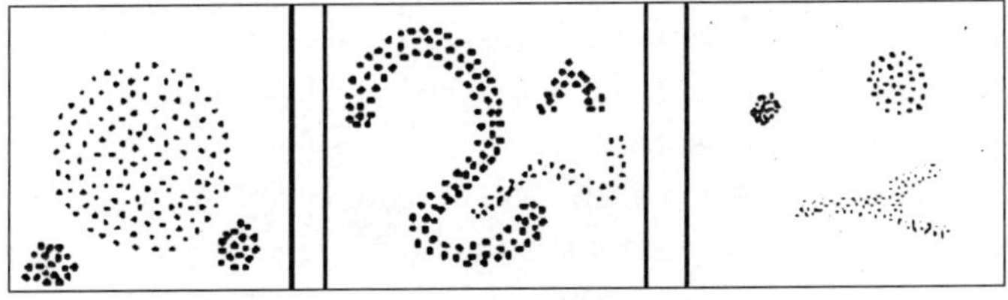

DBScan Method

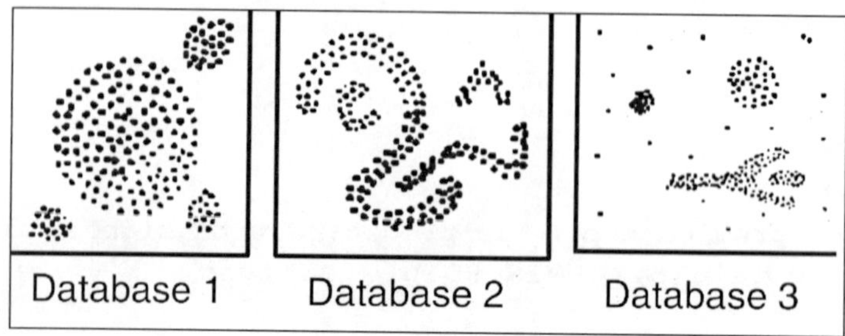

Clarans Method

Figure : The Input Dataset, DBSCAN Clustering, and Clarans Clustering

Obviously, the dbscan finds all clusters properly, independent of the size, shape, and location of clusters to each other, and is superior to a widely used Clarans method

Dbscan is based on two main concepts: *density reachability* and *density connectability.*

These both concepts depend on two input parameters of the dbscan clustering: *the size of epsilon neighbourhood e* and *the minimum points in a cluster m.* The impact of the dbscan parameters to the clustering with $m = 5$ and a give e).

The number of points parameter impacts detection of outliers. Points are declared to be outliers if there are few other points in the e-Eucledean neighbourhood. e parameter controls the size of the neighbourhood, as well as the size of the clusters. If the e is big enough, the would be one big cluster and no outliers.

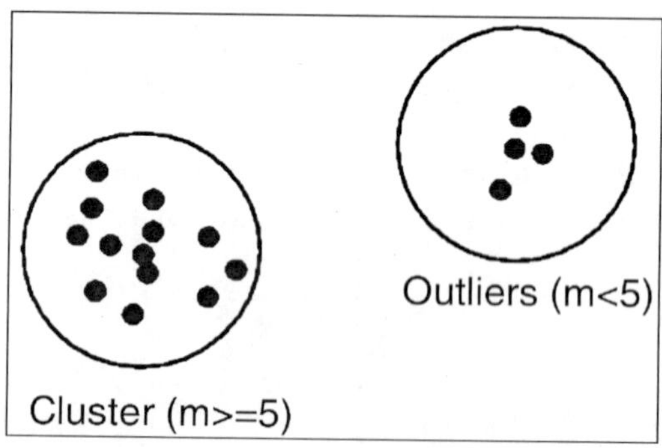

Figure: The Impact of DBSCAN Parameters

Density reachability is the first building block in dbscan. It defines whether two distance close points belong to the same cluster. Points $p1$ is density reachable from $p2$ if two conditions are satisfied:

- The points are close enough to each other: $distance\ (p1, p2) < e$,
- There are enough of points in is neighbourhood:
  $|\{ r : distance(r, p2)\}| > m$, where r is a database point.
  A density reachable point $p2$ from $p1$.

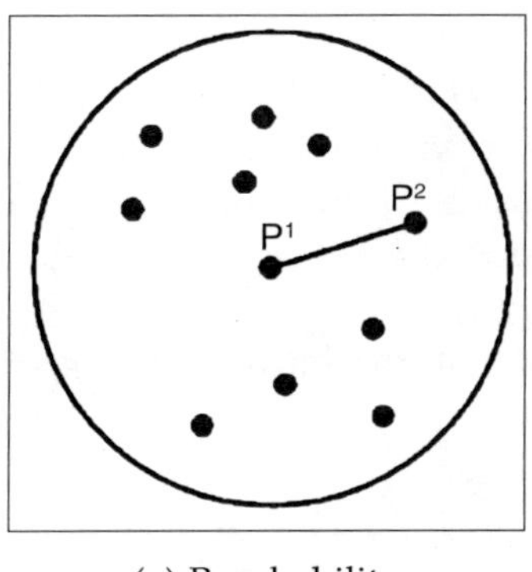

(a) Reachability

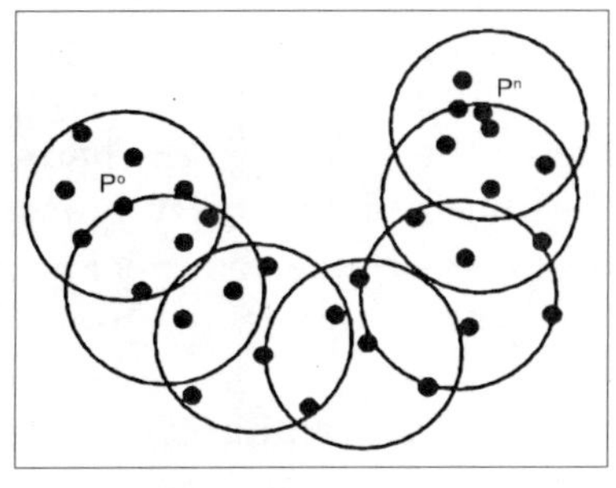

(b) Connectivity

Figure : Reachability and Connectivity Concepts of DBSCAN

Density connectivity is the last building step of dbscan. Points *p0* and *pn* are density connected, if there is a sequence of density reachable points *p1, i2,..., i (n - 1)* from *p0* to *pn* such that *p(i + 1)* is density reachable from *pi*.

A dbscan *cluster* is a set of all density connected points.

BASIC IDEA

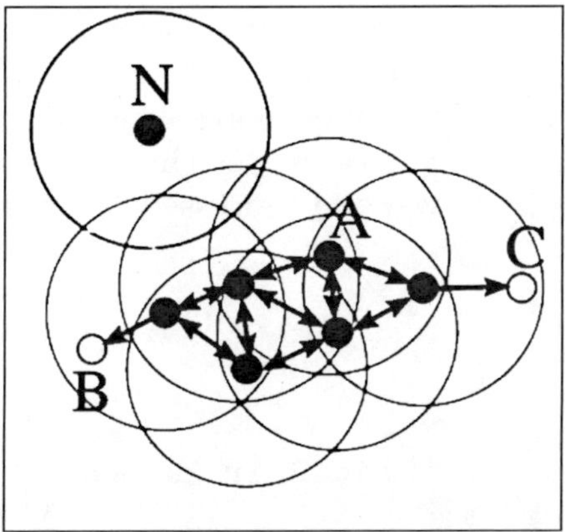

Figure: Points at A are Core Points. Points B and C are *Density-reachable* from A and thus *Density-connected* and belong to the Same Cluster. Point N is a Noise Point that is Neither a Core Point nor Density-reachable.

DBSCAN's definition of a cluster is based on the notion of *density reachability*. Basically, a point q is *directly density-reachable* from a point p if it is not farther away than a given distance ε (*i.e.*, is part of its ε-neighbourhood) and if p is surrounded by sufficiently many points such that one may consider p and q to be part of a cluster. q is called *density-reachable* (note the distinction from "*directly* density-reachable") from p if there is a sequence $p_1, ..., p_n$ of points with $p_1 = p$ and $p_n = q$ where each $p_i + 1$ is directly density-reachable from p_i.

Note that the relation of density-reachable is not symmetric. q might lie on the edge of a cluster, having insufficiently many neighbours to count as dense itself. This would halt the process of finding a path that stops with the first non-dense point. By contrast, starting the process with *q would* lead to *p* (though the process would halt there, *p* being the first non-dense point). Due to this asymmetry, the notion of *density-connected* is introduced: two points *p* and *q* are density-connected if there is a point such that both *p* and *q* are density-reachable from *o*. Density-connectedness *is* symmetric.

A cluster, which is a subset of the points of the database, satisfies two properties:

- All points within the cluster are mutually density-connected.
- If a point is density-connected to any point of the cluster, it is part of the cluster as well.

ALGORITHM

DBSCAN requires two parameters: ε (eps) and the minimum number of points required to form a cluster (minPts). It starts with an arbitrary starting point that has not been visited. This point's ε-neighbourhood is retrieved, and if it contains sufficiently many points, a cluster is started. Otherwise, the point is labelled as noise. Note that this point might later be found in a sufficiently sized ε-environment of a different point and hence be made part of a cluster.

If a point is found to be a dense part of a cluster, its ε-neighbourhood is also part of that cluster. Hence, all points that are found within the ε-neighbourhood are added, as is their own ε-neighbourhood when they are also dense. This process continues until the density-connected cluster is completely found. Then, a new unvisited point is retrieved and processed, leading to the discovery of a further cluster or noise.

Pseudocode

```
DBSCAN(D, eps, MinPts)
   C = 0
   for each unvisited point P in dataset D
      mark P as visited
      NeighborPts = regionQuery(P, eps)
      if sizeof(NeighborPts) < MinPts
         mark P as NOISE
      else
         C = next cluster
         expandCluster(P, NeighborPts, C, eps, MinPts)

expandCluster(P, NeighborPts, C, eps, MinPts)
   add P to cluster C
   for each point P' in NeighborPts
      if P' is not visited
         mark P' as visited
```

```
        NeighborPts' = regionQuery(P', eps)
        if sizeof(NeighborPts') >= MinPts
          NeighborPts = NeighborPts joined with NeighborPts'
      if P' is not yet member of any cluster
        add P' to cluster C

regionQuery(P, eps)
   return all points within P's eps-neighbourhood
```

Complexity

DBSCAN visits each point of the database, possibly multiple times (*e.g.*, as candidates to different clusters). For practical considerations, however, the time complexity is mostly governed by the number of regionQuery invocations. DBSCAN executes exactly one such query for each point, and if an indexing structure is used that executes such a neighbourhood query in $O(\log n)$, an overall runtime complexity of $O(n \cdot \log n)$ is obtained. Without the use of an accelerating index structure, the run time complexity is $O(n^2)$. Often the distance matrix of size $(n^2 - n)/2$ is materialized to avoid distance recomputations. This however also needs $O(n^2)$ memory.

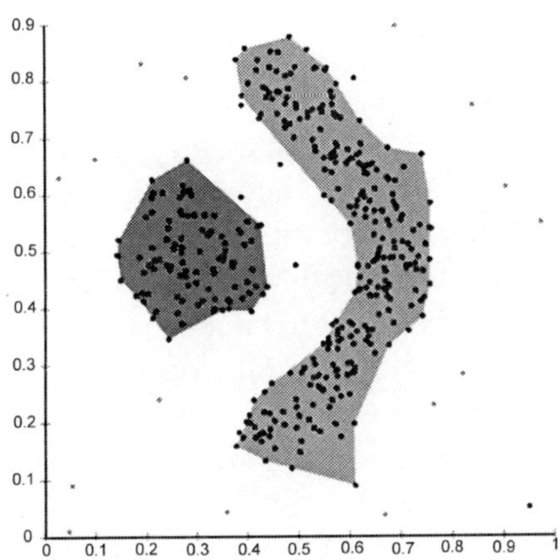

Figure: DBSCAN can find Non-linearly Separable Clusters. This Dataset cannot be Adequately Clustered with k-means or EM Clustering.

Advantages

- DBSCAN does not require one to specify the number of clusters in the data a priori, as opposed to k-means.
- DBSCAN can find arbitrarily shaped clusters. It can even find a cluster completely surrounded by (but not connected to) a different cluster. Due to the MinPts parameter, the so-called single-link effect (different clusters being connected by a thin line of points) is reduced.

- DBSCAN has a notion of noise.
- DBSCAN requires just two parameters and is mostly insensitive to the ordering of the points in the database. (However, points sitting on the edge of two different clusters might swap cluster membership if the ordering of the points is changed, and the cluster assignment is unique only up to isomorphism.)

Disadvantages

- The quality of DBSCAN depends on the distance measure used in the function regionQuery(P, ε). The most common distance metric used is Euclidean distance. Especially for high-dimensional data, this metric can be rendered almost useless due to the so-called "Curse of dimensionality", making it difficult to find an appropriate value for ε. This effect, however, is also present in any other algorithm based on Euclidean distance.
- DBSCAN cannot cluster data sets well with large differences in densities, since the minPts-ε combination cannot then be chosen appropriately for all clusters.

Parameter Estimation

Every data mining task has the problem of parameters. Every parameter influences the algorithm in specific ways. For DBSCAN, the parameters ε and MinPts are needed. The parameters must be specified by the user. An initial value for ε can be determined by a k-distance graph. As a rule of thumb, k can be derived from the number of dimensions D in the data set, as $k \geq D + 1$. However, larger values are usually better for data sets with noise.

Although this parameter estimation gives a sufficient initial parameter set, the resulting clustering can turn out not to be the expected partitioning. Therefore, research has been performed on incrementally optimizing the parameters against a specific target value. OPTICS can be seen as a generalization of DBSCAN that replaces the parameter with a maximum value that mostly affects performance. MinPts then essentially becomes the minimum cluster size to find. While the algorithm is much easier to parameterize than DBSCAN, the results are a bit more difficult to use, as it will usually produce a hierarchical clustering instead of the simple data partitioning that DBSCAN produces.

Generalization

Generalized DBSCAN or GDBSCAN is a generalization by the same authors to arbitrary "neighbourhood" and "dense" predicates. The ε and minpts parameters are removed from the original algorithm and moved to the predicates. For example on polygon data, the "neighbourhood" could be any intersecting polygon, whereas the density predicate uses the polygon areas instead of just the object count.

Extensions

The basic DBSCAN algorithm has been used as a base for many other developments, such as parallelisation by Domenica Arlia and Massimo Coppola or an enhancement of the data set background to support uncertain data presented by Dirk Habich and Peter Benjamin Volk. The basic idea has been extended to hierarchical clustering by the OPTICS algorithm. DBSCAN is also used as part of subspace clustering algorithms like PreDeCon and SUBCLU.

Availability

An implementation of DBSCAN is available in the ELKI framework. Notice that this implementation is not optimized for speed but for extensibility. Thus, this implementation can use various index structures for sub-quadratic performance and supports various distance functions and arbitrary data types, but it may be outperformed by low-level optimized implementations on small data sets.

GNU R contains DBSCAN in the "fpc" package with support for arbitrary distance functions via distance matrixes. However it does not have index support (and thus has quadratic runtime complexity).

Scikit-learn includes a Python implementation of DBSCAN with quadratic runtime and memory complexity due to the use of a materialized pair wise distance matrix.

DENSITY-BASED CLUSTERING ALGORITHMS –DBSCAN AND SNN

The problem of detecting clusters of points in data is challenging when the clusters are of different size, density and shape. Many of these issues become even more significant when the data is of very high dimensionality and when it includes noise and outliers.

DBSCAN ALGORITHM

The DBSCAN algorithm was first introduced by Ester, *et al.* [Ester1996], and relies on a density-based notion of clusters. Clusters are identified by looking at the density of points.

Regions with a high density of points depict the existence of clusters whereas regions with a low density of points indicate clusters of noise or clusters of outliers. This algorithm is particularly suited to deal with large datasets, with noise, and is able to identify clusters with different sizes and shapes.

The Algorithm

The key idea of the DBSCAN algorithm is that, for each point of a cluster, the neighbourhood of a given radius has to contain at least a minimum number of points, that is, the density in the neighbourhood has to exceed some predefined threshold. This algorithm needs three input parameters:

- k, the neighbour list size;
- Eps, the radius that delimitate the neighbourhood area of a point (Epsneighbourhood);
- MinPts, the minimum number of points that must exist in the Eps-neighbourhood.

The clustering process is based on the classification of the points in the dataset as *core points, border points* and *noise points,* and on the use of density relations between points (*directly density-reachable, density-reachable, density-connected*) to form the clusters.

Our Implementation

The DBSCAN algorithm was developed using Visual Basic 6.0. This implementation was adapted to deal with datasets consisting of lists of POIs. However, as the original algorithm, our implementation needs the same three input parameters: k, Eps and MinPts.

For this algorithm, two versions were developed:

- One that read/write the data from a .txt file (DBSCAN_File.vbp).
- The other that read/write the data from a geodatabase featureclass (DBSCAN_Geo.vbp).

The Algorithm

To clusters a dataset, our DBSCAN implementation starts by identifying the k nearest neighbours of each point and identify the farthest k nearest neighbour (in terms of Euclidean distance). The average of all this distance is then calculated. After that, for each point of the dataset the algorithm identifies the *directly density-reachable* points (using the Eps threshold provided by the user) and classifies the points into *core* or *border* points. It then loop trough all points of the dataset and for the *core* points it starts to construct a new cluster with the support of the GetDRPoints() procedure that follows the definition of *densityreachable* points. In this phase the value used as Eps threshold is the average distance calculated previously. At the end, the composition of the clusters is verified in order to check if there exist clusters that can be merged together. This can append if two points of different clusters are at a distance less than Eps.

VB Implementation

The main procedures of the module that implements the DBSCAN algorithm are:

CheckDDRPoints() that identify the *Directly Density-Reachable* points, FindClusters() that start to classify the points into clusters with the support of the GetDRPoints() procedure that identify the *Density-Reachable* points, and the VerifyClusters() procedure that verify the composition of the clusters.

Input Formats

As mentioned above, two different input formats can be used by our DBSCAN implementation:

Text file: the input dataset is a text file composed by three fields tab separated:

1150 -8.667331088 41.14964257
1151 -8.666030446 41.15305675
1152 -8.669282052 41.15273159
1153 -8.664242064 41.15045547
1154 -8.663266582 41.15289417
1155 -8.661640779 41.15061805
...

Each point is represented by an ID, an X coordinate (or longitude), and a Y coordinate (or latitude) with one point per line. In this file the decimal separator must be the dot. Geodatabase: the dataset is stored as a geodatabase *featureclass* (ESRI). This format is appropriate to integrate into the ESRI ArcView GIS. The structure of the *featureclass*.

OBJECTID	SHAPE	X	Y
1	ong binary data	-8,59435108	41,189216748
2	ong binary data	-8,593449387	41,195528599
3	ong binary data	-8,589842615	41,200758419
4	ong binary data	-8,586416181	41,199496049
5	ong binary data	-8,584432457	41,202742143
6	ong binary data	-8,588219567	41,195167922
7	ong binary data	-8,589662276	41,189216748
8	ong binary data	-8,589662276	41,183986928
9	ong binary data	-8,585334149	41,185609975
10	ong binary data	-8,585514488	41,190479118
11	ong binary data	-8,582809409	41,194987583
12	ong binary data	-8,579743652	41,19679097
13	ong binary data	-8,579563314	41,201660112
14	ong binary data	-8,575776203	41,198414016
15	ong binary data	-8,574874511	41,192643181
16	ong binary data	-8,579743652	41,191561150
17	ong binary data	-8,581366700	41,186872345
18	ong binary data	-8,582088055	41,182904896
19	ong binary data	-8,577038573	41,186872345

Record: 1 of 322

Figure : DBSCAN - Featureclass Format for Input

Output Formats

As the input format, here we can find two output formats each of one associated with the respective input format:

- Text file: after the process of clustering is finished, a new file is created with the name of the input file appended by "_results" and with a new field that stores the clustering results. This new file as the following structure:

1,-8.660345216,41.19695386,1
2,-8.665438916,41.20556176,1
3,-8.666897316,41.20563752,1
4,-8.668398458,41.20855247,0
...

The first three fields represents the point ID, the X coordinate and the Y coordinate and the fourth field represents the cluster number.

- Geodatabase: If a *featureclass* is used as input, the results are appended to the same featureclass by appending a field 'ClusterID' to store the clustering results.

OBJECTID	SHAPE	X	Y	ClusterID
10	ong binary data	-8,585514488	41,190479118	1
11	ong binary data	-8,582809409	41,194987583	1
12	ong binary data	-8,579743652	41,19679097	1
13	ong binary data	-8,579563314	41,201660112	1
14	ong binary data	-8,575776203	41,198414016	1
15	ong binary data	-8,574874511	41,192643181	1
16	ong binary data	-8,579743652	41,191561150	1
17	ong binary data	-8,581366700	41,186872345	1
18	ong binary data	-8,582088055	41,182904896	1
19	ong binary data	-8,577038573	41,186872345	1
20	ong binary data	-8,610040539	41,208873656	2
21	ong binary data	-8,615811374	41,202742143	2
22	ong binary data	-8,616893406	41,208512979	2
23	ong binary data	-8,624106950	41,209775349	2
24	ong binary data	-8,622303564	41,204906207	2
25	ong binary data	-8,623205258	41,200758419	2
26	ong binary data	-8,619598485	41,19805334	2
27	ong binary data	-8,611483248	41,193725213	2
28	ong binary data	-8,626631690	41,197873001	2

Record: 1 of 322

Figure : DBSCAN - Featureclass Format for Output

Usage

To use this VB6 implementation open the Visual Basic Project and change the variable 'Path' to the path where the file is. This path is complete, that is, it includes the file name at the end.

To use the 2nd version (Geodatabase version) edit the 'Path' variable to the directory where the geodatabase with the featureclass is and the variable 'FeatName' to the name of the featureclass with the dataset to cluster.

In both cases, after editing these variables, edit the input parameters k, Eps and MinPts. To run the algorithm press F5 or click on the menu Run – Start of the Visual Basic environment.

SNN ALGORITHM

The SNN algorithm [Ertoz2003], as DBSCAN, is a density-based clustering algorithm. The main difference between this algorithm and DBSCAN is that it defines the similarity between points by looking at the number of nearest neighbours that two points share. Using this similarity measure in the SNN algorithm, the density is defined as the sum of the similarities of the nearest neighbours of a point. Points with high density become *core points*, while points with low density represent *noise points*. All remainder points that are strongly similar to a specific core points will represent a new clusters.

The Algorithm

The SNN algorithm needs three inputs parameters:

- K, the neighbours' list size;
- Eps, the threshold density;
- MinPts, the threshold that define the core points.

After defining the input parameters, the SNN algorithm first finds the K nearest neighbours of each point of the dataset. Then the similarity between pairs of points is calculated in terms of how many nearest neighbours the two points share. Using this similarity measure, the density of each point can be calculated as being the numbers of neighbours with which the number of shared neighbours is equal or greater than Eps (density threshold). Next, the points are classified as being *core points*, if the density of the point is equal or greater than MinPts (core point threshold). At this point, the algorithm has all the information needed to start to build the clusters. Those start to be constructed around the core points. However, these clusters do not contain all points. They contain only points that come from regions of relatively uniform density. The points that are not classified into any cluster are classified as noise points.

Our Implementation

In the original SNN algorithm, the user must provide three parameters. However, in the implementation described here, the values of Eps and MinPts are dependent on the value of K3. In that sense, only the K parameter should be directly provided by the user. The remainder parameters are defined as a percentage of the K value. For example, we could have: Eps = 0.45 K and MinPts = 0.55 K.

The Algorithms

Two different approaches of the SNN algorithms were implemented. One that creates the clusters around the *core* points previously identified. In the other approach the clusters are identified by the points that are connected in a graph. The graph is constructed by linking all the points which similarity is higher than Eps. To facilitate the lecture of this document, let's call the 1st approach 'Core approach' and the 2nd 'Graph approach'.

'Core Approach'

The steps of the SNN clustering algorithm accordingly to our implementation are the following:

- Identify the k nearest neighbours for each point (the k points most similar to a given point, using a distance function to calculate the similarity).
- Calculate the SNN similarity between pairs of points as the number of nearest neighbours that the two points share. The SNN similarity is zero if the second point in not in its list of k nearest neighbours, and *vice-versa.*
- Calculate the SNN density of each point: number of nearest neighbours that share Eps or greater neighbours.
- Detect the core points. If the SNN density of the point is equal or greater than MinPts then classify the point as core.
- Form the cluster from the core points. Classify core points into the same cluster if they share Eps or greater neighbours.
- Identify the noise points. All non-core points that are not within a radius of Eps of a core point are classified as noise.
- Assign the remainder points to the cluster that contains the most similar core point.

'Graph Approach'

This approach includes the following steps:

- Identify the k nearest neighbours for each point (the k points most similar to a given point, using a distance function to calculate the similarity).
- Calculate the SNN similarity between pairs of points as the number of nearest neighbours that the two points share. The SNN similarity is zero if the second point in not in its list of k nearest neighbours, and *vice-versa.*
- Calculate the SNN density of each point: number of nearest neighbours that share Eps or greater neighbours.
- Detect the core points. If the SNN density of the point is equal or greater than MinPts then classify the point as core.
- Identify the noise points. All non-core points that are not within a radius of Eps of a core point are classified as noise.
- Cluster all non-noise points by building a graph where two points are connected if the SNN similarity between them is equal or greater than Eps. All sets of points that are connected constitute a cluster.

In both approaches, the algorithm will determine automatically the number of clusters. The results obtained with these two approaches are very similar.

These two approaches have been implemented in Mathematical (as a notebook) and in Visual Basic 6 (VB6).

ADDITIONAL ISSUES AND ALGORITHMS

With an enormous amount of data stored in databases and data warehouses, it is increasingly important to develop powerful tools for analysis of such data and mining interesting knowledge from it. Data mining is a process of inferring knowledge from such huge data. Data Mining has three major components Clustering or *Classification, Association Rules* and *Sequence Analysis.*

By simple definition, in classification/clustering we analyse a set of data and generate a set of grouping rules which can be used to classify future data. For example, one may classify diseases and provide the symptoms which describe each class or subclass. This has much in common with traditional work in statistics and machine learning. However, there are important new issues which arise because of the sheer size of the data. One of the important problem in data mining is the Classification-rule learning which involves finding rules that partition given data into predefined classes. In the data mining domain where millions of records and a large number of attributes are involved, the execution time of existing algorithms can become prohibitive, particularly in interactive applications.

An association rule is a rule which implies certain association relationships among a set of objects in a database. In this process we discover a set of association rules at multiple levels of abstraction from the relevant set(s) of data in a database. For example, one may discover a set of symptoms often occurring together with certain kinds of diseases and further study the reasons behind them. Since finding interesting association rules in databases may disclose some useful patterns for decision support, selective marketing, financial forecast, medical diagnosis, and many other applications, it has attracted a lot of attention in recent data mining research. Mining association rules may require iterative scanning of large transaction or relational databases which is quite costly in processing. Therefore, efficient mining of association rules in transaction and/or relational databases has been studied substantially.

In *sequential Analysis*, we seek to discover patterns that occur in sequence. This deals with data that appear in separate transactions (as opposed to data that appear in the same transaction in the case of association). For *e.g.*: If a shopper buys item A in the first week of the month, then s/he buys item B in the second week *etc.* There are many algorithms proposed that try to address the above aspects of data mining. Compiling a list of all algorithms suggested/used for these problems is an arduous task

CLASSIFICATION ALGORITHMS

In Data classification one develops a description or model for each class in a database, based on the features present in a set of class-labelled training data.

There have been many data classification methods studied, including decision-tree methods, such as C4.5, statistical methods, neural networks, rough sets, database-oriented methods *etc.*

DATA CLASSIFICATION METHODS

The *machine-learning* algorithms that have been successfully applied in the initial stages of this field. The other methods listed above are just being applied to data mining and have not been very successful.

Statistical Algorithms

Statistical analysis systems such as SAS and SPSS have been used by analysts to detect unusual patterns and explain patterns using statistical models such as linear models. Such systems have their place and will continue to be used.

Neural Networks

Artificial neural networks mimic the pattern-finding capacity of the human brain and hence some researchers have suggested applying Neural Network algorithms to pattern-mapping. Neural networks have been applied successfully in a few applications that involve classification.

Genetic Algorithms

Optimization techniques that use processes such as genetic combination, mutation, and natural selection in a design based on the concepts of natural evolution.

Nearest Neighbour Method

A technique that classifies each record in a dataset based on a combination of the classes of the k record(s) most similar to it in a historical dataset. Sometimes called the k-nearest neighbour technique.

Rule Induction

The extraction of useful *if-then* rules from data based on statistical significance.

Data Visualization

The visual interpretation of complex relationships in multidimensional data.

Data Abstraction

Many existing algorithms suggest abstracting the test data before classifying it into various classes. There are several alternatives for doing abstraction before classification: A data set can be generalized to either a minimally generalized abstraction level, an intermediate abstraction level, or a rather high abstraction level. Too low an abstraction level may result in scattered classes, bushy classification trees, and difficulty at concise semantic interpretation; whereas too high a level may result in the loss of classification accuracy. The generalization-based multi-level classification process has been implemented in the DB-Miner system.

Classification-rule Learning

Classification-rule learning involves finding rules or decision trees that partition given data into predefined classes. For any realistic problem domain of the classification-rule learning, the set of possible decision trees is too large to be searched exhaustively. In fact, the computational complexity of finding an optimal classification decision tree is NP hard.

Most of the existing induction-based algorithms use Hunt's method as the basic algorithm. Here is a recursive description of Hunt's method for constructing a decision tree from a set T of training cases with classes denoted $\{C_1, C_2, \ldots, C_k\}$.

Case 1 T contains one or more cases, all belonging to a single class C_j. The decision tree for T is a leaf identifying class C_j.

Case 2 T contains no cases: The decision tree for T is a leaf, but the class to be associated with the leaf must be determined from information other than T.

Case 3 T contains cases that belong to a mixture of classes: A test is chosen, based on a single attribute, that has one or more mutually exclusive outcomes $\{O_1, O_2, \ldots, O_n\}$. T is partitioned into subsets $T_1, T_2, \ldots, T_n$, where T_i contains all the cases in T that have outcome O_i of the chosen test. The decision tree for T consists of a decision node identifying the test, and one branch for each possible outcome. The same tree building machinery is applied recursively to each subset of training cases.

Table : A Small Training Data Set

Outlook	*Temp(F)*	*Humidity(%)*	*Windy?*	*Class*
sunny	75	70	true	Play
sunny	80	90	true	Don't Play
sunny	85	85	false	Don't Play
sunny	72	95	false	Don't Play
sunny	69	70	false	Play
overcast	72	90	true	Play
overcast	83	78	false	Play
overcast	64	65	true	Play
overcast	81	75	false	Play
rain	71	80	true	Don't Play
rain	65	70	true	Don't Play
rain	75	80	false	Play
rain	68	80	false	Play
rain	70	96	false	Play

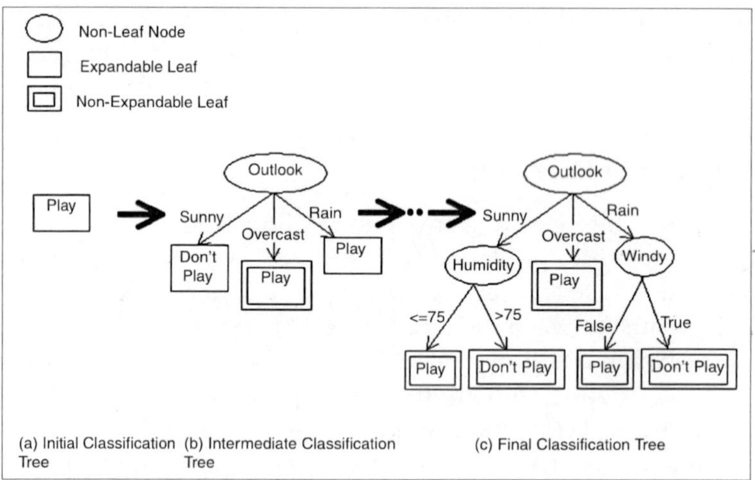

Figure: Demonstration of Hunt's Method

Table : Class Distribution Information of Attribute Outlook

Attribute Value	*Class*	
	Play	*Don't Play*
Sunny	2	3
Overcast	4	0
Rain	3	2

Table : Class Distribution Information of Attribute Humidity

Attribute Value	*Binary Test*	*Class*	
		Play	*Don't Play*
65		1	0
	>	8	5
70		3	1
	>	6	4
75		4	1
	>	5	4
78		5	1
	>	4	4
80		7	2
	>	2	3
85		7	3
	>	2	2
90		8	4
	>	1	1
95		8	5
	>	1	0
96		9	5
	>	0	0

A training data set with four data attributes and two classes. The Hunt's method works with the training data set. In the case 3 of the Hunt's method, a test based on a single attribute is chosen for expanding the current node. The choice of an attribute is normally based on the entropy gains of the attributes. The entropy of an attribute is calculated from class distribution information. For a discrete attribute, class distribution information of each value of the attribute is required. The class distribution information of data attribute Outlook. For a continuous attribute, binary test involving all the distinct values of the attribute is considered. The class distribution information of data attribute Humidity. Once the class distribution information of all the attributes are gathered, the entropy is calculated based on either information theory or Gini Index. One attribute with the most entropy gain is selected as a test for the node expansion.

ID3 Algorithm

The ID3 algorithm (Quinlan86) is a decision tree building algorithm which determines the classification of objects by testing the values of the their properties. It builds the tree in a top down fashion, starting from a set of objects and a specification of properties. At each node of the tree, a property is tested and the results used to partition the object set. This process is recursively done till the set in a given subtree is homogeneous with respect to the classification criteria - in other words it contains objects belonging to the same category. This then becomes a leaf node. At each node, the property to test is chosen based on information theoretic criteria that seek to maximize information gain and minimize entropy. In simpler terms, that property is tested which divides the candidate set in the most homogeneous subsets.

C4.5 Algorithm

This algorithm was proposed by Quinlan. The C4.5 algorithm generates a classification-decision tree for the given data-set by recursive partitioning of data. The decision is grown using Depth-first strategy. The algorithm considers all the possible tests that can split the data set and selects a test that gives the best information gain. For each discrete attribute, one test with outcomes as many as the number of distinct values of the attribute is considered. For each continuous attribute, binary tests involving every distinct values of the attribute are considered. In order to gather the entropy gain of all these binary tests efficiently, the training data set belonging to the node in consideration is sorted for the values of the continuous attribute and the entropy gains of the binary cut based on each distinct values are calculated in one scan of the sorted data. This process is repeated for each continuous attributes.

SLIQ Algorithm

SLIQ (Supervised Learning In Quest) developed by IBM's Quest project team, is a decision tree classifier designed to classify large training data. It uses a pre-sorting technique in the tree-growth phase. This helps avoid costly sorting at each node. SLIQ keeps a separate sorted list for each continuous attribute and a separate list called class list. An entry in the class list corresponds to a data item, and has a class label and name of the node it belongs in the decision tree. An entry in the sorted attribute list has an attribute value and the index of data item in the class list.

SLIQ grows the decision tree in breadth-first manner. For each attribute, it scans the corresponding sorted list and calculate entropy values of each distinct values of all the nodes in the frontier of the decision tree simultaneously. After the entropy values have been calculated for each attribute, one attribute is chosen for a split for each nodes in the current frontier, and they are expanded to have a new frontier. Then one more scan of the sorted attribute list is performed to update the class list for the new nodes.

While SLIQ handles disk-resident data that are too large to fit in memory, it still requires some information to stay memory-resident which grows in direct proportion to the number of input records, putting a hard-limit on the size of training data. The Quest team has recently designed a new decision-tree-based classification algorithm, called SPRINT (Scalable PaRallelizable INduction of decision Trees) that for the removes all of the memory restrictions.

Other Algorithms

There are many other machine learning algorithms; discussing all of them is outside the scope.

Nearest-neighbour

The classical nearest-neighbour with options for weight setting, normalizations and editing.

Naive-Bayes

A simple induction algorithm that assumes a conditional independence model of attributes given the label.

OODG

Oblivous read-Once Decision Graph induction algorithm described in Kohavi.

Lazy Decision Trees

An algorithm for building the "best" decision tree for every test instance described in Friedman, Kohavi & Yun.

Decision Table

A simple lookup table. A simple algorithm that is useful with feature subset selection

PARALLEL ALGORITHMS

Most of the existing algorithms use local heuristics to handle the computational complexity. The computational complexity of these algorithms ranges from O(AN logN) to $O(AN(\log N)^2)$ with N training data items and A attributes. These algorithms are fast enough for application domains where N is relatively small. However, in the data mining domain where millions of records and a large number of attributes are involved, the execution time of these algorithms can become prohibitive, particularly in interactive applications. Parallel algorithms have been suggested by many groups developing data mining algorithms. Two approaches that have been used.

Basic Idea

Initially N training data items are randomly distributed to P processors such that each processors has N=P data items. At this point, all the processors cooperate to expand the root node of a decision tree. For this, processors need to decide on an attribute to use to generate child nodes of the root. This can be done in three steps. In the first step, every processor collects the class distribution information of the local data. In the second step, the processors exchange the local class distribution information using global reduction. Finally, each processor can simultaneously compute entropy gains of the attributes and find the best attribute for splitting the root node. There are two approaches for further progress. In *Synchronous Tree Construction Approach,* the entire set of processors synchronously expand one node of the decision tree at a time. In *partitioned Tree Construction Approach,* each new generated node is expanded by a subset of processors that helped the expansion of the parent node.

Synchronous Tree Construction Approach

In this approach, all processors construct a decision tree synchronously by sending and receiving class distribution information of local data.

Major steps for the approach are :

- Select a node to expand according to a decision tree expansion strategy, and call that node as the current node.
- For each data attribute, collect class distribution information of the local data at the current node.
- Exchange the class distribution information with all other processors and add up the class distribution information to get a complete distribution of all the attributes.
- Calculate the entropy gains of each attribute and select the best attribute for child node expansion.
- Based on the attribute values, create child nodes and partition the data according to the values of the attribute chosen.
- Repeat the above steps until no more nodes are available for the expansion.

The advantage of this approach is that it does not require any movement of the training data items. However, this algorithm suffers from high communication cost and load imbalance. Load imbalance can be reduced if all the nodes on the frontier are expanded simultaneously, *i.e.* one pass of all the data at each processor is used to compute the class distribution information for all nodes on the frontier. Note that this improvement also reduces the number of times communications are done and reduces the message start-up overhead, but it does not reduce the overall volume of communications. Now the only source of load imbalance is when some leaf nodes become terminal nodes. This load imbalance can be further minimized if the training data set is distributed randomly.

Partitioned Tree Construction Approach

In this approach, each leaf node n of the frontier of the decision tree is handled by a distinct subset of processors $P_{(n)}$. Once the node n is expanded into child nodes, $n_1, n_2, \ldots, n_k$, the processor group $P_{(n)}$ is also partitioned into k parts, $P_1, P_2, \ldots, P_k$, such that P_i handle node n_i. All the data items are shuffled such that the processors in group P_i have data items that belong to the leaf n_i only. Major steps for the approach:

- Expand a node based on the method discussed in the beginning for expanding the root node.
- (a) If the number of leaf nodes is less than $|P_{(n)}|$,
  1. Assign a subset of processor to each leaf node such that number of processors assigned to a leaf node is proportional to the number of the data items contained in the node.
  2. Shuffle the training data such that each subset of processors has data item that belongs to the leaf nodes it is responsible for.
  3. Processor subsets assigned to different nodes develop subtrees of the responsible nodes independently, by following the above steps recursively.

  (b) Otherwise,
  1. Partition leaf nodes into $|P_{(n)}|$ groups such that each group has about the equal number of data items. Assign each processor to one node group.
  2. Shuffle the training data such that each processor has data item that belongs to the leaf nodes it is responsible for.
  3. Now the expansion of the subtrees rooted at a node group proceeds completely independently at each process.

At the end, the whole decision tree is constructed by combining subtrees of each processor.

The advantage of this approach is that once a processor becomes solely responsible for a node, it can develop a subtree of the decision tree independently without any communication overhead. There are a number of disadvantages of this approach. First disadvantage is that it requires data movement after each node expansion until one process becomes responsible for an entire subtree. The communication cost is particularly expensive in the expansion of the upper part of the decision tree. Second disadvantage is due to load balancing.

ASSOCIATION RULE ALGORITHMS

An association rule is a rule which implies certain association relationships among a set of objects (such as "occur together" or "one implies the other") in a database. Given a set of transactions, where each transaction is a set of literals (called items), an association rule is an expression of the form X Y, where X and Y are sets of items. The intuitive meaning of such a rule is that transactions of the database which contain X tend to contain Y. An example of an association rule is: "30% of transactions that contain beer also contain diapers; 2% of all transactions contain both of these items". Here 30% is called the confidence of the rule, and 2% the support of the rule. The problem is to find all association rules that satisfy user-specified minimum support and minimum confidence constraints.

APRIORI ALGORITHM

An association rule mining algorithm, Apriori has been developed for rule mining in large transaction databases by IBM's Quest project team. An *itemset* is a non-empty set of items.

They have decomposed the problem of mining association rules into two parts :

- Find all combinations of items that have transaction support above minimum support. Call those combinations frequent itemsets.
- Use the frequent itemsets to generate the desired rules. The general idea is that if, say, ABCD and AB are frequent itemsets, then we can determine if the rule AB CD holds by computing the ratio r = support(ABCD)/support(AB). The rule holds only if r > = minimum confidence. Note that the rule will have minimum support because ABCD is frequent. The Apriori algorithm used in Quest for finding all frequent itemsets is given below:

```
procedure AprioriAlg()
begin
 L1 := {frequent 1-itemsets};
 for (k := 2; Lk-1 0; k++) do {
      Ck= apriori-gen(Lk-1) ; // new candidates
 for all transactions t in the dataset do {
     for all candidates c Ck contained in t do
                 c:count++
     }
     Lk = { c Ck | c:count >= min-support}
 }
 Answer := k Lk
end
```

It makes multiple passes over the database. In the first pass, the algorithm simply counts item occurrences to determine the frequent 1-itemsets (itemsets with 1 item). A subsequent pass, say pass k, consists of two phases. First, the frequent itemsets L_{k-1} (the set of all frequent (k-1)-itemsets) found in the (k-1)th pass are used to generate the candidate itemsets C_k, using the apriori-gen() function. This function first joins L_{k-1} with L_{k-1}, the joining condition being that the lexicographically ordered first k-2 items are the same. Next, it deletes all those itemsets from the join result that have some (k-1)-subset that is not in L_{k-1} yielding C_k.

The algorithm now scans the database. For each transaction, it determines which of the candidates in C_k are contained in the transaction using a hash-tree data structure and increments the count of those candidates. At the end of the pass, C_k is examined to determine which of the candidates are frequent, yielding L_k. The algorithm terminates when L_k becomes empty.

DISTRIBUTED/PARALLEL ALGORITHMS

Databases or data warehouses may store a huge amount of data to be mined. Mining association rules in such databases may require substantial processing power. A possible solution to this problem can be a distributed system.. Moreover, many large databases are distributed in nature which may make it more feasible to use distributed algorithms.

Major cost of mining association rules is the computation of the set of large itemsets in the database. Distributed computing of large itemsets encounters some new problems.

One may compute locally large itemsets easily, but a locally large itemset may not be globally large. Since it is very expensive to broadcast the whole data set to other sites, one option is to broadcast all the counts of all the itemsets, no matter locally large or small, to other sites. However, a database may contain enormous combinations of itemsets, and it will involve passing a huge number of messages.

A distributed data mining algorithm FDM (Fast Distributed Mining of association rules) has been proposed by, which has the following distinct features.

- The generation of candidate sets is in the same spirit of Apriori. However, some relationships between locally large sets and globally large ones are explored to generate a smaller set of candidate sets at each iteration and thus reduce the number of messages to be passed.
- After the candidate sets have been generated, two pruning techniques, local pruning and global pruning, are developed to prune away some candidate sets at each individual sites.
- In order to determine whether a candidate set is large, this algorithm requires only O(n) messages for support count exchange, where n is the number of sites in the network. This is much less than a straight adaptation of Apriori, which requires $O(n^2)$ messages.

SEQUENTIAL ANALYSIS

The input data is a set of sequences, called data-sequences. Each data sequence is a ordered list of transactions (or itemsets), where each transaction is a sets of items (literals). Typically there is a transaction-time associated with each transaction. A sequential pattern also consists of a list of sets of items. The problem is to find all sequential patterns with a user-specified minimum support, where the support of a sequential pattern is the percentage of data sequences that contain the pattern.

An example of such a pattern is that customers typically rent "Star Wars", then "Empire Strikes Back", and then "Return of the Jedi". Note that these rentals need not be consecutive. Customers who rent some other videos in between also support this sequential pattern. Elements of a sequential pattern need not be simple items. "Fitted Sheet and flat sheet and pillow cases", followed by "comforter", followed by "drapes and ruffles" is an example of a sequential pattern in which the elements are sets of items. This problem was initially motivated by applications in the retailing industry, including attached mailing, add-on sales, and customer satisfaction. But the results apply to many scientific and business domains. For instance, in the medical domain, a data-sequence may correspond to the symptoms or diseases of a patient, with a transaction corresponding to the symptoms exhibited or diseases diagnosed during a visit to the doctor. The patterns discovered using this data could be used in disease research to help identify symptoms/diseases that precede certain diseases.

ALGORITHMS FOR FINDING SEQUENTIAL PATTERNS

Various groups working in this field have suggested algorithms for mining sequential patterns. Two algorithms proposed by IBM's Quest data team.

Terminology : The length of a sequence is the number of itemsets in the sequence. A sequence of length k is called a k-sequence. The sequence formed by the concatenation of two sequences x and y is denoted as x.y. The support for an itemset i is defined as the fraction of customers who bought the items in i in a single transaction. Thus the itemset i and the 1-sequence i have the same support. An itemset with minimum support is called a large itemset or *litemset*. Note that each itemset in a large sequence must have minimum support. Hence, any large sequence must be a list of litemsets. In the algorithms, L_k denotes the set of all large k-sequences, and C_k the set of candidate k-sequences.

Algorithm

The problem of mining sequential patterns can be split into the following phases:

- *Sort Phase*. This step implicitly converts the original transaction database into a database of sequences.

- *Litemset Phase*. In this phase we find the set of all litemsets L. We are also simultaneously finding the set of all large 1-sequences, since this set is just *l* | *l* L.
- *Transformation Phase*. We need to repeatedly determine which of a given set of large sequences are contained in a customer sequence. To make this test fast, we transform each customer sequence into an alternative representation. In a transformed customer sequence, each transaction is replaced by the set of all litemsets contained in that transaction. If a transaction does not contain any litemset, it is not retained in the transformed sequence. If a customer sequence does not contain any litemset, this sequence is dropped from the transformed database. However, it still contributes to the count of total number of customers. A customer sequence is now represented by a list of sets of litemsets.
- *Sequence Phase*. Use the set of litemsets to find the desired sequences.
- *Maximal Phase*. Find the maximal sequences among the set of large sequences. In some algorithms this phase is combined with the sequence phase to reduce the time wasted in counting non maximal sequences.

The general structure of the algorithms for the sequence phase is that they make multiple passes over the data. In each pass, we start with a seed set of large sequences. We use the seed set for generating new potentially large sequences, called *candidate sequences*. We find the support for these candidate sequences during the pass over the data. At the end of the pass, we determine which of the candidate sequences are actually large. These large candidates become the seed for the next pass. In the first pass, all 1-sequences with minimum support, obtained in the litemset phase, form the seed set.

There are two families of algorithms- *count-all* and *count-some*. The count-all algorithms count all the large sequences, including non-maximal sequences. The non-maximal sequences must then be pruned out (in the maximal phase). All algorithm, based on the Apriori algorithm for finding large itemsets. Apriori-Some is a count-some algorithm. The intuition behind these algorithms is that since we are only interested in maximal sequences, we can avoid counting sequences which are contained in a longer sequence if we first count longer sequences. However, we have to be careful not to count a lot of longer sequences that do not have minimum support. Otherwise, the time saved by not counting sequences contained in a longer sequence may be less than the time wasted counting sequences without minimum support that would never have been counted because their subsequences were not large.

Algorithm AprioriAll

```
L_1 = large 1-sequences; // Result of litemset phase
for (k = 2; L_{k-1} 0; k++) do
begin
 C_k = New Candidates generated from L_{k-1}
```

```
 foreach customer-sequence c in the database do
     Increment the count of all candidates in Ck that are
contained in c.
 Lk = Candidates in Ck with minimum support.
end
 Answer = Maximal Sequences in k Lk ;
```

AprioriAll Algorithm

In each pass, we use the large sequences from the previous pass to generate the candidate sequences and then measure their support by making a pass over the database. At the end of the pass, the support of the candidates is used to determine the large sequences. In the first pass, the output of the litemset phase is used to initialize the set of large 1-sequences. The candidates are stored in *hash-tree* to quickly find all candidates contained in a customer sequence.

Apriori Candidate Generation

The apriori-generate function takes as argument L_{k-1}, the set of all large (k-1)-sequences. It works as follows. First join L_{k-1} with L_{k-1}

```
insert into Ck
select p.litemset1, ..., p.litemsetk-1, q.litemsetk-1
from Lk-1 p, Lk-1 q
where p.litemset1 = q.litemset1,...,
p.litemsetk-2 = q.litemsetk-2 ;
```

Next delete all sequences c C_k such that some (k-1)-subsequence of c is not in L_{k-1}.

Example

Consider a database with the customer-sequences. We have not shown the original database in this example. The customer sequences are in transformed form where each transaction has been replaced by the set of litemsets contained in the transaction and the litemsets have been replaced by integers. The minimum support has been specified to be 40% (*i.e.* 2 customer sequences). The first pass over the database is made in the litemset phase, and we determine the large 1-sequences. The large sequences together with their support at the end of the second, third, and fourth passes are also shown in the same figure. No candidate is generated for the fifth pass. The maximal large sequences would be the three sequences 1 2 3 4, 1 3 5 and 4 5.

1 5 2 3 4

1 3 4 3 5

1} 2} 3} 4}

1} 3} 5}

4} 5}

Figure: Customer Sequences.

Algorithm AprioriSome

In the forward pass, we only count sequences of certain lengths. For example, we might count sequences of length 1, 2, 4 and 6 in the forward phase and count sequences of length 3 and 5 in the backward phase. The function next takes as parameter the length of sequences counted in the last pass and returns the length of sequences to be counted in the next pass. Thus, this function determines exactly which sequences are counted, and balances the tradeoff between the time wasted in counting non-maximal sequences versus counting extensions of small candidate sequences. One extreme is next(k) = k + 1 (k is the length for which candidates were counted last), when all non-maximal sequences are counted, but no extensions of small candidate sequences are counted. In this case, AprioriSome degenerates into AprioriAll. The other extreme is a function like next(k) = 100 * k, when almost no non-maximal large sequence is counted, but lots of ex- tensions of small candidates are counted.

```
// Forward Phase
L1 = large 1-sequences; // Result of litemset phase
C1 = L1 ; // so that we have a nice loop condition
last = 1; // we last counted Clast
for (k = 2; Ck-1 0 and Llast 0; k++) do
begin
if (Lk-1 known) then
Ck= New candidates generated from Lk-1 ;
else
Ck= New candidates generated from Ck-1 ;
if (k == next(last)) then begin
foreach customer-sequence c in the database do
Increment the count of all candidates in Ck that are contained in c.
Lk = Candidates in Ck with minimum support.
last = k;
end
end
// Backward Phase
for (k– ; k >=1; k==) do
if (Lk not found in forward phase) then begin
Delete all sequences in Ck contained in some Li, i>k;
foreach customer-sequence in DT do
Increment the count of all candidates in Ck that are contained
in c.
Lk = Candidates in Ck with minimum support.
end
else // Lk already known
Delete all sequences in Lk contained in some Li, i > k.
Answer = k Lk ;
```

AprioriSome Algorithm

Let hit_k denote the ratio of the number of large k-sequences to the number of candidate k-sequences (*i.e.*, $|L_k|/|C_k|$). The *next* function we used in the experiments. The intuition behind the heuristic is that as the percentage of candidates counted in the current pass which had minimum support increases, the time wasted by counting extensions of small candidates when we skip a length goes down.

```
function next(k: integer)
begin
if (hit_k < 0.666) return k + 1;
elsif (hit_k <0.75) return k + 2;
elsif (hit_k < 0.80) return k + 3;
elsif (hit_k < 0.85) return k + 4;
else return k + 5;
end
```

We use the apriori-generate function to generate new candidate sequences. However, in the kth pass, we may not have the large sequence set L_{k-1} available as we did not count the (k-1)-candidate sequences. In that case, we use the candidate set C_{k-1} to generate C_k. Correctness is maintained because C_{k-1} L_{k-1}

In the backward phase, we count sequences for the lengths we skipped over during the forward phase, after first deleting all sequences contained in some large sequence.

These smaller sequences cannot be in the answer because we are only interested in maximal sequences. We also delete the large sequences found in the forward phase that are non-maximal.

Example

Using again the database used in the example for the AprioriAll algorithm, we find the large 1-sequences (L_1) in the litemset phase (during the first pass over the database).

Take for illustration simplicity, f (k) = 2k. In the second pass, we count C_2 to get L_2. After the third pass, apriori-generate is called with L_2 as argument to get C_3. We do not count C_3, and hence do not generate L_3. Next, apriori-generate is called with C_3 to get C_4. After counting C_4 to get L_4, we try generating C_5, which turns out to be empty.

We then start the backward phase. Nothing gets deleted from L_4 since there are no longer sequences. We had skipped counting the support for sequences in C_3 in the forward phase. After deleting those sequences in C_3 that are subsequences of sequences in L_4, *i.e.*, subsequences of 1 2 3 4, we are left with the sequences 1 3 5 and 3 4 5. These would be counted to get 1 3 5 as a maximal large 3-sequence. Next, all the sequences in L_2 except 4 5 are deleted since they are contained in some longer sequence. For the same reason, all sequences in L_1 are also deleted.

L 1

1-Sequences	Support
1	4
2	2
3	4
4	4
5	4

L 2

2-Sequences	Support
1 2	2
1 3	4
1 4	3
1 5	3
2 3	2
2 4	2
3 4	3
3 5	2
4 5	2

L 3

3-Sequences	Support
1 2 3	2
1 2 4	2
1 3 4	3
1 3 5	2
2 3 4	2

L 4

4-Sequences	Support
1 2 3 4	2

Figure: Large Sequences

Relative Performance of the Two Algorithms

As expected, the execution times of all the algorithms increase as the support is decreased because of a large increase in the number of large sequences in the result. The apriori-generate does not count any candidate sequence that contains any subsequence which is not large. The major advantage of AprioriSome over AprioriAll is that it avoids counting many non-maximal sequences. However, this advantage is reduced because of two reasons. First, candidates C_k in AprioriAll are generated using L_{k-1}, whereas AprioriSome sometimes uses C_{k-1} for this purpose. Since C_{k-1} L_{k-1}, the number of candidates generated using AprioriSome can be larger. Second, although AprioriSome skips over counting candidates of some lengths, they are generated nonetheless and stay memory resident. If memory gets filled up, AprioriSome is forced to count the last set of candidates generated even if the heuristic suggests skipping some more candidate sets. This effect decreases the skipping distance between the two candidate sets that are indeed counted, and AprioriSome starts behaving more like AprioriAll. For lower supports, there are longer large sequences, and hence more non-maximal sequences, and AprioriSome does better.

4

Data Mining Techniques

There are several major *data mining techniques* have been developed and used in data mining projects recently including association, classification, clustering, prediction and sequential patterns. We will briefly examine those data mining techniques with example to have a good overview of them.

ASSOCIATION

Association is one of the best known data mining technique. In association, a pattern is discovered based on a relationship of a particular item on other items in the same transaction. For example, the association technique is used in *market basket analysis* to identify what products that customers frequently purchase together. Based on this data businesses can have corresponding marketing campaign to sell more products to make more profit.

CLASSIFICATION

Classification is a classic data mining technique based on machine learning. Basically classification is used to classify each item in a set of data into one of predefined set of classes or groups. Classification method makes use of mathematical techniques such as decision trees, linear programming, neural network and statistics. In classification, we make the software that can learn how to classify the data items into groups. For example, we can apply classification in application that "given all past records of employees who left the company, predict which current employees are probably to leave in the future." In this case, we divide the employee's records into two groups that are "leave" and "stay". And then we can ask our data mining software to classify the employees into each group.

CLUSTERING

Clustering is a data mining technique that makes meaningful or useful cluster of objects that have similar characteristic using automatic technique. Different from classification, clustering technique also defines the classes and put objects in them, while in classification objects are assigned into predefined classes. To make the concept clearer, we can take library as an example. In a library, books have a wide range of topics available. The challenge is how to keep those books in a way that readers can take several books in a specific topic without hassle. By using clustering technique, we can keep books that have some kind of similarities in one cluster or one shelf and label it with a meaningful name. If readers want to grab books in a topic, he or she would only go to that shelf instead of looking the whole in the whole library.

Prediction

The prediction as it name implied is one of a data mining techniques that discovers relationship between independent variables and relationship between dependent and independent variables. For instance, prediction analysis technique can be used in sale to predict profit for the future if we consider sale is an independent variable, profit could be a dependent variable. Then based on the historical sale and profit data, we can draw a fitted regression curve that is used for profit prediction.

Sequential Patterns

Sequential patterns analysis in one of data mining technique that seeks to discover similar patterns in data transaction over a business period. The uncover patterns are used for further business analysis to recognize relationships among data.

AN OVERVIEW OF DATA MINING TECHNIQUES

This overview provides a description of some of the most common data mining algorithms in use today. We have broken the discussion into two sections, each with a specific theme:

- Classical Techniques: Statistics, Neighbourhoods and Clustering
- Next Generation Techniques: Trees, Networks and Rules.

A number of data mining algorithms at a high level, focusing on the "big picture" so that the reader will be able to understand how each algorithm fits into the landscape of data mining techniques. Overall, six broad classes of data mining algorithms are covered. Although there are a number of other algorithms and many variations of the techniques described, one of the algorithms from this group of six is almost always used in real world deployments of data mining systems.

CLASSICAL TECHNIQUES: STATISTICS, NEIGHBORHOODS AND CLUSTERING

The Classics

These two sections have been broken up based on when the data mining technique was developed and when it became technically mature enough to be used for business, especially for aiding in the optimization of customer relationship management systems. Thus this section contains descriptions of techniques that have classically been used for decades represents techniques that have only been widely used since the early 1980s. This section should help the user to understand the rough differences in the techniques and at least enough information to be dangerous and well armed enough to not be baffled by the vendors of different data mining tools.

The main techniques that we will discuss here are the ones that are used 99.9% of the time on existing business problems. There are certainly many other ones as well as proprietary techniques from particular vendors - but in general the industry is converging to those techniques that work consistently and are understandable and explainable.

Statistics

By strict definition "statistics" or statistical techniques are not data mining. They were being used long before the term data mining was coined to apply to business applications. However, statistical techniques are driven by the data and are used to discover patterns and build predictive models. And from the users perspective you will be faced with a conscious choice when solving a "data mining" problem as to whether you wish to attack it with statistical methods or other data mining techniques. For this reason it is important to have some idea of how statistical techniques work and how they can be applied.

Difference between Statistics and Data Mining

Recently a professor from one the Boston area Universities. He has discussed the drosophila (fruit flies) genetic makeup to a pharmaceutical company in New Jersey. He had compiled the world's largest database on the genetic makeup of the fruit fly and had made it available to other researchers on the internet through Java applications accessing a larger relational database.

He explained to me that they not only now were storing the information on the flies but also were doing "data mining" adding as an aside "which seems to be very important these days whatever that is".

The techniques used in data mining, when successful, are successful for precisely the same reasons that statistical techniques are successful (*e.g.* clean data, a well defined target to predict and good validation to avoid overfitting). And for the most part the techniques are used in the same places for the same types of problems (prediction, classification discovery). In fact some of the techniques that are classical defined as "data mining" such as CART and CHAID arose from statisticians.

So what is the difference? Why aren't we as excited about "statistics" as we are about data mining? There are several reasons. The first is that the classical data mining techniques such as CART, neural networks and nearest neighbour techniques tend to be more robust to both messier real world data and also more robust to being used by less expert users. But that is not the only reason. The other reason is that the time is right. Because of the use of computers for closed loop business data storage and generation there now exists large quantities of data that is available to users. IF there were no data - there would be no interest in mining it. Likewise the fact that computer hardware has dramatically upped the ante by several orders of magnitude in storing and processing the data makes some of the most powerful data mining techniques feasible today. The bottom line though, from an academic standpoint at least, is that there is little practical difference between a statistical technique and a classical data mining technique. Hence we have included a description of some of the most useful in this section.

Statistics

Statistics is a branch of mathematics concerning the collection and the description of data. Usually statistics is considered to be one of those scary topics in college right up there with chemistry and physics. However, statistics is probably a much friendlier branch of mathematics because it really can be used every day.

Statistics was in fact born from very humble beginnings of real world problems from business, biology, and gambling! Knowing statistics in your everyday life will help the average business person make better decisions by allowing them to figure out risk and uncertainty when all the facts either aren't known or can't be collected. Even with all the data stored in the largest of data warehouses business decisions still just become more informed guesses. The more and better the data and the better the understanding of statistics the better the decision that can be made. Statistics has been around for a long time easily a century and arguably many centuries when the ideas of probability began to gel. It could even be argued that the data collected by the ancient Egyptians, Babylonians, and Greeks were all statistics long before the field was officially recognized. Today data mining has been defined independently of statistics though "mining data" for patterns and predictions is really what statistics is all about. Some of the techniques that are classified under data mining such as CHAID and CART really grew out of the statistical profession more than anywhere else, and the basic ideas of probability, independence and causality and overfitting are the foundation on which both data mining and statistics are built.

Data, Counting and Probability

One thing that is always true about statistics is that there is always data involved, and usually enough data so that the average person cannot keep track of all the data in their heads. This is certainly more true today than it was when the basic ideas of probability and statistics were being formulated and refined early this century. Today people have to deal with up to terabytes of data and have to make sense of it and glean the important patterns from it. Statistics can help greatly in this process by helping to answer several important questions about your data:

- What patterns are there in my database?
- What is the chance that an event will occur?
- Which patterns are significant?
- What is a high level summary of the data that gives me some idea of what is contained in my database?

Certainly statistics can do more than answer these questions but for most people today these are the questions that statistics can help answer. Consider for example that a large part of statistics is concerned with summarizing data, and more often than not, this summarization has to do with counting. One of the great values of statistics is in presenting a high level view of the database that provides some useful information without requiring every record to be understood. This aspect of statistics is the part that people run into every day when they read the daily newspaper and see, for example, a pie chart reporting the number of US citizens of different eye colours, or the average number of annual doctor visits for people of different ages. Statistics at this level is used in the reporting of important information from which people may be able to make useful decisions. There are many different parts of statistics but the idea of collecting data and counting it is often at the base of even these more sophisticated techniques. The first step then in understanding statistics is to understand how the data is collected into a higher level form - one of the most notable ways of doing this is with the histogram.

Histograms

One of the best ways to summarize data is to provide a histogram of the data. In the simple example database, we can create a histogram of eye colour by counting the number of occurrences of different colours of eyes in our database. For this example database of 10 records this is fairly easy to do and the results are only slightly more interesting than the database itself. However, for a database of many more records this is a very useful way of getting a high level understanding of the database.

Table : An Example Database of Customers with Different Predictor Types

ID	*Name*	*Prediction*	*Age*	*Balance*	*Income*	*Eyes*	*Gender*
1	Amy	No	62	$0	Medium	Brown	F
2	Al	No	53	$1,800	Medium	Green	M
3	Betty	No	47	$16,543	High	Brown	F
4	Bob	Yes	32	$45	Medium	Green	M
5	Carla	Yes	21	$2,300	High	Blue	F
6	Carl	No	27	$5,400	High	Brown	M
7	Donna	Yes	50	$165	Low	Blue	F
8	Don	Yes	46	$0	High	Blue	M
9	Edna	Yes	27	$500	Low	Blue	F
10	Ed	No	68	$1,200	Low	Blue	M

This histogram depicts a simple predictor (eye colour) which will have only a few different values no matter if there are 100 customer records in the database or 100 million. There are, however, other predictors that have many more distinct values and can create a much more complex histogram. Consider, for instance, the histogram of ages of the customers in the population. In this case the histogram can be more complex but can also be enlightening. Consider if you found that the histogram of your customer data.

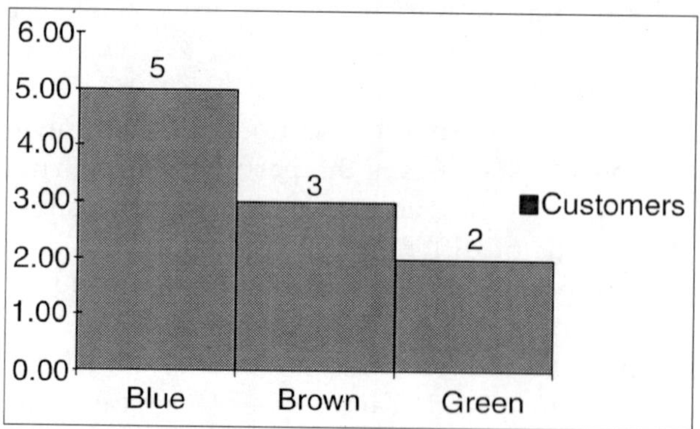

Figure : This Histogram Shows the Number of Customers with Various Eye Colours. This Summary can Quickly Show Important Information about the Database such as that Blue Eyes are the Most Frequent.

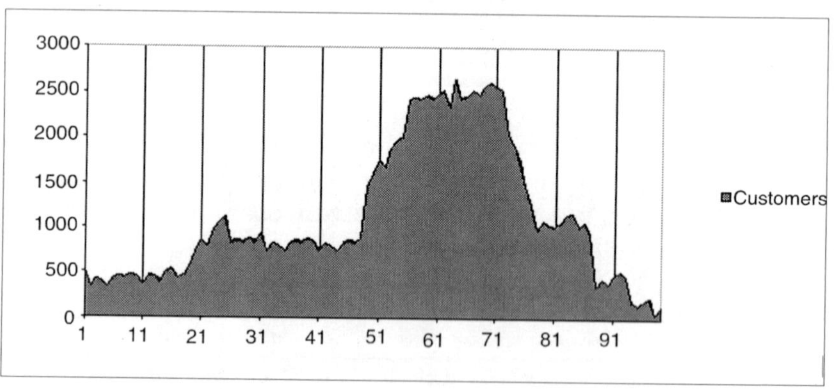

Figure : This Histogram Shows the Number of Customers of Different ages and Quickly Tells the Viewer that the Majority of Customers are over the Age of 50.

By looking at this second histogram the viewer is in many ways looking at all of the data in the database for a particular predictor or data column. By looking at this histogram it is also possible to build an intuition about other important factors. Such as the average age of the population, the maximum and minimum age. All of which are important. These values are called summary statistics. Some of the most frequently used summary statistics include:

- Max - the maximum value for a given predictor.

- Min - the minimum value for a given predictor.
- Mean - the average value for a given predictor.
- Median - the value for a given predictor that divides the database as nearly as possible into two databases of equal numbers of records.
- Mode - the most common value for the predictor.
- Variance - the measure of how spread out the values are from the average value.

When there are many values for a given predictor the histogram begins to look smoother and smoother. Sometimes the shape of the distribution of data can be calculated by an equation rather than just represented by the histogram. This is what is called a data distribution. Like a histogram a data distribution can be described by a variety of statistics. In classical statistics the belief is that there is some "true" underlying shape to the data distribution that would be formed if all possible data was collected. The shape of the data distribution can be calculated for some simple examples. The statistician's job then is to take the limited data that may have been collected and from that make their best guess at what the "true" or at least most likely underlying data distribution might be.

Many data distributions are well described by just two numbers, the mean and the variance. The mean is something most people are familiar with, the variance, however, can be problematic. The easiest way to think about it is that it measures the average distance of each predictor value from the mean value over all the records in the database. If the variance is high it implies that the values are all over the place and very different. If the variance is low most of the data values are fairly close to the mean. To be precise the actual definition of the variance uses the square of the distance rather than the actual distance from the mean and the average is taken by dividing the squared sum by one less than the total number of records. In terms of prediction a user could make some guess at the value of a predictor without knowing anything else just by knowing the mean and also gain some basic sense of how variable the guess might be based on the variance.

STATISTICS FOR PREDICTION

In this book the term "prediction" is used for a variety of types of analysis that may elsewhere be more precisely called regression. We have done so in order to simplify some of the concepts and to emphasize the common and most important aspects of predictive modelling. Nonetheless regression is a powerful and commonly used tool in statistics.

Linear Regression

In statistics prediction is usually synonymous with regression of some form. There are a variety of different types of regression in statistics but the basic idea is that a model is created that maps values from predictors in such a way that the lowest error occurs in making a prediction. The simplest form of regression is simple linear regression that just contains one predictor and a prediction. The relationship between the two can be mapped on a two dimensional space and the records plotted for the prediction values along the Y axis and the predictor values along the X axis. The simple linear regression model then could be viewed as the line that minimized the error rate between the actual prediction value and the point on the line (the prediction from the model). The simplest form of regression seeks to build a predictive model that is a line that maps between each predictor value to a prediction value. Of the many possible lines that could be drawn through the data the one that minimizes the distance between the line and the data points is the one that is chosen for the predictive model.

On average if you guess the value on the line it should represent an acceptable compromise amongst all the data at that point giving conflicting answers. Likewise if there is no data available for a particular input value the line will provide the best guess at a reasonable answer based on similar data.

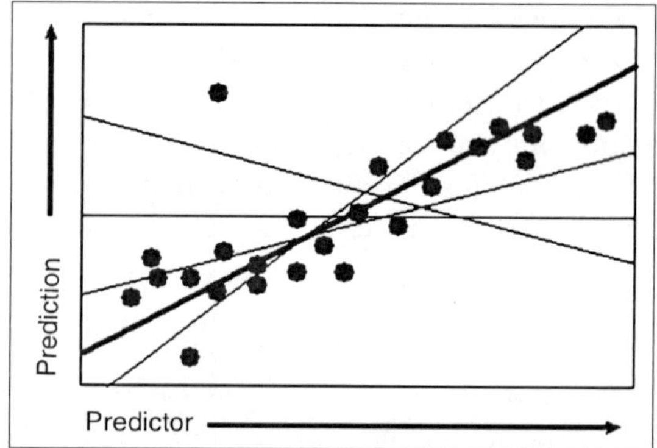

Figure : Linear Regression is Similar to the Task of Finding the Line that Minimizes the Total Distance to a Set of Data.

The predictive model is the line. The line will take a given value for a predictor and map it into a given value for a prediction. The actual equation would look something like: Prediction = a + b * Predictor. Which is just the equation for a line Y = a + bX. As an example for a bank the predicted average consumer bank balance might equal $1,000 + 0.01 * customer's annual income. The trick, as always with predictive modelling, is to find the model that best minimizes the error. The most common way to calculate the error is the square of the difference between the predicted value and the actual value. Calculated this way points that are very far from the line will have a great effect on moving the choice of line towards themselves in order to reduce the error. The values of a and b in the regression equation that minimize this error can be calculated directly from the data relatively quickly.

What if the Pattern in My Data doesn't Look Like a Straight Line?

Regression can become more complicated than the simple linear regression we've introduced so far. It can get more complicated in a variety of different ways in order to better model particular database problems. There are, however, three main modifications that can be made:

- More predictors than just one can be used.
- Transformations can be applied to the predictors.
- Predictors can be multiplied together and used as terms in the equation.
- Modifications can be made to accommodate response predictions that just have yes/no or 0/1 values.

Adding more predictors to the linear equation can produce more complicated lines that take more information into account and hence make a better prediction. This is called multiple linear regression and might have an equation like the following if 5 predictors were used (X1, X2, X3, X4, X5):

$$Y = a + b1(X1) + b2(X2) + b3(X3) + b4(X4) + b5(X5)$$

This equation still describes a line but it is now a line in a 6 dimensional space rather than the two dimensional space.

By transforming the predictors by squaring, cubing or taking their square root it is possible to use the same general regression methodology and now create much more complex models that are no longer simple shaped like lines. This is called non-linear regression. A model of just one predictor might look like this: $Y = a + b1(X1) + b2\ (X12)$. In many real world cases analysts will perform a wide variety of transformations on their data just to try them out. If they do not contribute to a useful model their coefficients in the equation will tend towards zero and then they can be removed. The other transformation of predictor values that is often performed is multiplying them together. For instance a new predictor created by dividing hourly wage by the minimum wage might be a much more effective predictor than hourly wage by itself.

When trying to predict a customer response that is just yes or no (*e.g.* they bought the product or they didn't or they defaulted or they didn't) the standard form of a line doesn't work. Since there are only two possible values to be predicted it is relatively easy to fit a line through them. However, that model would be the same no matter what predictors were being used or what particular data was being used. Typically in these situations a transformation of the prediction values is made in order to provide a better predictive model. This type of regression is called logistic regression and because so many business problems are response problems, logistic regression is one of the most widely used statistical techniques for creating predictive models.

Nearest Neighbour

Clustering and the Nearest Neighbour prediction technique are among the oldest techniques used in data mining. Most people have an intuition that they understand what clustering is - namely that like records are grouped or clustered together. Nearest neighbour is a prediction technique that is quite similar to clustering - its essence is that in order to predict what a prediction value is in one record look for records with similar predictor values in the historical database and use the prediction value from the record that it "nearest" to the unclassified record.

A Simple Example of Clustering

A simple example of clustering would be the clustering that most people perform when they do the laundry - grouping the permanent press, dry cleaning, whites and brightly coloured clothes is important because they have similar characteristics. And it turns out they have important attributes in common about the way they behave (and can be ruined) in the wash. To "cluster" your laundry most of your decisions are relatively straightforward. There are of course difficult decisions to be made about which cluster your white shirt with red stripes goes into (since it is mostly white but has some colour and is permanent press). When clustering is used in business the clusters are often much more dynamic - even changing weekly to monthly and many more of the decisions concerning which cluster a record falls into can be difficult.

A Simple Example of Nearest Neighbour

A simple example of the nearest neighbour prediction algorithm is that if you look at the people in your neighbourhood (in this case those people that are in fact geographically near to you). You may notice that, in general, you all have somewhat similar incomes. Thus if your neighbour has an income greater than \$100,000 chances are good that you too have a high income. Certainly the chances that you have a high income are greater when all of your neighbours have incomes over \$100,000 than if all of your neighbours have incomes of \$20,000. Within your neighbourhood there may still be a wide variety of incomes possible among even your "closest" neighbours but if you had to predict someone's income based on only knowing their neighbours you're best chance of being right would be to predict the incomes of the neighbours who live closest to the unknown person.

The nearest neighbour prediction algorithm works in very much the same way except that "nearness" in a database may consist of a variety of factors not just where the person lives. It may, for instance, be far more important to know which school someone attended and what degree they attained when predicting income. The better definition of "near" might in fact be other people that you graduated from college with rather than the people that you live next to.

Nearest Neighbour techniques are among the easiest to use and understand because they work in a way similar to the way that people think - by detecting closely matching examples. They also perform quite well in terms of automation, as many of the algorithms are robust with respect to dirty data and missing data. Lastly they are particularly adept at performing complex ROI calculations because the predictions are made at a local level where business simulations could be performed in order to optimize ROI. As they enjoy similar levels of accuracy compared to other techniques the measures of accuracy such as lift are as good as from any other.

How to use Nearest Neighbour for Prediction

One of the essential elements underlying the concept of clustering is that one particular object (whether they be cars, food or customers) can be closer to another object than can some third object. It is interesting that most people have an innate sense of ordering placed on a variety of different objects. Most people would agree that an apple is closer to an orange than it is to a tomato and that a Toyota Corolla is closer to a Honda Civic than to a Porsche. This sense of ordering on many different objects helps us place them in time and space and to make sense of the world. It is what allows us to build clusters - both in databases on computers as well as in our daily lives. This definition of nearness that seems to be ubiquitous also allows us to make predictions.

The nearest neighbour prediction algorithm simply stated is:

Objects that are "near" to each other will have similar prediction values as well. Thus if you know the prediction value of one of the objects you can predict it for it's nearest neighbours.

Use of the Nearest Neighbour Technique in Business

One of the classical places that nearest neighbour has been used for prediction has been in text retrieval. The problem to be solved in text retrieval is one where the end user defines a document (*e.g.* Wall Street Journal article, technical conference paper *etc.*) that is interesting to them and they solicit the system to "find more documents like this one". Effectively defining a target of: "this is the interesting document" or "this is not interesting". The prediction problem is that only a very few of the documents in the database actually have values for this prediction field (namely only the documents that the reader has had a chance to look at so far). The nearest neighbour technique is used to find other documents that share important characteristics with those documents that have been marked as interesting.

Using Nearest Neighbour for Stock Market Data

As with almost all prediction algorithms, nearest neighbour can be used in a variety of places. Its successful use is mostly dependent on the pre-formatting of the data so that nearness can be calculated and where individual records can be defined. In the text retrieval example this was not too difficult - the objects were documents. This is not always as easy as it is for text retrieval. Consider what it might be like in a time series problem - say for predicting the stock market. In this case the input data is just a long series of stock prices over time without any particular record that could be considered to be an object. The value to be predicted is just the next value of the stock price. The way that this problem is solved for both nearest neighbour techniques and for some other types of prediction algorithms is to create training records by taking, for instance, 10 consecutive stock prices and using the first 9 as predictor values and the 10th as the prediction value. Doing things this way, if you had 100 data points in your time series you could create 10 different training records.

You could create even more training records than 10 by creating a new record starting at every data point. For instance in the you could take the first 10 data points and create a record. Then you could take the 10 consecutive data points starting at the second data point, then the 10 consecutive data point starting at the third data point. Even though some of the data points would overlap from one record to the next the prediction value would always be different. In our example of 100 initial data points 90 different training records could be created this way as opposed to the 10 training records created via the other method.

Why Voting is Better - K Nearest Neighbours

One of the improvements that is usually made to the basic nearest neighbour algorithm is to take a vote from the "K" nearest neighbours rather than just relying on the sole nearest neighbour to the unclassified record. We can see that unclassified example C has a nearest neighbour that is a defaulter and yet is surrounded almost exclusively by records that are good credit risks. In this case the nearest neighbour to record C is probably an outlier - which may be incorrect data or some non-repeatable idiosyncrasy. In either case it is more than likely that C is a non-defaulter yet would be predicted to be a defaulter if the sole nearest neighbour were used for the prediction.

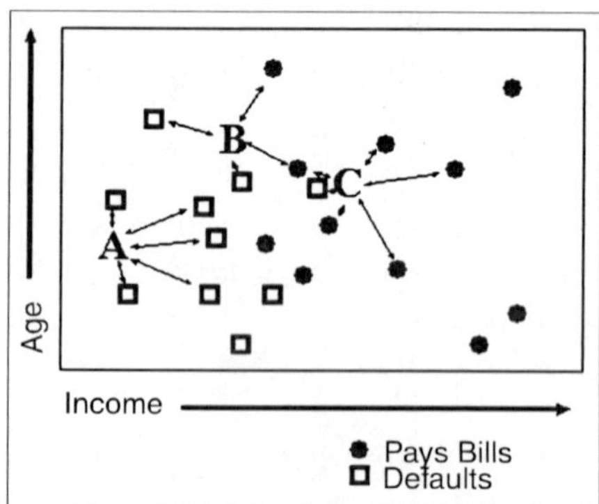

Figure : The Nearest Neighbours are Shown Graphically for Three Unclassified Records: A, B, and C.

In cases like these a vote of the 9 or 15 nearest neighbours would provide a better prediction accuracy for the system than would just the single nearest neighbour. Usually this is accomplished by simply taking the majority or plurality of predictions from the K nearest neighbours if the prediction column is a binary or categorical or taking the average value of the prediction column from the K nearest neighbours.

How can the Nearest Neighbour Tell you How Confident it is in the Prediction?

Another important aspect of any system that is used to make predictions is that the user be provided with, not only the prediction, but also some sense of the confidence in that prediction (*e.g.* the prediction is defaulter with the chance of being correct 60% of the time). The nearest neighbour algorithm provides this confidence information in a number of ways:

The distance to the nearest neighbour provides a level of confidence. If the neighbour is very close or an exact match then there is much higher confidence in the prediction than if the nearest record is a great distance from the unclassified record.

The degree of homogeneity amongst the predictions within the K nearest neighbours can also be used. If all the nearest neighbours make the same prediction then there is much higher confidence in the prediction than if half the records made one prediction and the other half made another prediction.

Clustering

Clustering for Clarity

Clustering is the method by which like records are grouped together. Usually this is done to give the end user a high level view of what is going on in the database. Clustering is sometimes used to mean segmentation - which most marketing people will tell you is useful for coming up with a birds eye view of the business. Two of these clustering systems are the PRIZM™ system from Claritas corporation and MicroVision™ from Equifax corporation. These companies have grouped the population by demographic information into segments that they believe are useful for direct marketing and sales. To build these groupings they use information such as income, age, occupation, housing and race collect in the US Census. Then they assign memorable "nicknames" to the clusters.

Table : Some Commercially Available Cluster Tags

Name	*Income*	*Age*	*Education*	*Vendor*
Blue Blood Estates	Wealthy	35-54	College	Claritas Prizm™
Shotguns and Pickups	Middle	35-64	High School	Claritas Prizm™
Southside City	Poor	Mix	Grade School	Claritas Prizm™
Living Off the Land	Middle-Poor	School Age Families	Low	Equifax MicroVision™
University USA	Very low	Young - Mix		Medium to High Equifax MicroVision™
Sunset Years	Medium	Seniors	Medium	Equifax MicroVision™

This clustering information is then used by the end user to tag the customers in their database. Once this is done the business user can get a quick high level view of what is happening within the cluster. Once the business user has worked with these codes for some time they also begin to build intuitions about how these different customers clusters will react to the marketing offers particular to their business.

For instance some of these clusters may relate to their business and some of them may not.

But given that their competition may well be using these same clusters to structure their business and marketing offers it is important to be aware of how you customer base behaves in regard to these clusters.

Finding the Ones that don't Fit in - Clustering for Outliers

Sometimes clustering is performed not so much to keep records together as to make it easier to see when one record sticks out from the rest. For instance: Most wine distributors selling inexpensive wine in Missouri and that ship a certain volume of product produce a certain level of profit. There is a cluster of stores that can be formed with these characteristics. One store stands out, however, as producing significantly lower profit. On closer examination it turns out that the distributor was delivering product to but not collecting payment from one of their customers.

A sale on men's suits is being held in all branches of a department store for southern California. All stores with these characteristics have seen at least a 100% jump in revenue since the start of the sale except one. It turns out that this store had, unlike the others, advertised via radio rather than television.

How is Clustering Like the Nearest Neighbour Technique?

The nearest neighbour algorithm is basically a refinement of clustering in the sense that they both use distance in some feature space to create either structure in the data or predictions.

The nearest neighbour algorithm is a refinement since part of the algorithm usually is a way of automatically determining the weighting of the importance of the predictors and how the distance will be measured within the feature space. Clustering is one special case of this where the importance of each predictor is considered to be equivalent.

How to put Clustering and Nearest Neighbour to Work for Prediction

To see clustering and nearest neighbour prediction in use let's go back to our example database and now look at it in two ways. First let's try to create our own clusters - which if useful we could use internally to help to simplify and clarify large quantities of data (and maybe if we did a very good job sell these new codes to other business users). Secondly let's try to create predictions based on the nearest neighbour.

First take a look at the data. How would you cluster the data in Table?

Table : A Simple Example Database

ID	*Name*	*Prediction*	*Age*	*Balance*	*Income*	*Eyes*	*Gender*
1	Amy	No	62	$0	Medium	Brown	F
2	Al	No	53	$1,800	Medium	Green	M
3	Betty	No	47	$16,543	High	Brown	F
4	Bob	Yes	32	$45	Medium	Green	M
5	Carla	Yes	21	$2,300	High	Blue	F
6	Carl	No	27	$5,400	High	Brown	M
7	Donna	Yes	50	$165	Low	Blue	F
8	Don	Yes	46	$0	High	Blue	M
9	Edna	Yes	27	$500	Low	Blue	F
10	Ed	No	68	$1,200	Low	Blue	M

If these were your friends rather than your customers (hopefully they could be both) and they were single, you might cluster them based on their compatibility with each other. Creating your own mini dating service. If you were a pragmatic person you might cluster your database as follows because you think that marital happiness is mostly dependent on financial compatibility and create three clusters as shown in Table.

Table : A Simple Clustering of the Example Database

ID	*Name*	*Prediction*	*Age*	*Balance*	*Income*	*Eyes*	*Gender*
3	Betty	No	47	$16,543	High	Brown	F
5	Carla	Yes	21	$2,300	High	Blue	F
6	Carl	No	27	$5,400	High	Brown	M
8	Don	Yes	46	$0	High	Blue	M
1	Amy	No	62	$0	Medium	Brown	F
2	Al	No	53	$1,800	Medium	Green	M
4	Bob	Yes	32	$45	Medium	Green	M
7	Donna	Yes	50	$165	Low	Blue	F
9	Edna	Yes	27	$500	Low	Blue	F
10	Ed	No	68	$1,200	Low	Blue	M

Is the Another "Correct" Way to Cluster?

If on the other hand you are more of a romantic you might note some incompatibilities between 46 year old Don and 21 year old Carla (even though they both make very good incomes). You might instead consider age and some physical characteristics to be most important in creating clusters of friends. Another way you could cluster your friends would be based on their ages and on the colour of their eyes. Here three clusters are created where each person in the cluster is about the same age and some attempt has been made to keep people of like eye colour together in the same cluster.

Table : A More "Romantic" Clustering of the Example Database to Optimize for Your Dating Service

ID	*Name*	*Prediction*	*Age*	*Balance*	*Income*	*Eyes*	*Gender*
5	Carla	Yes	21	$2,300	High	Blue	F
9	Edna	Yes	27	$500	Low	Blue	F
6	Carl	No	27	$5,400	High	Brown	M
4	Bob	Yes	32	$45	Medium	Green	M
8	Don	Yes	46	$0	High	Blue	M
7	Donna	Yes	50	$165	Low	Blue	F
10	Ed	No	68	$1,200	Low	Blue	M
3	Betty	No	47	$16,543	High	Brown	F
2	Al	No	53	$1,800	Medium	Green	M
1	Amy	No	62	$0	Medium	Brown	F

There is no best way to cluster. This example, though simple, points up some important questions about clustering. For instance: Is it possible to say whether the first clustering that was performed above (by financial status) was better or worse than the second clustering (by age and eye colour)? Probably not since the clusters were constructed for no particular purpose except to note similarities between some of the records and that the view of the database could be somewhat simplified by using clusters. But even the differences that were created by the two different clusterings were driven by slightly different motivations (financial vs. Romantic). In general the reasons for clustering are just this ill defined because clusters are used more often than not for exploration and summarization as much as they are used for prediction.

How are Tradeoffs made when Determining which Records Fall into which Clusters?

Notice that for the first clustering example there was a pretty simple rule by which the records could be broken up into clusters - namely by income. In the second clustering example there were less clear dividing lines since two predictors were used to form the clusters (age and eye colour). Thus the first cluster is dominated by younger people with somewhat mixed eye colours whereas the latter two clusters have a mix of older people where eye colour has been used to separate them out (the second cluster is entirely blue eyed people). In this case these tradeoffs were made arbitrarily but when clustering much larger numbers of records these tradeoffs are explicitly defined by the clustering algorithm.

Clustering is the happy medium between homogeneous clusters and the fewest number of clusters. In the best possible case clusters would be built where all records within the cluster had identical values for the particular predictors that were being clustered on. This would be the optimum in creating a high level view since knowing the predictor values for any member of the cluster would mean knowing the values for every member of the cluster no matter how large the cluster was. Creating homogeneous clusters where all values for the predictors are the same is difficult to do when there are many predictors and/or the predictors have many different values (high cardinality).

It is possible to guarantee that homogeneous clusters are created by breaking apart any cluster that is inhomogeneous into smaller clusters that are homogeneous. In the extreme, though, this usually means creating clusters with only one record in them which usually defeats the original purpose of the clustering. For instance in our 10 record database above 10 perfectly homogeneous clusters could be formed of 1 record each, but not much progress would have been made in making the original database more understandable.

The second important constraint on clustering is then that a reasonable number of clusters are formed. Where, again, reasonable is defined by the user but is difficult to quantify beyond that except to say that just one cluster is unacceptable (too much generalization) and that as many clusters and original records is also unacceptable Many clustering algorithms either let the user choose the number of clusters that they would like to see created from the database or they provide the user a "knob" by which they can create fewer or greater numbers of clusters interactively after the clustering has been performed.

What is the difference between clustering and nearest neighbour prediction? The main distinction between clustering and the nearest neighbour technique is that clustering is what is called an unsupervised learning technique and nearest neighbour is generally used for prediction or a supervised learning technique. Unsupervised learning techniques are unsupervised in the sense that when they are run there is not particular reason for the creation of the models the way there is for supervised learning techniques that are trying to perform prediction. In prediction, the patterns that are found in the database and presented in the model are always the most important patterns in the database for performing some particular prediction. In clustering there is no particular sense of why certain records are near to each other or why they all fall into the same cluster. Some of the differences between clustering and nearest neighbour prediction can be summarized in Table.

Table : Some of the Differences Between the Nearest-Neighbour Data Mining Technique and Clustering

Nearest Neighbor	Clustering
Used for prediction as well as consolidation.	Used mostly for consolidating data into a high-level view and general grouping of records into like behaviors.
Space is defined by the problem to be solved (supervised learning).	Space is defined as default n-dimensional space, or is defined by the user, or is a predefined space driven by past experience (unsupervised learning).
Generally only uses distance metrics to determine nearness.	Can use other metrics besides distance to determine nearness of two records - for example linking two points together.

What is an n-dimensional space? Do I really need to know this?

When people talk about clustering or nearest neighbour prediction they will often talk about a "space" of "N" dimensions. What they mean is that in order to define what is near and what is far away it is helpful to have a "space" defined where distance can be calculated. Generally these spaces behave just like the three dimensional space that we are familiar with where distance between objects is defined by euclidean distance.

What goes for three dimensions works pretty well for more dimensions as well. Which is a good thing since most real world problems consists of many more than three dimensions. In fact each predictor (or database column) that is used can be considered to be a new dimension. In the example above the five predictors: age, income, balance, eyes and gender can all be construed to be dimensions in an n dimensional space where n, in this case, equal 5. It is sometimes easier to think about these and other data mining algorithms in terms of n-dimensional spaces because it allows for some intuitions to be used about how the algorithm is working.

Moving from three dimensions to five dimensions is not too large a jump but there are also spaces in real world problems that are far more complex. In the credit card industry credit card issuers typically have over one thousand predictors that could be used to create an n-dimensional space. For text retrieval (*e.g.* finding useful Wall Street Journal articles from a large database, or finding useful web sites on the internet) the predictors (and hence the dimensions) are typically words or phrases that are found in the document records. In just one year of the Wall Street Journal there are more than 50,000 different words used - which translates to a 50,000 dimensional space in which nearness between records must be calculated.

How is the space for clustering and nearest neighbour defined? For clustering the n-dimensional space is usually defined by assigning one predictor to each dimension. For the nearest neighbour algorithm predictors are also mapped to dimensions but then those dimensions are literally stretched or compressed based on how important the particular predictor is in making the prediction. The stretching of a dimension effectively makes that dimension (and hence predictor) more important than the others in calculating the distance.

For instance if you are a mountain climber and someone told you that you were 2 miles from your destination the distance is the same whether it's 1 mile north and 1 mile up the face of the mountain or 2 miles north on level ground but clearly the former route is much different from the latter. The distance travelled straight upward is the most important if figuring out how long it will really take to get to the destination and you would probably like to consider this "dimension" to be more important than the others. In fact you, as a mountain climber, could "weight" the importance of the vertical dimension in calculating some new distance by reasoning that every mile upward is equivalent to 10 miles on level ground.

If you used this rule of thumb to weight the importance of one dimension over the other it would be clear that in one case you were much "further away" from your destination ("11 miles") than in the second ("2 miles"). The nearest neighbour algorithm uses distance measure that similarly weight the important dimensions more heavily when calculating a distance measure.

Hierarchical and Non-Hierarchical Clustering

There are two main types of clustering techniques, those that create a hierarchy of clusters and those that do not. The hierarchical clustering techniques create a hierarchy of clusters from small to big. The main reason for this is that, as was already stated, clustering is an unsupervised learning technique, and as such, there is no absolutely correct answer. For this reason and depending on the particular application of the clustering, fewer or greater numbers of clusters may be desired. With a hierarchy of clusters defined it is possible to choose the number of clusters that are desired.

At the extreme it is possible to have as many clusters as there are records in the database. In this case the records within the cluster are optimally similar to each other (since there is only one) and certainly different from the other clusters. But of course such a clustering technique misses the point in the sense that the idea of clustering is to find useful patters in the database that summarize it and make it easier to understand. Any clustering algorithm that ends up with as many clusters as there are records has not helped the user understand the data any better. Thus one of the main points about clustering is that there be many fewer clusters than there are original records. Exactly how many clusters should be formed is a matter of interpretation. The advantage of hierarchical clustering methods is that they allow the end user to choose from either many clusters or only a few.

The hierarchy of clusters is usually viewed as a tree where the smallest clusters merge together to create the next highest level of clusters and those at that level merge together to create the next highest level of clusters. How several clusters might form a hierarchy. When a hierarchy of clusters like this is created the user can determine what the right number of clusters is that adequately summarizes the data while still providing useful information (at the other extreme a single cluster containing all the records is a great summarization but does not contain enough specific information to be useful).

This hierarchy of clusters is created through the algorithm that builds the clusters. There are two main types of hierarchical clustering algorithms:

- Agglomerative - Agglomerative clustering techniques start with as many clusters as there are records where each cluster contains just one record. The clusters that are nearest each other are merged together to form the next largest cluster. This merging is continued until a hierarchy of clusters is built with just a single cluster containing all the records at the top of the hierarchy.

- Divisive - Divisive clustering techniques take the opposite approach from agglomerative techniques. These techniques start with all the records in one cluster and then try to split that cluster into smaller pieces and then in turn to try to split those smaller pieces.

Of the two the agglomerative techniques are the most commonly used for clustering and have more algorithms developed for them. The non-hierarchical techniques in general are faster to create from the historical database but require that the user make some decision about the number of clusters desired or the minimum "nearness" required for two records to be within the same cluster. These non-hierarchical techniques often times are run multiple times starting off with some arbitrary or even random clustering and then iteratively improving the clustering by shuffling some records around. Or these techniques some times create clusters that are created with only one pass through the database adding records to existing clusters when they exist and creating new clusters when no existing cluster is a good candidate for the given record. Because the definition of which clusters are formed can depend on these initial choices of which starting clusters should be chosen or even how many clusters these techniques can be less repeatable than the hierarchical techniques and can sometimes create either too many or too few clusters because the number of clusters is predetermined by the user not determined solely by the patterns inherent in the database.

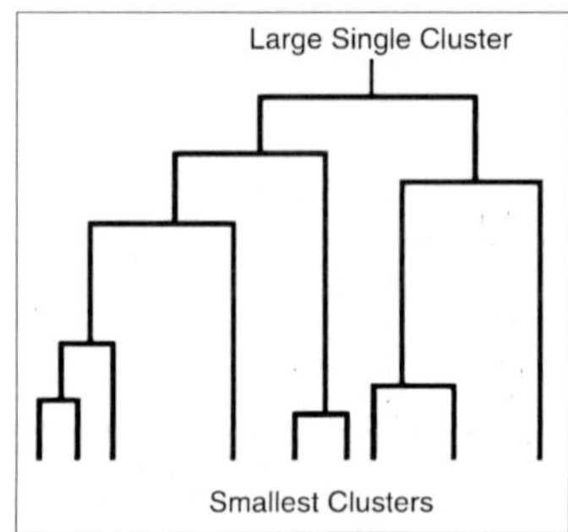

Figure : Diagram Showing a Hierarchy of Clusters. Clusters at the Lowest Level are Merged Together to Form Larger Clusters at the Next Level of the Hierarchy.

Non-Hierarchical Clustering

There are two main non-hierarchical clustering techniques. Both of them are very fast to compute on the database but have some drawbacks. The first are the single pass methods. They derive their name from the fact that the database must only be passed through once in order to create the clusters (*i.e.* each record is only read from the database once). The other class of techniques are called reallocation methods. They get their name from the movement or "reallocation" of records from one cluster to another in order to create better clusters. The reallocation techniques do use multiple passes through the database but are relatively fast in comparison to the hierarchical techniques.

Some techniques allow the user to request the number of clusters that they would like to be pulled out of the data. Predefining the number of clusters rather than having them driven by the data might seem to be a bad idea as there might be some very distinct and observable clustering of the data into a certain number of clusters which the user might not be aware of.

For instance the user may wish to see their data broken up into 10 clusters but the data itself partitions very cleanly into 13 clusters. These non-hierarchical techniques will try to shoe horn these extra three clusters into the existing 10 rather than creating 13 which best fit the data. The saving grace for these methods, however, is that, as we have seen, there is no one right answer for how to cluster so it is rare that by arbitrarily predefining the number of clusters that you would end up with the wrong answer. One of the advantages of these techniques is that often times the user does have some predefined level of summarization that they are interested in (*e.g.* "25 clusters is too confusing, but 10 will help to give me an insight into my data"). The fact that greater or fewer numbers of clusters would better match the data is actually of secondary importance.

Hierarchical Clustering

Hierarchical clustering has the advantage over non-hierarchical techniques in that the clusters are defined solely by the data (not by the users predetermining the number of clusters) and that the number of clusters can be increased or decreased by simple moving up and down the hierarchy.

The hierarchy is created by starting either at the top (one cluster that includes all records) and subdividing (divisive clustering) or by starting at the bottom with as many clusters as there are records and merging (agglomerative clustering). Usually the merging and subdividing are done two clusters at a time.

The main distinction between the techniques is their ability to favour long, scraggly clusters that are linked together record by record, or to favour the detection of the more classical, compact or spherical cluster that was shown at the beginning of this section. It may seem strange to want to form these long snaking chain like clusters, but in some cases they are the patters that the user would like to have detected in the database. These are the times when the underlying space looks quite different from the spherical clusters and the clusters that should be formed are not based on the distance from the centre of the cluster but instead based on the records being "linked" together. In these cases there are two clusters that are not very spherical in shape but could be detected by the single link technique.

When looking at the layout of the data, there appears to be two relatively flat clusters running parallel to each along the income axis. Neither the complete link nor Ward's method would, however, return these two clusters to the user. These techniques rely on creating a "centre" for each cluster and picking these centres so that they average distance of each record from this centre is minimized.

Points that are very distant from these centres would necessarily fall into a different cluster. What makes these clusters "visible" in this simple two dimensional space is the fact that each point in a cluster is tightly linked to some other point in the cluster.

For the two clusters we see the maximum distance between the nearest two points within a cluster is less than the minimum distance of the nearest two points in different clusters. That is to say that for any point in this space, the nearest point to it is always going to be another point in the same cluster. Now the centre of gravity of a cluster could be quite distant from a given point but that every point is linked to every other point by a series of small distances.

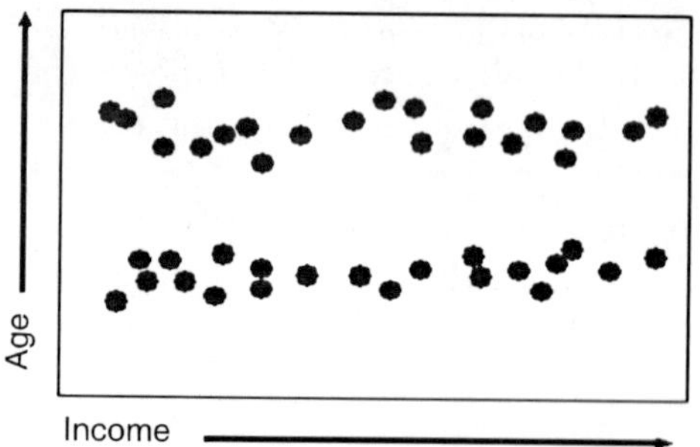

Figure : An Example of Elongated Clusters which would not be Recovered by the Complete Link or Ward's Methods but Would be by the Single-link Method.

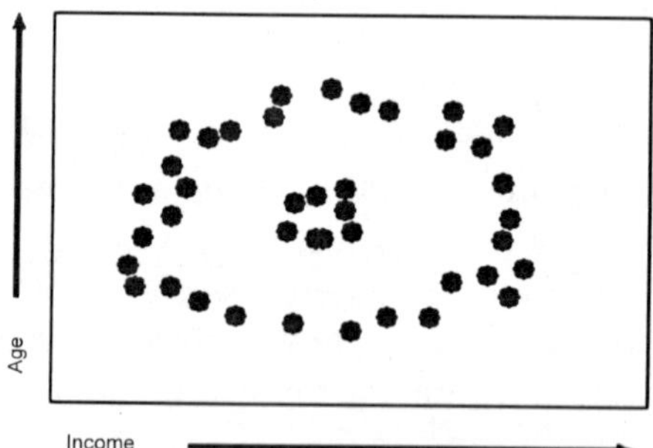

Figure : An Example of Nested Clusters which would not be Recovered by the Complete Link or Ward's Methods but would be By the Single-link Method.

CHOOSING THE CLASSICS

There is no particular rule that would tell you when to choose a particular technique over another one. Sometimes those decisions are made relatively arbitrarily based on the availability of data mining analysts who are most experienced in one technique over another. And even choosing classical techniques over some of the newer techniques is more dependent on the availability of good tools and good analysts. Whichever techniques are chosen whether classical or next generation all of the techniques presented here have been available and tried for more than two decades. So even the next generation is a solid bet for implementation.

NEXT GENERATION TECHNIQUES: TREES, NETWORKS AND RULES

THE NEXT GENERATION

The data mining techniques in this section represent the most often used techniques that have been developed over the last two decades of research. They also represent the vast majority of the techniques that are being spoken about when data mining is mentioned in the popular press. These techniques can be used for either discovering new information within large databases or for building predictive models. Though the older decision tree techniques such as CHAID are currently highly used the new techniques such as CART are gaining wider acceptance.

DECISION TREES

What is a Decision Tree?

A decision tree is a predictive model that, as its name implies, can be viewed as a tree. Specifically each branch of the tree is a classification question and the leaves of the tree are partitions of the dataset with their classification. For instance if we were going to classify customers who churn (don't renew their phone contracts) in the Cellular Telephone Industry a decision tree might look something like that found in Figure.

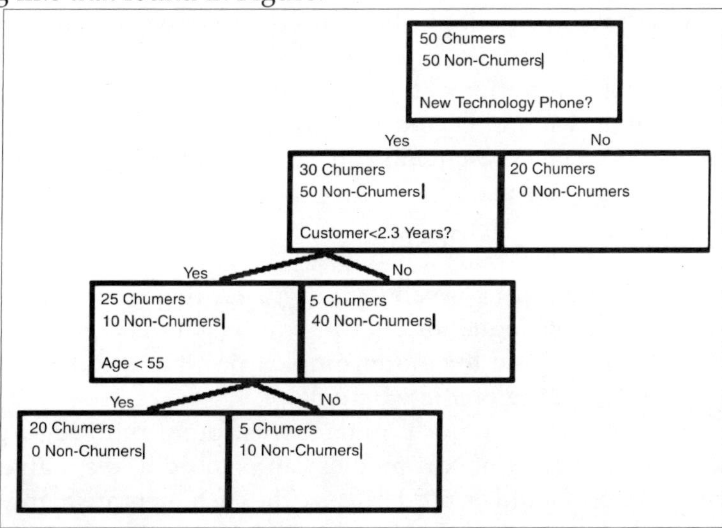

Figure : A Decision Tree is a Predictive Model that Makes a Prediction on the Basis of a Series of Decision Much Like the Game of 20 Questions.

You may notice some interesting things about the tree:

- It divides up the data on each branch point without losing any of the data (the number of total records in a given parent node is equal to the sum of the records contained in its two children).
- The number of churners and non-churners is conserved as you move up or down the tree
- It is pretty easy to understand how the model is being built (in contrast to the models from neural networks or from standard statistics).
- It would also be pretty easy to use this model if you actually had to target those customers that are likely to churn with a targeted marketing offer.

You may also build some intuitions about your customer base *e.g.* "customers who have been with you for a couple of years and have up to date cellular phones are pretty loyal".

Viewing Decision Trees as Segmentation with a Purpose

From a business perspective decision trees can be viewed as creating a segmentation of the original dataset (each segment would be one of the leaves of the tree). Segmentation of customers, products, and sales regions is something that marketing managers have been doing for many years. In the past this segmentation has been performed in order to get a high level view of a large amount of data - with no particular reason for creating the segmentation except that the records within each segmentation were somewhat similar to each other.

In this case the segmentation is done for a particular reason - namely for the prediction of some important piece of information. The records that fall within each segment fall there because they have similarity with respect to the information being predicted - not just that they are similar - without similarity being well defined. These predictive segments that are derived from the decision tree also come with a description of the characteristics that define the predictive segment. Thus the decision trees and the algorithms that create them may be complex, the results can be presented in an easy to understand way that can be quite useful to the business user.

Applying Decision Trees to Business

Because of their tree structure and ability to easily generate rules decision trees are the favoured technique for building understandable models. Because of this clarity they also allow for more complex profit and ROI models to be added easily in on top of the predictive model.

For instance once a customer population is found with high predicted likelihood to attrite a variety of cost models can be used to see if an expensive marketing intervention should be used because the customers are highly valuable or a less expensive intervention should be used because the revenue from this sub-population of customers is marginal. Because of their high level of automation and the ease of translating decision tree models into SQL for deployment in relational databases the technology has also proven to be easy to integrate with existing IT processes, requiring little preprocessing and cleansing of the data, or extraction of a special purpose file specifically for data mining.

Where can Decision Trees be Used?

Decision trees are data mining technology that has been around in a form very similar to the technology of today for almost twenty years now and early versions of the algorithms date back in the 1960s.

Often times these techniques were originally developed for statisticians to automate the process of determining which fields in their database were actually useful or correlated with the particular problem that they were trying to understand.

Partially because of this history, decision tree algorithms tend to automate the entire process of hypothesis generation and then validation much more completely and in a much more integrated way than any other data mining techniques.

They are also particularly adept at handling raw data with little or no pre-processing. Perhaps also because they were originally developed to mimic the way an analyst interactively performs data mining they provide a simple to understand predictive model based on rules (such as "90% of the time credit card customers of less than 3 months who max out their credit limit are going to default on their credit card loan.").

Because decision trees score so highly on so many of the critical features of data mining they can be used in a wide variety of business problems for both exploration and for prediction. They have been used for problems ranging from credit card attrition prediction to time series prediction of the exchange rate of different international currencies. There are also some problems where decision trees will not do as well. Some very simple problems where the prediction is just a simple multiple of the predictor can be solved much more quickly and easily by linear regression. Usually the models to be built and the interactions to be detected are much more complex in real world problems and this is where decision trees excel.

Using Decision Trees for Exploration

The decision tree technology can be used for exploration of the dataset and business problem. This is often done by looking at the predictors and values that are chosen for each split of the tree. Often times these predictors provide usable insights or propose questions that need to be answered. For instance if you ran across the following in your database for cellular phone churn you might seriously wonder about the way your telesales operators were making their calls and maybe change the way that they are compensated: "IF customer lifetime < 1.1 years AND sales channel = telesales THEN chance of churn is 65%.

Using decision trees for Data Preprocessing

Another way that the decision tree technology has been used is for preprocessing data for other prediction algorithms. Because the algorithm is fairly robust with respect to a variety of predictor types (*e.g.* number, categorical *etc.*) and because it can be run relatively quickly decision trees can be used on the first pass of a data mining run to create a subset of possibly useful predictors that can then be fed into neural networks, nearest neighbour and normal statistical routines - which can take a considerable amount of time to run if there are large numbers of possible predictors to be used in the model.

Decision Trees for Prediction

Although some forms of decision trees were initially developed as exploratory tools to refine and preprocess data for more standard statistical techniques like logistic regression. They have also been used and more increasingly often being used for prediction. This is interesting because many statisticians will still use decision trees for exploratory analysis effectively building a predictive model as a by product but then ignore the predictive model in favour of techniques that they are most comfortable with. Sometimes veteran analysts will do this even excluding the predictive model when it is superior to that produced by other techniques. With a host of new products and skilled users now appearing this tendency to use decision trees only for exploration now seems to be changing.

The First Step is Growing the Tree

The first step in the process is that of growing the tree. Specifically the algorithm seeks to create a tree that works as perfectly as possible on all the data that is available. Most of the time it is not possible to have the algorithm work perfectly. There is always noise in the database to some degree (there are variables that are not being collected that have an impact on the target you are trying to predict).

The name of the game in growing the tree is in finding the best possible question to ask at each branch point of the tree. At the bottom of the tree you will come up with nodes that you would like to be all of one type or the other. Thus the question: "Are you over 40?" probably does not sufficiently distinguish between those who are churners and those who are not - let's say it is 40%/60%. On the other hand there may be a series of questions that do quite a nice job in distinguishing those cellular phone customers who will churn and those who won't. Maybe the series of questions would be something like: "Have you been a customer for less than a year, do you have a telephone that is more than two years old and were you originally landed as a customer via telesales rather than direct sales?" This series of questions defines a segment of the customer population in which 90% churn. These are then relevant questions to be asking in relation to predicting churn.

The Difference between a Good Question and a Bad Question

The difference between a good question and a bad question has to do with how much the question can organize the data - or in this case, change the likelihood of a churner appearing in the customer segment. If we started off with our population being half churners and half non-churners then we would expect that a question that didn't organize the data to some degree into one segment that was more likely to churn than the other then it wouldn't be a very useful question to ask.

On the other hand if we asked a question that was very good at distinguishing between churners and non-churners - say that split 100 customers into one segment of 50 churners and another segment of 50 non-churners then this would be considered to be a good question. In fact it had decreased the "disorder" of the original segment as much as was possible.

The process in decision tree algorithms is very similar when they build trees. These algorithms look at all possible distinguishing questions that could possibly break up the original training dataset into segments that are nearly homogeneous with respect to the different classes being predicted. Some decision tree algorithms may use heuristics in order to pick the questions or even pick them at random. CART picks the questions in a very unsophisticated way: It tries them all. After it has tried them all CART picks the best one uses it to split the data into two more organized segments and then again asks all possible questions on each of those new segments individually.

When does the Tree Stop Growing?

If the decision tree algorithm just continued growing the tree like this it could conceivably create more and more questions and branches in the tree so that eventually there was only one record in the segment. To let the tree grow to this size is both computationally expensive but also unnecessary. Most decision tree algorithms stop growing the tree when one of three criteria are met:

- The segment contains only one record. (There is no further question that you could ask which could further refine a segment of just one.)
- All the records in the segment have identical characteristics. (There is no reason to continue asking further questions segmentation since all the remaining records are the same.)
- The improvement is not substantial enough to warrant making the split.

Why would a Decision Tree Algorithm Stop Growing the Tree if there wasn't Enough Data?

Consider the following example of a segment that we might want to split further which has just two examples. It has been created out of a much larger customer database by selecting only those customers aged 27 with blue eyes and salaries between $80,000 and $81,000.

Table : Decision Tree Algorithm Segment. This Segment cannot be Split Further Except by using the Predictor "Name".

Name	*Age*	*Eyes*	*Salary*	*Churned?*
Steve	27	Blue	$80,000	Yes
Alex	27	Blue	$80,000	No

In this case all of the possible questions that could be asked about the two customers turn out to have the same value (age, eyes, salary) except for name. It would then be possible to ask a question like: "Is the customer's name Steve?" and create the segments which would be very good at breaking apart those who churned from those who did not:

The problem is that we all have an intuition that the name of the customer is not going to be a very good indicator of whether that customer churns or not. It might work well for this particular 2 record segment but it is unlikely that it will work for other customer databases or even the same customer database at a different time. This particular example has to do with overfitting the model - in this case fitting the model too closely to the idiosyncrasies of the training data. This can be fixed later on but clearly stopping the building of the tree short of either one record segments or very small segments in general is a good idea.

Decision Trees aren't Necessarily Finished after the Tree is Grown

After the tree has been grown to a certain size (depending on the particular stopping criteria used in the algorithm) the CART algorithm has still more work to do. The algorithm then checks to see if the model has been overfit to the data. It does this in several ways using a cross validation approach or a test set validation approach. Basically using the same mind numbingly simple approach it used to find the best questions in the first place - namely trying many different simpler versions of the tree on a held aside test set. The tree that does the best on the held aside data is selected by the algorithm as the best model. The nice thing about CART is that this testing and selection is all an integral part of the algorithm as opposed to the after the fact approach that other techniques use.

ID3 and an Enhancement - C4.5

In the late 1970s J. Ross Quinlan introduced a decision tree algorithm named ID3. It was one of the first decision tree algorithms yet at the same time built solidly on work that had been done on inference systems and concept learning systems from that decade as well as the preceding decade. Initially ID3 was used for tasks such as learning good game playing strategies for chess end games. Since then ID3 has been applied to a wide variety of problems in both academia and industry and has been modified, improved and borrowed from many times over.

ID3 picks predictors and their splitting values based on the gain in information that the split or splits provide. Gain represents the difference between the amount of information that is needed to correctly make a prediction before a split is made and after the split has been made. If the amount of information required is much lower after the split is made then that split has decreased the disorder of the original single segment. Gain is defined as the difference between the entropy of the original segment and the accumulated entropies of the resulting split segments.

ID3 was later enhanced in the version called C4.5. C4.5 improves on ID3 in several important areas:

- Predictors with missing values can still be used
- Predictors with continuous values can be used
- Pruning is introduced
- Rule derivation.

Many of these techniques appear in the CART algorithm plus some others so we will go through this introduction in the CART algorithm.

CART - Growing a Forest and Picking the Best Tree

CART stands for Classification and Regression Trees and is a data exploration and prediction algorithm developed by Leo Breiman, Jerome Friedman, Richard Olshen and Charles Stone and is nicely detailed in their 1984 book "Classification and Regression Trees". These researchers from Stanford University and the University of California at Berkeley showed how this new algorithm could be used on a variety of different problems from to the detection of Chlorine from the data contained in a mass spectrum.

Predictors are picked as they decrease the disorder of the data. In building the CART tree each predictor is picked based on how well it teases apart the records with different predictions. For instance one measure that is used to determine whether a given split point for a give predictor is better than another is the entropy metric. The measure originated from the work done by Claude Shannon and Warren Weaver on information theory in 1949. They were concerned with how information could be efficiently communicated over telephone lines. Interestingly, their results also prove useful in creating decision trees.

CART Automatically Validates the Tree

One of the great advantages of CART is that the algorithm has the validation of the model and the discovery of the optimally general model built deeply into the algorithm. CART accomplishes this by building a very complex tree and then pruning it back to the optimally general tree based on the results of cross validation or test set validation. The tree is pruned back based on the performance of the various pruned version of the tree on the test set data. The most complex tree rarely fares the best on the held aside data as it has been overfitted to the training data. By using cross validation the tree that is most likely to do well on new, unseen data can be chosen.

CART Surrogates Handle Missing Data

The CART algorithm is relatively robust with respect to missing data. If the value is missing for a particular predictor in a particular record that record will not be used in making the determination of the optimal split when the tree is being built. In effect CART will utilizes as much information as it has on hand in order to make the decision for picking the best possible split. When CART is being used to predict on new data, missing values can be handled via surrogates. Surrogates are split values and predictors that mimic the actual split in the tree and can be used when the data for the preferred predictor is missing. For instance though shoe size is not a perfect predictor of height it could be used as a surrogate to try to mimic a split based on height when that information was missing from the particular record being predicted with the CART model.

CHAID

Another equally popular decision tree technology to CART is CHAID or Chi-Square Automatic Interaction Detector. CHAID is similar to CART in that it builds a decision tree but it differs in the way that it chooses its splits. Instead of the entropy or Gini metrics for choosing optimal splits the technique relies on the chi square test used in contingency tables to determine which categorical predictor is furthest from independence with the prediction values.

Because CHAID relies on the contingency tables to form its test of significance for each predictor all predictors must either be categorical or be coerced into a categorical form via binning (*e.g.* break up possible people ages into 10 bins from 0-9, 10-19, 20-29 *etc.*). Though this binning can have deleterious consequences the actual accuracy performances of CART and CHAID have been shown to be comparable in real world direct marketing response models.

NEURAL NETWORKS

What is a Neural Network?

When data mining algorithms are talked about these days most of the time people are talking about either decision trees or neural networks. Of the two neural networks have probably been of greater interest through the formative stages of data mining technology. As we will see neural networks do have disadvantages that can be limiting in their ease of use and ease of deployment, but they do also have some significant advantages. Foremost among these advantages is their highly accurate predictive models that can be applied across a large number of different types of problems.

To be more precise with the term "neural network" one might better speak of an "artificial neural network". True neural networks are biological systems (a k a brains) that detect patterns, make predictions and learn. The artificial ones are computer programmes implementing sophisticated pattern detection and machine learning algorithms on a computer to build predictive models from large historical databases. Artificial neural networks derive their name from their historical development which started off with the premise that machines could be made to "think" if scientists found ways to mimic the structure and functioning of the human brain on the computer. Thus historically neural networks grew out of the community of Artificial Intelligence rather than from the discipline of statistics. Despite the fact that scientists are still far from understanding the human brain let alone mimicking it, neural networks that run on computers can do some of the things that people can do.

It is difficult to say exactly when the first "neural network" on a computer was built. During World War II a seminal paper was published by McCulloch and Pitts which first outlined the idea that simple processing units (like the individual neurons in the human brain) could be connected together in large networks to create a system that could solve difficult problems and display behaviour that was much more complex than the simple pieces that made it up. Since that time much progress has been made in finding ways to apply artificial neural networks to real world prediction problems and in improving the performance of the algorithm in general. In many respects the greatest breakthroughs in neural networks in recent years have been in their application to more mundane real world problems like customer response prediction or fraud detection rather than the loftier goals that were originally set out for the techniques such as overall human learning and computer speech and image understanding.

Don't Neural Networks Learn to Make Better Predictions?

Because of the origins of the techniques and because of some of their early successes the techniques have enjoyed a great deal of interest. To understand how neural networks can detect patterns in a database an analogy is often made that they "learn" to detect these patterns and make better predictions in a similar way to the way that human beings do. This view is encouraged by the way the historical training data is often supplied to the network - one record (example) at a time. Neural networks do "learn" in a very real sense but under the hood the algorithms and techniques that are being deployed are not truly different from the techniques found in statistics or other data mining algorithms. It is for instance, unfair to assume that neural networks could outperform other techniques because they "learn" and improve over time while the other techniques are static. The other techniques if fact "learn" from historical examples in exactly the same way but often times the examples (historical records) to learn from a processed all at once in a more efficient manner than neural networks which often modify their model one record at a time.

Are Neural Networks Easy to Use?

A common claim for neural networks is that they are automated to a degree where the user does not need to know that much about how they work, or predictive modelling or even the database in order to use them. The implicit claim is also that most neural networks can be unleashed on your data straight out of the box without having to rearrange or modify the data very much to begin with.

Just the opposite is often true. There are many important design decisions that need to be made in order to effectively use a neural network such as:

- How should the nodes in the network be connected?
- How many neuron like processing units should be used?
- When should "training" be stopped in order to avoid overfitting?

There are also many important steps required for preprocessing the data that goes into a neural network - most often there is a requirement to normalize numeric data between 0.0 and 1.0 and categorical predictors may need to be broken up into virtual predictors that are 0 or 1 for each value of the original categorical predictor. And, as always, understanding what the data in your database means and a clear definition of the business problem to be solved are essential to ensuring eventual success. The bottom line is that neural networks provide no short cuts.

APPLYING NEURAL NETWORKS TO BUSINESS

Neural networks are very powerful predictive modelling techniques but some of the power comes at the expense of ease of use and ease of deployment. Neural networks, create very complex models that are almost always impossible to fully understand even by experts. The model itself is represented by numeric values in a complex calculation that requires all of the predictor values to be in the form of a number. The output of the neural network is also numeric and needs to be translated if the actual prediction value is categorical (*e.g.* predicting the demand for blue, white or black jeans for a clothing manufacturer requires that the predictor values blue, black and white for the predictor colour to be converted to numbers). Because of the complexity of these techniques much effort has been expended in trying to increase the clarity with which the model can be understood by the end user. These efforts are still in there infancy but are of tremendous importance since most data mining techniques including neural networks are being deployed against real business problems where significant investments are made based on the predictions from the models (*e.g.* consider trusting the predictive model from a neural network that dictates which one million customers will receive a $1 mailing).

There are two ways that these shortcomings in understanding the meaning of the neural network model have been successfully addressed:

- The neural network is package up into a complete solution such as fraud prediction. This allows the neural network to be carefully crafted for one particular application and once it has been proven successful it can be used over and over again without requiring a deep understanding of how it works.

- The neural network is package up with expert consulting services. Here the neural network is deployed by trusted experts who have a track record of success. Either the experts are able to explain the models or they are trusted that the models do work.

The first tactic has seemed to work quite well because when the technique is used for a well defined problem many of the difficulties in preprocessing the data can be automated (because the data structures have been seen before) and interpretation of the model is less of an issue since entire industries begin to use the technology successfully and a level of trust is created. There are several vendors who have deployed this strategy (*e.g.* HNC's Falcon system for credit card fraud prediction and Advanced Software Applications ModelMAX package for direct marketing).

Packaging up neural networks with expert consultants is also a viable strategy that avoids many of the pitfalls of using neural networks, but it can be quite expensive because it is human intensive.

One of the great promises of data mining is, after all, the automation of the predictive modelling process.

These neural network consulting teams are little different from the analytical departments many companies already have in house. Since there is not a great difference in the overall predictive accuracy of neural networks over standard statistical techniques the main difference becomes the replacement of the statistical expert with the neural network expert. Either with statistics or neural network experts the value of putting easy to use tools into the hands of the business end user is still not achieved.

Where to Use Neural Networks

Neural networks are used in a wide variety of applications. They have been used in all facets of business from detecting the fraudulent use of credit cards and credit risk prediction to increasing the hit rate of targeted mailings. They also have a long history of application in other areas such as the military for the automated driving of an unmanned vehicle at 30 miles per hour on paved roads to biological simulations such as learning the correct pronunciation of English words from written text.

Neural Networks for Clustering

Neural networks of various kinds can be used for clustering and prototype creation. The Kohonen network is probably the most common network used for clustering and segmentation of the database. Typically the networks are used in a unsupervised learning mode to create the clusters. The clusters are created by forcing the system to compress the data by creating prototypes or by algorithms that steer the system towards creating clusters that compete against each other for the records that they contain, thus ensuring that the clusters overlap as little as possible.

Neural Networks for Outlier Analysis

Sometimes clustering is performed not so much to keep records together as to make it easier to see when one record sticks out from the rest. For instance:

Most wine distributors selling inexpensive wine in Missouri and that ship a certain volume of product produce a certain level of profit. There is a cluster of stores that can be formed with these characteristics. One store stands out, however, as producing significantly lower profit. On closer examination it turns out that the distributor was delivering product to but not collecting payment from one of their customers.

A sale on men's suits is being held in all branches of a department store for southern California. All stores with these characteristics have seen at least a 100% jump in revenue since the start of the sale except one. It turns out that this store had, unlike the others, advertised via radio rather than television.

Neural Networks for Feature Extraction

One of the important problems in all of data mining is that of determining which predictors are the most relevant and the most important in building models that are most accurate at prediction. These predictors may be used by themselves or they may be used in conjunction with other predictors to form "features". A simple example of a feature in problems that neural networks are working on is the feature of a vertical line in a computer image. The predictors, or raw input data are just the coloured pixels that make up the picture. Recognizing that the predictors (pixels) can be organized in such a way as to create lines, and then using the line as the input predictor can prove to dramatically improve the accuracy of the model and decrease the time to create it.

Some features like lines in computer images are things that humans are already pretty good at detecting, in other problem domains it is more difficult to recognize the features. One novel way that neural networks have been used to detect features is the idea that features are sort of a compression of the training database. For instance you could describe an image to a friend by rattling off the colour and intensity of each pixel on every point in the picture or you could describe it at a higher level in terms of lines, circles - or maybe even at a higher level of features such as trees, mountains *etc.* In either case your friend eventually gets all the information that they need in order to know what the picture looks like, but certainly describing it in terms of high level features requires much less communication of information than the "paint by numbers" approach of describing the colour on each square millimeter of the image.

If we think of features in this way, as an efficient way to communicate our data, then neural networks can be used to automatically extract them. The neural network is used to extract features by requiring the network to learn to recreate the input data at the output nodes by using just 5 hidden nodes. Consider that if you were allowed 100 hidden nodes, that recreating the data for the network would be rather trivial - simply pass the input node value directly through the corresponding hidden node and on to the output node. But as there are fewer and fewer hidden nodes, that information has to be passed through the hidden layer in a more and more efficient manner since there are less hidden nodes to help pass along the information.

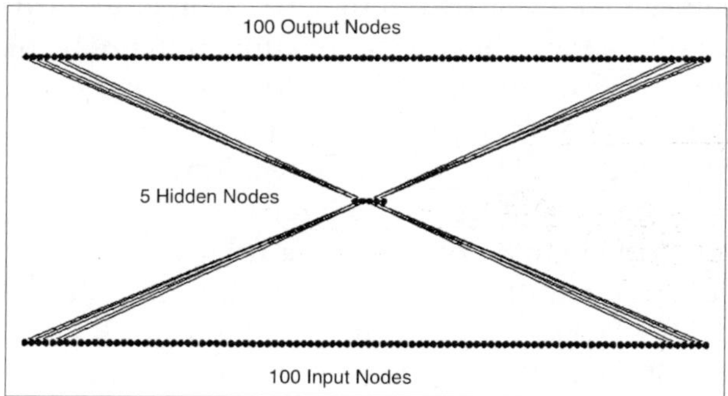

Figure : Neural Networks can be used for Data Compression and Feature Extraction.

In order to accomplish this the neural network tries to have the hidden nodes extract features from the input nodes that efficiently describe the record represented at the input layer. This forced "squeezing" of the data through the narrow hidden layer forces the neural network to extract only those predictors and combinations of predictors that are best at recreating the input record. The link weights used to create the inputs to the hidden nodes are effectively creating features that are combinations of the input nodes values.

What does a neural net look like? A neural network is loosely based on how some people believe that the human brain is organized and how it learns. Given that there are two main structures of consequence in the neural network:

The node - which loosely corresponds to the neuron in the human brain. The link - which loosely corresponds to the connections between neurons (axons, dendrites and synapses) in the human brain.

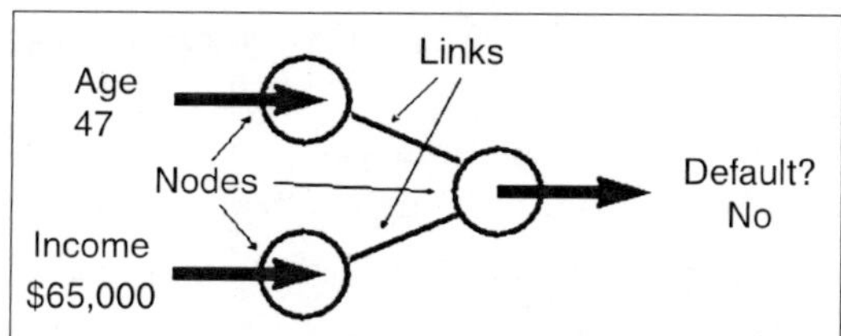

Figure : A Simplified View of a Neural Network for Prediction of Loan Default.

There is a drawing of a simple neural network. The round circles represent the nodes and the connecting lines represent the links. The neural network functions by accepting predictor values at the left and performing calculations on those values to produce new values in the node at the far right. The value at this node represents the prediction from the neural network model. In this case the network takes in values for predictors for age and income and predicts whether the person will default on a bank loan.

How does a neural net make a prediction? In order to make a prediction the neural network accepts the values for the predictors on what are called the input nodes. These become the values for those nodes those values are then multiplied by values that are stored in the links (sometimes called links and in some ways similar to the weights that were applied to predictors in the nearest neighbour method). These values are then added together at the node at the far right (the output node) a special thresholding function is applied and the resulting number is the prediction. In this case if the resulting number is 0 the record is considered to be a good credit risk (no default) if the number is 1 the record is considered to be a bad credit risk (likely default).

A simplified version of the calculations made. Here the value age of 47 is normalized to fall between 0.0 and 1.0 and has the value 0.47 and the income is normalized to the value 0.65. This simplified neural network makes the prediction of no default for a 47 year old making $65,000. The links are weighted at 0.7 and 0.1 and the resulting value after multiplying the node values by the link weights is 0.39. The network has been trained to learn that an output value of 1.0 indicates default and that 0.0 indicates non-default. The output value calculated here (0.39) is closer to 0.0 than to 1.0 so the record is assigned a non-default prediction.

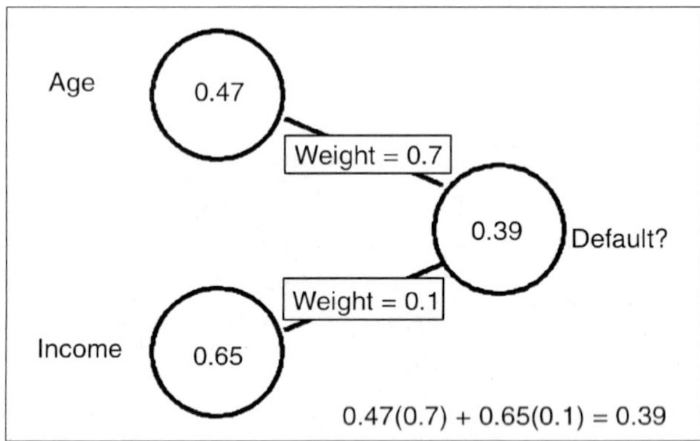

Figure : The Normalized Input Values are Multiplied by the Link Weights and Added Together at the Output.

How is the neural net model created? The neural network model is created by presenting it with many examples of the predictor values from records in the training set (in this example age and income are used) and the prediction value from those same records. By comparing the correct answer obtained from the training record and the predicted answer from the neural network it is possible to slowly change the behaviour of the neural network by changing the values of the link weights. In some ways this is like having a grade school teacher ask questions of her student (a.k.a. the neural network) and if the answer is wrong to verbally correct the student. The greater the error the harsher the verbal correction. So that large errors are given greater attention at correction than are small errors.

For the actual neural network it is the weights of the links that actually control the prediction value for a given record. Thus the particular model that is being found by the neural network is in fact fully determined by the weights and the architectural structure of the network. For this reason it is the link weights that are modified each time an error is made.

How complex can the neural network model become? The models shown in the figures above have been designed to be as simple as possible in order to make them understandable. In practice no networks are as simple as these. Networks with many more links and many more nodes are possible. This was the case in the architecture of a neural network system called NETtalk that learned how to pronounce written English words. Each node in this network was connected to every node in the level above it and below it resulting in 18,629 link weights that needed to be learned in the network.

In this network there was a row of nodes in between the input nodes and the output nodes. These are called hidden nodes or the hidden layer because the values of these nodes are not visible to the end user the way that the output nodes are (that contain the prediction) and the input nodes (which just contain the predictor values). There are even more complex neural network architectures that have more than one hidden layer. In practice one hidden layer seems to suffice however.

Hidden Nodes are Like Trusted Advisors to the Output Nodes

The meaning of the input nodes and the output nodes are usually pretty well understood - and are usually defined by the end user based on the particular problem to be solved and the nature and structure of the database. The hidden nodes, however, do not have a predefined meaning and are determined by the neural network as it trains. Which poses two problems:

- It is difficult to trust the prediction of the neural network if the meaning of these nodes is not well understood.
- The prediction is made at the output layer and the difference between the prediction and the actual value is calculated there, how is this error correction fed back through the hidden layers to modify the link weights that connect them?

The meaning of these hidden nodes is not necessarily well understood but sometimes after the fact they can be looked at to see when they are active and when they are not and derive some meaning from them.

The learning that goes on in the hidden nodes. The learning procedure for the neural network has been defined to work for the weights in the links connecting the hidden layer. A good metaphor for how this works is to think of a military operation in some war where there are many layers of command with a general ultimately responsible for making the decisions on where to advance and where to retreat. The general probably has several lieutenant generals advising him and each lieutenant general probably has several major generals advising him. This hierarchy continuing downward through colonels and privates at the bottom of the hierarchy.

This is not too far from the structure of a neural network with several hidden layers and one output node. You can think of the inputs coming from the hidden nodes as advice. The link weight corresponds to the trust that the general has in his advisors. Some trusted advisors have very high weights and some advisors may no be trusted and in fact have negative weights. The other part of the advice from the advisors has to do with how competent the particular advisor is for a given situation. The general may have a trusted advisor but if that advisor has no expertise in aerial invasion and the question at hand has to do with a situation involving the air force this advisor may be very well trusted but the advisor himself may not have any strong opinion one way or another.

In this analogy the link weight of a neural network to an output unit is like the trust or confidence that a commander has in his advisors and the actual node value represents how strong an opinion this particular advisor has about this particular situation. To make a decision the general considers how trustworthy and valuable the advice is and how knowledgeable and confident each advisor is in making their suggestion and then taking all of this into account the general makes the decision to advance or retreat.

In the same way the output node will make a decision (a prediction) by taking into account all of the input from its advisors (the nodes connected to it). In the case of the neural network this decision is reach by multiplying the link weight by the output value of the node and summing these values across all nodes. If the prediction is incorrect the nodes that had the most influence on making the decision have their weights modified so that the wrong prediction is less likely to be made the next time.

This learning in the neural network is very similar to what happens when the wrong decision is made by the general. The confidence that the general has in all of those advisors that gave the wrong recommendation is decreased - and all the more so for those advisors who were very confident and vocal in their recommendation. On the other hand any advisors who were making the correct recommendation but whose input was not taken as seriously would be taken more seriously the next time. Likewise any advisor that was reprimanded for giving the wrong advice to the general would then go back to his advisors and determine which of them he had trusted more than he should have in making his recommendation and who he should have listened more closely to.

SHARING THE BLAME AND THE GLORY THROUGHOUT THE ORGANIZATION

This feedback can continue in this way down throughout the organization- at each level giving increased emphasis to those advisors who had advised correctly and decreased emphasis to those who had advised incorrectly. In this way the entire organization becomes better and better and supporting the general in making the correct decision more of the time.

A very similar method of training takes place in the neural network. It is called "back propagation" and refers to the propagation of the error backwards from the output nodes (where the error is easy to determine the difference between the actual prediction value from the training database and the prediction from the neural network) through the hidden layers and to the input layers. At each level the link weights between the layers are updated so as to decrease the chance of making the same mistake again.

DIFFERENT TYPES OF NEURAL NETWORKS

There are literally hundreds of variations on the back propagation feed forward neural networks that have been briefly described here. Most having to do with changing the architecture of the neural network to include recurrent connections where the output from the output layer is connected back as input into the hidden layer. These recurrent nets are some times used for sequence prediction where the previous outputs from the network need to be stored some place and then fed back into the network to provide context for the current prediction. Recurrent networks have also been used for decreasing the amount of time that it takes to train the neural network.

Another twist on the neural net theme is to change the way that the network learns. Back propagation is effectively utilizing a search technique called gradient descent to search for the best possible improvement in the link weights to reduce the error. There are, however, many other ways of doing search in a high dimensional space including Newton's methods and conjugate gradient as well as simulating the physics of cooling metals in a process called simulated annealing or in simulating the search process that goes on in biological evolution and using genetic algorithms to optimize the weights of the neural networks. It has even been suggested that creating a large number of neural networks with randomly weighted links and picking the one with the lowest error rate would be the best learning procedure.

Despite all of these choices, the back propagation learning procedure is the most commonly used. It is well understand, relatively simple, and seems to work in a large number of problem domains. There are, however, two other neural network architectures that are used relatively often. Kohonen feature maps are often used for unsupervised learning and clustering and Radial Basis Function networks are used for supervised learning and in some ways represent a hybrid between nearest neighbour and neural network classification.

Kohonen Feature Maps

Kohonen feature maps were developed in the 1970's and as such were created to simulate certain brain function. Today they are used mostly to perform unsupervised learning and clustering. Kohonen networks are feed forward neural networks generally with no hidden layer. The networks generally contain only an input layer and an output layer but the nodes in the output layer compete amongst themselves to display the strongest activation to a given record. What is sometimes called "winner take all".

The networks originally came about when some of the puzzling yet simple behaviours of the real neurons were taken into effect. Namely that physical locality of the neurons seems to play an important role in the behaviour and learning of neurons. When these networks were run, in order to simulate the real world visual system it became that the organization that was automatically being constructed on the data was also very useful for segmenting and clustering the training database. Each output node represented a cluster and nearby clusters were nearby in the two dimensional output layer. Each record in the database would fall into one and only one cluster (the most active output node) but the other clusters in which it might also fit would be shown and likely to be next to the best matching cluster.

How much like a human brain is the neural network? Since the inception of the idea of neural networks the ultimate goal for these techniques has been to have them recreate human thought and learning. This has once again proved to be a difficult task - despite the power of these new techniques and the similarities of their architecture to that of the human brain. Many of the things that people take for granted are difficult for neural networks - like avoiding overfitting and working with real world data without a lot of preprocessing required. There have also been some exciting successes.

COMBATTING OVERFITTING - GETTING A MODEL YOU CAN USE SOMEWHERE ELSE

As with all predictive modelling techniques some care must be taken to avoid overfitting with a neural network. Neural networks can be quite good at overfitting training data with a predictive model that does not work well on new data. This is particularly problematic for neural networks because it is difficult to understand how the model is working. In the early days of neural networks the predictive accuracy that was often mentioned first was the accuracy on the training set and the vaulted or validation set database was reported as a footnote.

This is in part due to the fact that unlike decision trees or nearest neighbour techniques, which can quickly achieve 100% predictive accuracy on the training database, neural networks can be trained forever and still not be 100% accurate on the training set. While this is an interesting fact it is not terribly relevant since the accuracy on the training set is of little interest and can have little bearing on the validation database accuracy. Perhaps because overfitting was more obvious for decision trees and nearest neighbour approaches more effort was placed earlier on to add pruning and editing to these techniques. For neural networks generalization of the predictive model is accomplished via rules of thumb and sometimes in a more methodically way by using cross validation as is done with decision trees.

One way to control overfitting in neural networks is to limit the number of links. Since the number of links represents the complexity of the model that can be produced, and since more complex models have the ability to overfit while less complex ones cannot, overfitting can be controlled by simply limiting the number of links in the neural network. Unfortunately there is no god theoretical grounds for picking a certain number of links.

Test set validation can be used to avoid overfitting by building the neural network on one portion of the training database and using the other portion of the training database to detect what the predictive accuracy is on vaulted data. This accuracy will peak at some point in the training and then as training proceeds it will decrease while the accuracy on the training database will continue to increase. The link weights for the network can be saved when the accuracy on the held aside data peaks. The NeuralWare product, and others, provide an automated function that saves out the network when it is best performing on the test set and even continues to search after the minimum is reached.

Explaining the Network

One of the indictments against neural networks is that it is difficult to understand the model that they have built and also how the raw data effects the output predictive answer. With nearest neighbour techniques prototypical records are provided to "explain" why the prediction is made, and decision trees provide rules that can be translated in to English to explain why a particular prediction was made for a particular record. The complex models of the neural network are captured solely by the link weights in the network which represent a very complex mathematical equation.

There have been several attempts to alleviate these basic problems of the neural network. The simplest approach is to actually look at the neural network and try to create plausible explanations for the meanings of the hidden nodes. Some times this can be done quite successfully. In the example given at the beginning of this section the hidden nodes of the neural network seemed to have extracted important distinguishing features in predicting the relationship between people by extracting information like country of origin. Features that it would seem that a person would also extract and use for the prediction. But there were also many other hidden nodes, even in this particular example that were hard to explain and didn't seem to have any particular purpose. Except that they aided the neural network in making the correct prediction.

RULE INDUCTION

Rule induction is one of the major forms of data mining and is perhaps the most common form of knowledge discovery in unsupervised learning systems.

It is also perhaps the form of data mining that most closely resembles the process that most people think about when they think about data mining, namely "mining" for gold through a vast database. The gold in this case would be a rule that is interesting - that tells you something about your database that you didn't already know and probably weren't able to explicitly articulate (aside from saying "show me things that are interesting").

Rule induction on a data base can be a massive undertaking where all possible patterns are systematically pulled out of the data and then an accuracy and significance are added to them that tell the user how strong the pattern is and how likely it is to occur again. In general these rules are relatively simple such as for a market basket database of items scanned in a consumer market basket you might find interesting correlations in your database such as:

- If bagels are purchased then cream cheese is purchased 90% of the time and this pattern occurs in 3% of all shopping baskets.
- If live plants are purchased from a hardware store then plant fertilizer is purchased 60% of the time and these two items are bought together in 6% of the shopping baskets.

The rules that are pulled from the database are extracted and ordered to be presented to the user based on the percentage of times that they are correct and how often they apply.

The bane of rule induction systems is also its strength - that it retrieves all possible interesting patterns in the database. This is a strength in the sense that it leaves no stone unturned but it can also be viewed as a weakness because the user can easily become overwhelmed with such a large number of rules that it is difficult to look through all of them. You almost need a second pass of data mining to go through the list of interesting rules that have been generated by the rule induction system in the first place in order to find the most valuable gold nugget amongst them all. This overabundance of patterns can also be problematic for the simple task of prediction because all possible patterns are culled from the database there may be conflicting predictions made by equally interesting rules. Automating the process of culling the most interesting rules and of combing the recommendations of a variety of rules are well handled by many of the commercially available rule induction systems on the market today and is also an area of active research.

Applying Rule Induction to Business

Rule induction systems are highly automated and are probably the best of data mining techniques for exposing all possible predictive patterns in a database. They can be modified to for use in prediction problems but the algorithms for combining evidence from a variety of rules comes more from rules of thumbs and practical experience.

In comparing data mining techniques along an axis of explanation neural networks would be at one extreme of the data mining algorithms and rule induction systems at the other end. Neural networks are extremely proficient and saying exactly what must be done in a prediction task (*e.g.* who do I give credit to/ who do I deny credit to) with little explanation. Rule induction systems when used for prediction on the other hand are like having a committee of trusted advisors each with a slightly different opinion as to what to do but relatively well grounded reasoning and a good explanation for why it should be done.

The business value of rule induction techniques reflects the highly automated way in which the rules are created which makes it easy to use the system but also that this approach can suffer from an overabundance of interesting patterns which can make it complicated in order to make a prediction that is directly tied to return on investment (ROI).

What is a Rule?

In rule induction systems the rule itself is of a simple form of "if this and this and this then this". For example a rule that a supermarket might find in their data collected from scanners would be: "if pickles are purchased then ketchup is purchased'. Or

- If paper plates then plastic forks
- If dip then potato chips
- If salsa then tortilla chips.

In order for the rules to be useful there are two pieces of information that must be supplied as well as the actual rule:

- Accuracy - How often is the rule correct?
- Coverage - How often does the rule apply?

Just because the pattern in the data base is expressed as rule does not mean that it is true all the time. Thus just like in other data mining algorithms it is important to recognize and make explicit the uncertainty in the rule. This is what the accuracy of the rule means. The coverage of the rule has to do with how much of the database the rule "covers" or applies to. Examples of these two measure for a variety of rules.

In some cases accuracy is called the confidence of the rule and coverage is called the support. Accuracy and coverage appear to be the preferred ways of naming these two measurements.

Table : Examples of Rule Accuracy and Coverage

Rule	*Accuracy*	*Coverage*
If breakfast cereal purchased then milk purchased.	85%	20%
If bread purchased then swiss cheese purchased.	15%	6%
If 42 years old and purchased pretzels and purchased dry roasted peanuts then beer will be purchased.	95%	0.01%

The rules themselves consist of two halves. The left hand side is called the antecedent and the right hand side is called the consequent. The antecedent can consist of just one condition or multiple conditions which must all be true in order for the consequent to be true at the given accuracy. Generally the consequent is just a single condition (prediction of purchasing just one grocery store item) rather than multiple conditions. Thus rules such as: "if *x* and *y* then *a* and *b* and *c*".

What to do with a Rule

When the rules are mined out of the database the rules can be used either for understanding better the business problems that the data reflects or for performing actual predictions against some predefined prediction target. Since there is both a left side and a right side to a rule (antecedent and consequent) they can be used in several ways for your business.

Target the antecedent. In this case all rules that have a certain value for the antecedent are gathered and displayed to the user. For instance a grocery store may request all rules that have nails, bolts or screws as the antecedent in order to try to understand whether discontinuing the sale of these low margin items will have any effect on other higher margin. For instance maybe people who buy nails also buy expensive hammers but wouldn't do so at the store if the nails were not available.

Target the consequent. In this case all rules that have a certain value for the consequent can be used to understand what is associated with the consequent and perhaps what affects the consequent. For instance it might be useful to know all of the interesting rules that have "coffee" in their consequent. These may well be the rules that affect the purchases of coffee and that a store owner may want to put close to the coffee in order to increase the sale of both items. Or it might be the rule that the coffee manufacturer uses to determine in which magazine to place their next coupons.

Target based on accuracy. Some times the most important thing for a user is the accuracy of the rules that are being generated. Highly accurate rules of 80% or 90% imply strong relationships that can be exploited even if they have low coverage of the database and only occur a limited number of times. For instance a rule that only has 0.1% coverage but 95% can only be applied one time out of one thousand but it will very likely be correct. If this one time is highly profitable that it can be worthwhile. This, for instance, is how some of the most successful data mining applications work in the financial markets - looking for that limited amount of time where a very confident prediction can be made.

Target based on coverage. Some times user want to know what the most ubiquitous rules are or those rules that are most readily applicable. By looking at rules ranked by coverage they can quickly get a high level view of what is happening within their database most of the time.

Target based on "interestingness". Rules are interesting when they have high coverage and high accuracy and deviate from the norm. There have been many ways that rules have been ranked by some measure of interestingness so that the trade off between coverage and accuracy can be made.Since rule induction systems are so often used for pattern discovery and unsupervised learning it is less easy to compare them.

For example it is very easy for just about any rule induction system to generate all possible rules, it is, however, much more difficult to devise a way to present those rules (which could easily be in the hundreds of thousands) in a way that is most useful to the end user. When interesting rules are found they usually have been created to find relationships between many different predictor values in the database not just one well defined target of the prediction. For this reason it is often much more difficult to assign a measure of value to the rule aside from its interestingness. For instance it would be difficult to determine the monetary value of knowing that if people buy breakfast sausage they also buy eggs 60% of the time. For data mining systems that are more focused on prediction for things like customer attrition, targeted marketing response or risk it is much easier to measure the value of the system and compare it to other systems and other methods for solving the problem.

Caveat: Rules do not Imply Causality

It is important to recognize that even though the patterns produced from rule induction systems are delivered as if then rules they do not necessarily mean that the left hand side of the rule (the "if" part) causes the right hand side of the rule (the "then" part) to happen. Purchasing cheese does not cause the purchase of wine even though the rule if cheese then wine may be very strong.

This is particularly important to remember for rule induction systems because the results are presented as if this then that as many causal relationships are presented.

TYPES OF DATABASES USED FOR RULE INDUCTION

Typically rule induction is used on databases with either fields of high cardinality (many different values) or many columns of binary fields. The classical case of this is the super market basket data from store scanners that contains individual product names and quantities and may contain tens of thousands of different items with different packaging that create hundreds of thousands of SKU identifiers (Stock Keeping Units).

Sometimes in these databases the concept of a record is not easily defined within the database - consider the typical Star Schema for many data warehouses that store the supermarket transactions as separate entries in the fact table. Where the columns in the fact table are some unique identifier of the shopping basket (so all items can be noted as being in the same shopping basket), the quantity, the time of purchase, whether the item was purchased with a special promotion (sale or coupon). Thus each item in the shopping basket has a different row in the fact table. This layout of the data is not typically the best for most data mining algorithms which would prefer to have the data structured as one row per shopping basket and each column to represent the presence or absence of a given item. This can be an expensive way to store the data, however, since the typical grocery store contains 60,000 SKUs or different items that could come across the checkout counter. This structure of the records can also create a very high dimensional space (60,000 binary dimensions) which would be unwieldy for many classical data mining algorithms like neural networks and decision trees. Several tricks are played to make this computationally feasible for the data mining algorithm while not requiring a massive reorganization of the database.

Discovery

The claim to fame of these ruled induction systems is much more so for knowledge discovers in unsupervised learning systems than it is for prediction. These systems provide both a very detailed view of the data where significant patterns that only occur a small portion of the time and only can be found when looking at the detail data as well as a broad overview of the data where some systems seek to deliver to the user an overall view of the patterns contained n the database. These systems thus display a nice combination of both micro and macro views:

- Macro Level - Patterns that cover many situations are provided to the user that can be used very often and with great confidence and can also be used to summarize the database.
- Micro Level - Strong rules that cover only a very few situations can still be retrieved by the system and proposed to the end user. These may be valuable if the situations that are covered are highly valuable (maybe they only apply to the most profitable customers) or represent a small but growing subpopulation which may indicate a market shift or the emergence of a new competitor (*e.g.* customers are only being lost in one particular area of the country where a new competitor is emerging).

Prediction

After the rules are created and their interestingness is measured there is also a call for performing prediction with the rules. Each rule by itself can perform prediction - the consequent is the target and the accuracy of the rule is the accuracy of the prediction. But because rule induction systems produce many rules for a given antecedent or consequent there can be conflicting predictions with different accuracies. This is an opportunity for improving the overall performance of the systems by combining the rules. This can be done in a variety of ways by summing the accuracies as if they were weights or just by taking the prediction of the rule with the maximum accuracy.

How a given consequent or antecedent can be part of many rules with different accuracies and coverages. From this example consider the prediction problem of trying to predict whether milk was purchased based solely on the other items that were in the shopping basket. If the shopping basket contained only bread then from the table we would guess that there was a 35% chance that milk was also purchased. If, however, bread and butter and eggs and cheese were purchased what would be the prediction for milk then? 65% chance of milk because the relationship between butter and milk is the greatest at 65%? Or would all of the other items in the basket increase even further the chance of milk being purchased to well beyond 65%? Determining how to combine evidence from multiple rules is a key part of the algorithms for using rules for prediction.

Table : Accuracy and Coverage in Rule Antecedents and Consequents

Antecedent	*Consequent*	*Accuracy*	*Coverage*
bagels	cream cheese	80%	5%
bagels	orange juice	40%	3%
bagels	coffee	40%	2%
bagels	eggs	25%	2%
bread	milk	35%	30%
butter	milk	65%	20%
eggs	milk	35%	15%
cheese	milk	40%	8%

The General Idea

The general idea of a rule classification system is that rules are created that show the relationship between events captured in your database. These rules can be simple with just one element in the antecedent or they might be more complicated with many column value pairs in the antecedent all joined together by a conjunction (item1 and item2 and item3 ... must all occur for the antecedent to be true).

The rules are used to find interesting patterns in the database but they are also used at times for prediction. There are two main things that are important to understanding a rule:

Accuracy - Accuracy refers to the probability that if the antecedent is true that the precedent will be true. High accuracy means that this is a rule that is highly dependable.

Coverage - Coverage refers to the number of records in the database that the rule applies to. High coverage means that the rule can be used very often and also that it is less likely to be a spurious artifact of the sampling technique or idiosyncrasies of the database.

THE BUSINESS IMPORTANCE OF ACCURACY AND COVERAGE

From a business perspective accurate rules are important because they imply that there is useful predictive information in the database that can be exploited - namely that there is something far from independent between the antecedent and the consequent. The lower the accuracy the closer the rule comes to just random guessing. If the accuracy is significantly below that of what would be expected from random guessing then the negation of the antecedent may well in fact be useful (for instance people who buy denture adhesive are much less likely to buy fresh corn on the cob than normal).

From a business perspective coverage implies how often you can use a useful rule. For instance you may have a rule that is 100% accurate but is only applicable in 1 out of every 100,000 shopping baskets. You can rearrange your shelf space to take advantage of this fact but it will not make you much money since the event is not very likely to happen. Displays the trade off between coverage and accuracy.

Table : Rule Coverage Versus Accuracy.

	Accuracy Low	*Accuracy High*
Coverage High	Rule is rarely correct but can be used often.	Rule is often correct and can be used often.
Coverage Low	Rule is rarely correct and can be only rarely used.	Rule is often correct but can be only rarely used.

Trading Off Accuracy and Coverage is like Betting at the Track

An analogy between coverage and accuracy and making money is the following from betting on horses. Having a high accuracy rule with low coverage would be like owning a race horse that always won when he raced but could only race once a year. In betting, you could probably still make a lot of money on such a horse. In rule induction for retail stores it is unlikely that finding that one rule between mayonnaise, ice cream and sardines that seems to always be true will have much of an impact on your bottom line.

How to Evaluate the Rule

One way to look at accuracy and coverage is to see how they relate so some simple statistics and how they can be represented graphically. From statistics coverage is simply the a priori probability of the antecedent and the consequent occurring at the same time. The accuracy is just the probability of the consequent conditional on the precedent. So, for instance the if we were looking at the following database of super market basket scanner data we would need the following information in order to calculate the accuracy and coverage for a simple rule (let's say milk purchase implies eggs purchased).

T = 100 = Total number of shopping baskets in the database.

E = 30 = Number of baskets with eggs in them.

M = 40 = Number of baskets with milk in them.

B = 20 = Number of baskets with both eggs and milk in them.

Accuracy is then just the number of baskets with eggs and milk in them divided by the number of baskets with milk in them. In this case that would be

20/40 = 50%. The coverage would be the number of baskets with milk in them divided by the total number of baskets. This would be 40/100 = 40%.

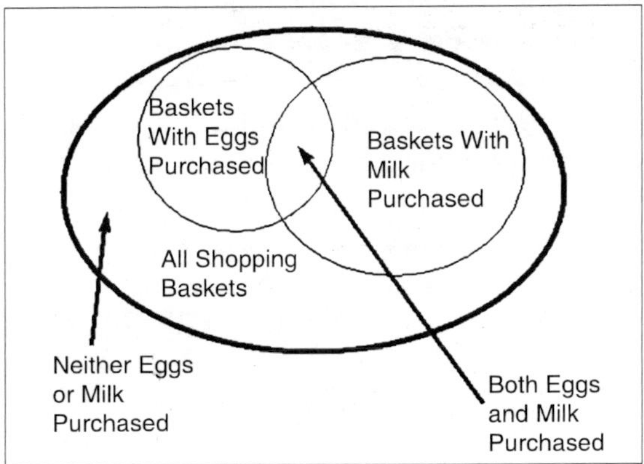

Figure : Graphically the Total Number of Shopping Baskets can be Represented in a Space and the Number of Baskets Containing Eggs or Milk Can be Represented by the Area of a Circle. The Coverage of the Rule "If Milk Then Eggs" is Just The Relative Size of the Circle Corresponding to Milk. The Accuracy is the Relative Size of the Overlap Between the Two to the Circle Representing Milk Purchased.

Notice that we haven't used E the number of baskets with eggs in these calculations. One way that eggs could be used would be to calculate the expected number of baskets with eggs and milk in them based on the independence of the events.

This would give us some sense of how unlikely and how special the event is that 20% of the baskets have both eggs and milk in them. Remember from the statistics section that if two events are independent (have no effect on one another) that the product of their individual probabilities of occurrence should equal the probability of the occurrence of them both together.

If the purchase of eggs and milk were independent of each other one would expect that $0.3 \times 0.4 = 0.12$ or 12% of the time we would see shopping baskets with both eggs and milk in them. The fact that this combination of products occurs 20% of the time is out of the ordinary if these events were independent. That is to say there is a good chance that the purchase of one effects the other and the degree to which this is the case could be calculated through statistical tests and hypothesis testing.

Defining "Interestingness"

One of the biggest problems with rule induction systems is the sometimes overwhelming number of rules that are produced. Most of which have no practical value or interest. Some of the rules are so inaccurate that they cannot be used, some have so little coverage that though they are interesting they have little applicability, and finally many of the rules capture patterns and information that the user is already familiar with. To combat this problem researchers have sought to measure the usefulness or interestingness of rules. Certainly any measure of interestingness would have something to do with accuracy and coverage. We might also expect it to have at least the following four basic behaviours:

- Interestingness = 0 if the accuracy of the rule is equal to the background accuracy (a priori probability of the consequent). Where a rule for attrition is no better than just guessing the overall rate of attrition.
- Interestingness increases as accuracy increases (or decreases with decreasing accuracy) if the coverage is fixed.
- Interestingness increases or decreases with coverage if accuracy stays fixed
- Interestingness decreases with coverage for a fixed number of correct responses (remember accuracy equals the number of correct responses divided by the coverage).

Table : Uninteresting Rules

Antecedent	*Consequent*	*Accuracy*	*Coverage*
<no constraints>	then customer will attrite	10%	100%
If customer balance > $3,000	then customer will attrite	10%	60%
If customer eyes = blue	then customer will attrite	10%	30%
If customer social security number = 144 30 8217	then customer will attrite	100%	0.000001%

There are a variety of measures of interestingness that are used that have these general characteristics. They are used for pruning back the total possible number of rules that might be generated and then presented to the user.

Other Measures of Usefulness

Another important measure is that of simplicity of the rule. This is an important solely for the end user. As complex rules, as powerful and as interesting as they might be, may be difficult to understand or to confirm via intuition.

Thus the user has a desire to see simpler rules and consequently this desire can be manifest directly in the rules that are chosen and supplied automatically to the user. Finally a measure of novelty is also required both during the creation of the rules - so that rules that are redundant but strong are less favoured to be searched than rules that may not be as strong but cover important examples that are not covered by other strong rules.

For instance there may be few historical records to provide rules on a little sold grocery item (*e.g.* mint jelly) and they may have low accuracy but since there are so few possible rules even though they are not interesting they will be "novel" and should be retained and presented to the user for that reason alone.

Rules vs. Decision Trees

Decision trees also produce rules but in a very different way than rule induction systems. The main difference between the rules that are produced by decision trees and rule induction systems is as follows:

Decision trees produce rules that are mutually exclusive and collectively exhaustive with respect to the training database while rule induction systems produce rules that are not mutually exclusive and might be collectively exhaustive.

In plain English this means that for a given record there will be a rule to cover it and there will only be one rule for rules that come from decision trees. There may be many rules that match a given record from a rule induction system and for many systems it is not guaranteed that a rule will exist for each and every possible record that might be encountered (though most systems do create very general default rules to capture these records).

The reason for this difference is the way in which the two algorithms operate. Rule induction seeks to go from the bottom up and collect all possible patterns that are interesting and then later use those patterns for some prediction target. Decisions trees on the other hand work from a prediction target downward in what is known as a "greedy" search. Looking for the best possible split on the next step (*i.e.* greedily picking the best one without looking any further than the next step). Though the greedy algorithm can make choices at the higher levels of the tree which are less than optimal at the lower levels of the tree it is very good at effectively squeezing out any correlations between predictors and the prediction. Rule induction systems on the other hand retain all possible patterns even if they are redundant or do not aid in predictive accuracy.

For instance, consider that in a rule induction system that if there were two columns of data that were highly correlated (or in fact just simple transformations of each other) they would result in two rules whereas in a decision tree one predictor would be chosen and then since the second one was redundant it would not be chosen again. An example might be the two predictors annual charges and average monthly charges (average monthly charges being the annual charges divided by 12). If the amount charged was predictive then the decision tree would choose one of the predictors and use it for a split point somewhere in the tree. The decision tree effectively "squeezed" the predictive value out of the predictor and then moved onto the next. A rule induction system would on the other hand create two rules. Perhaps something like:

If annual charges > 12,000 then default = true 90% accuracy

If average monthly charges > 1,000 the default = true 90% accuracy.

In this case we've shown an extreme case where two predictors were exactly the same, but there can also be less extreme cases. For instance height might be used rather than shoe size in the decision tree whereas in a rule induction system both would be presented as rules. Neither one technique or the other is necessarily better though having a variety of rules and predictors helps with the prediction when there are missing values. For instance if the decision tree did choose height as a split point but that predictor was not captured in the record (a null value) but shoe size was the rule induction system would still have a matching rule to capture this record. Decision trees do have ways of overcoming this difficulty by keeping "surrogates" at each split point that work almost as well at splitting the data as does the chosen predictor. In this case shoe size might have been kept as a surrogate for height at this particular branch of the tree.

Another Commonality between Decision Trees and Rule Induction Systems

One other thing that decision trees and rule induction systems have in common is the fact that they both need to find ways to combine and simplify rules. In a decision tree this can be as simple as recognizing that if a lower split on a predictor is more constrained than a split on the same predictor further up in the tree that both don't need to be provided to the user but only the more restrictive one. For instance if the first split of the tree is age <= 50 years and the lowest split for the given leaf is age <= 30 years then only the latter constraint needs to be captured in the rule for that leaf.

Rules from rule induction systems are generally created by taking a simple high level rule and adding new constraints to it until the coverage gets so small as to not be meaningful. This means that the rules actually have families or what is called "cones of specialization" where one more general rule can be the parent of many more specialized rules. These cones then can be presented to the user as high level views of the families of rules and can be viewed in a hierarchical manner to aid in understanding.

Which Technique and When?

Clearly one of the hardest things to do when deciding to implement a data mining system is to determine which technique to use when. When are neural networks appropriate and when are decision trees appropriate? When is data mining appropriate at all as opposed to just working with relational databases and reporting? When would just using OLAP and a multidimensional database be appropriate?

Some of the criteria that are important in determining the technique to be used are determined by trial and error. There are definite differences in the types of problems that are most conducive to each technique but the reality of real world data and the dynamic way in which markets, customers and hence the data that represents them is formed means that the data is constantly changing. These dynamics mean that it no longer makes sense to build the "perfect" model on the historical data since whatever was known in the past cannot adequately predict the future because the future is so unlike what has gone before.

In some ways this situation is analogous to the business person who is waiting for all information to come in before they make their decision. They are trying out different scenarios, different formulae and researching new sources of information. But this is a task that will never be accomplished - at least in part because the business the economy and even the world is changing in unpredictable and even chaotic ways that could never be adequately predicted. Better to take a robust model that perhaps is an under-performer compared to what some of the best data mining tools could provide with a great deal of analysis and execute it today rather than to wait until tomorrow when it may be too late.

Balancing Exploration and Exploitation

There is always the trade off between exploration (learning more and gathering more facts) and exploitation (taking immediate advantage of everything that is currently known). This theme of exploration versus exploitation is echoed also at the level of collecting data in a targeted marketing system: from a limited population of prospects/customers to choose from how many to you sacrifice to exploration (trying out new promotions or messages at random) versus optimizing what you already know.

There was for instance no reasonable way that Barnes and Noble bookstores could in 1995 look at past sales figures and foresee the impact that Amazon books and others would have based on the internet sales model.

Compared to historic sales and marketing data the event of the internet could not be predicted based on the data alone. Instead perhaps data mining could have been used to detect trends of decreased sales to certain customer sub-populations - such as to those involved in the high tech industry that were the first to begin to buy books online at Amazon.

So caveat emptor - use the data mining tools well but strike while the iron is hot. The performance of predictive model provided by data mining tools have a limited half life of decay. Unlike a good bottle of wine they do not increase in value with age.

5

Practical Applications of Data Mining

MINING OBJECT, SPATIAL, MULTIMEDIA, TEXT AND WEB DATA

An important feature of object-relational and object-oriented databases is their capability of storing, accessing, and modelling complex structure-valued data, such as set- and list-valued data and data with nested structures. A set-valued attribute may be of homogeneous or heterogeneous type. Typically, set-valued data can be generalized by

- Generalization of each value in the set to its corresponding higher-level concept
- Derivation of the general behaviour of the set, such as the number of elements in the set, the types or value ranges in the set, the weighted average for numerical data, or the major clusters formed by the set.

Example: Generalization of a set-valued attribute. Suppose that the expertise of a person is a set-valued attribute containing the set of values {tennis, hockey, NFS, violin, prince of persia}. This set can be generalized to a set of high-level concepts, such as {sports, music, computer games} or into the number 5 (*i.e.*, the number of activities in the set). Moreover, a count can be associated with a generalized value to indicate how many elements are generalized to that value, as in {sports(3), music(1), computer games(1)}, where sports(3) indicates three kinds of sports, and so on.

AGGREGATION AND APPROXIMATION IN SPATIAL AND MULTIMEDIA DATA GENERALIZATION

Aggregation and approximation are another important means of generalization. They are especially useful for generalizing attributes with large sets of values, complex structures, and spatial or multimedia data.

Example: Spatial aggregation and approximation. Suppose that we have different pieces of land for various purposes of agricultural usage, such as the planting of vegetables, grains, and fruits. These pieces can be merged or aggregated into one large piece of agricultural land by a spatial merge. However, such a piece of agricultural land may contain highways, houses, and small stores. If the majority of the land is used for agriculture, the scattered regions for other purposes can be ignored, and the whole region can be claimed as an agricultural area by approximation.

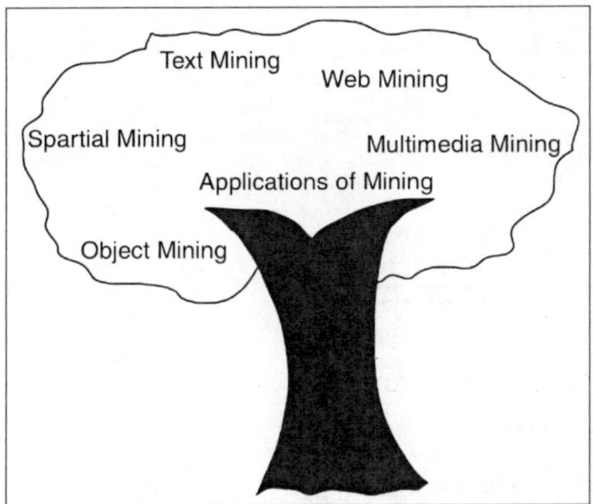

Figure: Multidimensional Analysis and Descriptive Mining of Complex Data Objects Generalization of Structured Data

GENERALIZATION OF OBJECT IDENTIFIERS AND CLASS/SUBCLASS HIERARCHIES

An object identifier can be generalized as follows. First, the object identifier is generalized to the identifier of the lowest subclass to which the object belongs. The identifier of this subclass can then, in turn, be generalized to a higherlevel class/subclass identifier by climbing up the class/subclass hierarchy. Similarly, a class or a subclass can be generalized to its corresponding superclass(es) by climbing up its associated class/subclass hierarchy.

Generalization of Class Composition Hierarchies

An attribute of an object may be composed of or described by another object, some of whose attributes may be in turn composed of or described by other objects, thus forming a class composition hierarchy. Generalization on a class composition hierarchy can be viewed as generalization on a set of nested structured data (which are possibly infinite, if the nesting is recursive).

Construction and Mining of Object Cubes

In an object database, data generalization and multidimensional analysis are not applied to individual objects but to classes of objects. Since a set of objects in a class may share many attributes and methods, and the generalization of each attribute and method may apply a sequence of generalization operators, the major issue becomes how to make the generalization processes cooperate among different attributes and methods in the class(es).

Generalization-Based Mining of Plan Databases by Divide-and-Conquer

A plan consists of a variable sequence of actions. A plan database, or simply a planbase, is a large collection of plans.

Plan mining is the task of mining significant patterns or knowledge from a planbase.

SPATIAL DATA MINING

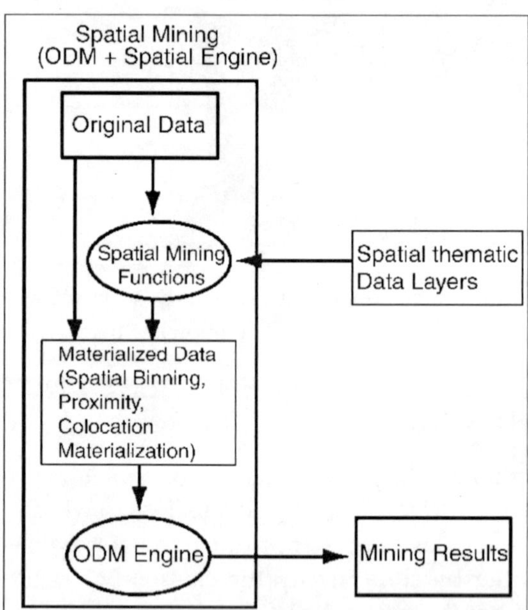

Figure: A Spatial Database stores a Large Amount of Space-related Data, such as Maps, Preprocessed Remote Sensing or Medical Imaging data, and VLSI Chip Layout Data.

Spatial data mining refers to the extraction of knowledge, spatial relationships, or other interesting patterns not explicitly stored in spatial databases.

Spatial Data Cube Construction and Spatial OLAP

As with relational data, we can integrate spatial data to construct a data warehouse that facilitates spatial data mining. A spatial data warehouse is a subject-oriented, integrated, timevariant, and nonvolatile collection of both spatial and nonspatial data in support of spatial data mining and spatial-data-related decision-making processes.

There are three types of dimensions in a spatial data cube:

- A nonspatial dimension
- A spatial-to-nonspatial dimension
- A spatial-to-spatial dimension.

We can distinguish two types of measures in a spatial data cube:

- A numerical measure contains only numerical data
- A spatial measure contains a collection of pointers to spatial objects

Mining Spatial Association and Co-location Patterns

- For mining spatial associations related to the spatial predicate close to, we can first collect the candidates that pass the minimum support threshold by
- Applying certain rough spatial evaluation algorithms, for example, using an MBR structure (which registers only two spatial points rather than a set of complex polygons),
- Evaluating the relaxed spatial predicate, g close to, which is a generalized close to covering a broader context that includes close to, touch, and intersect.

Spatial Clustering Methods : Spatial data clustering identifies clusters, or densely populated regions, according to some distance measurement in a large, multidimensional data set. Spatial Classification and Spatial Trend Analysis Spatial classification analyses spatial objects to derive classification schemes in relevance to certain spatial properties, such as the neighbourhood of a district, highway, or river.

Example: Spatial classification. Suppose that you would like to classify regions in a province into rich versus poor according to the average family income. In doing so, you would like to identify the important spatial-related factors that determine a region's classification. Many properties are associated with spatial objects, such as hosting a university, containing interstate highways, being near a lake or ocean, and so on. These properties can be used for relevance analysis and to find interesting classification schemes. Such classification schemes may be represented in the form of decision trees or rules, for example.

MINING RASTER DATABASES

Spatial database systems usually handle vector data that consist of points, lines, polygons (regions), and their compositions, such as networks or partitions. Typical examples of such data include maps, design graphs, and 3-D representations of the arrangement of the chains of protein molecules.

MULTIMEDIA DATA MINING

A multimedia database system stores and manages a large collection of multimedia data, such as audio, video, image, graphics, speech, text, document, and hypertext data, which contain text, text markups, and linkages Similarity Search in Multimedia Data When searching for similarities in multimedia data, we can search on either the data description or the data content approaches:

- Colour histogram–based signature
- Multifeature composed signature
- Wavelet-based signature
- Wavelet-based signature with region-based granularity.

MULTIDIMENSIONAL ANALYSIS OF MULTIMEDIA DATA

To facilitate the multidimensional analysis of large multimedia databases, multimedia data cubes can be designed and constructed in a manner similar to that for traditional data cubes from relational data.

A multimedia data cube can contain additional dimensions and measures for multimedia information, such as colour, texture, and shape.

CLASSIFICATION AND PREDICTION ANALYSIS OF MULTIMEDIA DATA

Classification and predictive modelling can be used for mining multimedia data, especially in scientific research, such as astronomy, seismology, and geoscientific research example:

Classification and prediction analysis of astronomy data. Taking sky images that have been carefully classified by astronomers as the training set, we can construct models for the recognition of galaxies, stars, and other stellar objects, based on properties like magnitudes, areas, intensity, image moments, and orientation. A large number of sky images taken by telescopes or space probes can then be tested against the constructed models in order to identify new celestial bodies. Similar studies have successfully been performed to identify volcanoes on Venus.

Mining Associations in Multimedia Data

- Associations between image content and nonimage content features:
- Associations among image contents that are not related to spatial relationships
- Associations among image contents related to spatial relationships:

Audio and Video Data Mining

An incommensurable amount of audiovisual information is becoming available in digital form, in digital archives, on the World Wide Web, in broadcast data streams, and in personal and professional databases, and hence a need to mine them.

TEXT MINING

Precision: This is the percentage of retrieved documents that are in fact relevant to the query (*i.e.*, "correct" responses). It is formally defined as

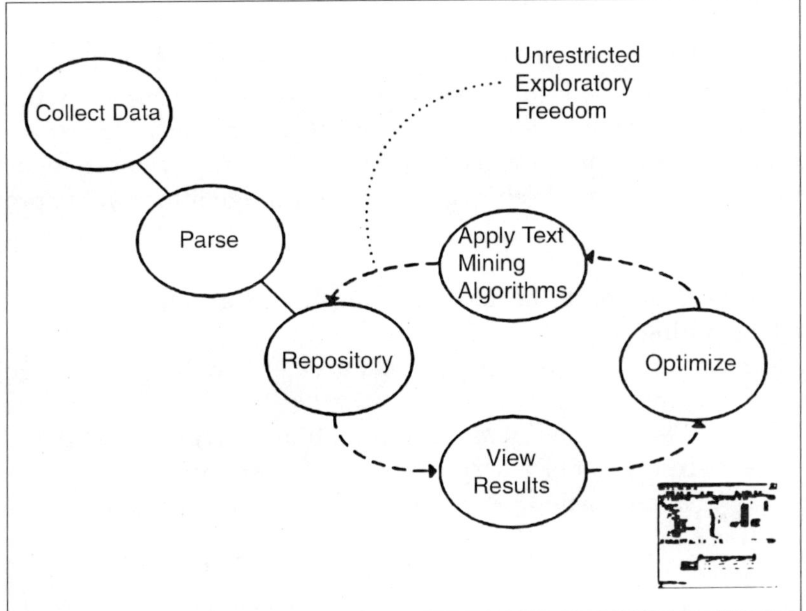

Figure: Text Data Analysis and Information Retrieval Information Retrieval (IR) is a Field that has been Developing in Parallel with Database Systems for many Years. Basic Measures for Text Retrieval: Precision and Recall

Recall: This is the percentage of documents that are relevant to the query and were, in fact, retrieved.

It is formally defined as Text Retrieval Methods:

- Document selection methods
- Document ranking methods.

Text Indexing Techniques:

- Inverted indices
- Signature files.

Query Processing Techniques

Once an inverted index is created for a document collection, a retrieval system can answer a keyword query quickly by looking up which documents contain the query keywords.

Ways of Dimensionality Reduction for Text

- Latent Semantic Indexing
- Locality Preserving Indexing
- Probabilistic Latent Semantic Indexing.

Probabilistic Latent Semantic Indexing schemas :

- Keyword-Based Association Analysis
- Document Classification Analysis
- Document Clustering Analysis.

MINING THE WORLD WIDE WEB

The World Wide Web serves as a huge, widely distributed, global information service centre for news, advertisements, consumer information, financial management, education, government, e-commerce, and many other information services. The Web also contains a rich and dynamic collection of hyperlink information and Web page access and usage information, providing rich sources for data mining.

Challenges:

- The Web seems to be too huge for effective data warehousing and data mining
- The complexity of Web pages is far greater than that of any traditional text document collection
- The Web is a highly dynamic information source
- The Web serves a broad diversity of user communities
- Only a small portion of the information on the Web is truly relevant or useful.

Authoritative Web pages:

Suppose you would like to search for Web pages relating to a given topic, such as financial investing. In addition to retrieving pages that are relevant, you also hope that the pages retrieved will be of high quality, or authoritative on the topic.

APPLICATIONS AND TRENDS IN DATA MINING

Data Mining for Financial Data Analysis few typical cases:

- Design and construction of data warehouses for multidimensional data analysis and data mining
- Loan payment prediction and customer credit policy analysis
- Classification and clustering of customers for targeted marketing
- Detection of money laundering and other financial crimes
- Data Mining for the Retail Industry.

A few examples of data mining in the retail industry:

- Design and construction of data warehouses based on the benefits of data mining
- Multidimensional analysis of sales, customers, products, time, and region
- Analysis of the effectiveness of sales campaigns
- Customer retention—analysis of customer loyalty
- Product recommendation and cross-referencing of items.

Data Mining for the Telecommunication Industry

- Multidimensional analysis of telecommunication data
- Fraudulent pattern analysis and the identification of unusual patterns

- Multidimensional association and sequential pattern analysis:
- Mobile telecommunication services
- Use of visualization tools in telecommunication data analysis.

Data Mining for Biological Data Analysis

- Semantic integration of heterogeneous, distributed genomic and proteomic databases
- Alignment, indexing, similarity search, and comparative analysis of multiple nucleotide/protein sequences
- Discovery of structural patterns and analysis of genetic networks and protein pathways
- Association and path analysis: identifying co-occurring gene sequences and linking genes to different stages of disease development
- Visualization tools in genetic data analysis.

DATA MINING IN OTHER SCIENTIFIC APPLICATIONS

Data collection and storage technologies have recently improved, so that today, scientific data can be amassed at much higher speeds and lower costs. This has resulted in the accumulation of huge volumes of high-dimensional data, stream data, and heterogenous data, containing rich spatial and temporal information. Consequently, scientific applications are shifting from the "hypothesize-and-test" paradigm towards a "collect and store data, mine for new hypotheses, confirm with data or experimentation" process. This shift brings about new challenges for data mining

Challenges:

- Data warehouses and data preprocessing
- Mining complex data types
- Graph-based mining
- Visualization tools and domain-specific knowledge.

Data Mining for Intrusion Detection

The security of our computer systems and data is at continual risk. The extensive growth of the Internet and increasing availability of tools and tricks for intruding and attacking networks have prompted intrusion detection to become a critical component of network administration.

The following are areas in which data mining technology may be applied or further developed for intrusion detection:

- Development of data mining algorithms for intrusion detection
- Association and correlation analysis, and aggregation to help select and build discriminating attributes
- Analysis of stream data
- Distributed data mining
- Visualization and querying tools.

Data Mining System Products and Research Prototypes data mining systems should be assessed based on the following multiple features:

- Data types
- System issues
- Data sources
- Data mining functions and methodologies.
- Coupling data mining with database and/or data warehouse systems.
- Scalability
- Visualization tools
- Data mining query language and graphical user interface:

Additional Themes on Data Mining : Theoretical Foundations of Data Mining:

- Data reduction: In this theory, the basis of data mining is to reduce the data representation
- Data compression: According to this theory, the basis of data mining is to compress the given data by encoding in terms of bits, association rules, decision trees, clusters, and so on
- Pattern discovery: In this theory, the basis of data mining is to discover patterns occurring in the database, such as associations, classification models, sequential patterns, and so on
- Probability theory: This is based on statistical theory. In this theory, the basis of data mining is to discover joint probability distributions of random variables, for example, Bayesian belief networks or hierarchical Bayesian models.
- Microeconomic view: The microeconomic view considers data mining as the task of finding patterns that are interesting only to the extent that they can be used in the decision making process of some enterprise (*e.g.*, regarding marketing strategies and production plans).
- Inductive databases: According to this theory, a database schema consists of data and patterns that are stored in the database.

Statistical Data Mining Techniques

- Regression
- Generalized linear model
- Analysis of variance
- Mixed effect model
- Factor analysis
- Discriminant analysis
- Time series analysis
- Survival analysis
- Quality control.

VISUAL AND AUDIO DATA MINING

Visual data mining discovers implicit and useful knowledge from large data sets using data and/or knowledge visualization techniques.

In general, data visualization and data mining can be integrated in the following ways:

- Data visualization
- Data mining result visualization
- Data mining process visualization
- Interactive visual data mining.

Data Mining and Collaborative Filtering

A collaborative filtering approach is commonly used, in which products are recommended based on the opinions of other customers. Collaborative recommender systems may employ data mining or statistical techniques to search for similarities among customer preferences.

Security of Data Mining

Data security–enhancing techniques have been developed to help protect data. Databases can employ a multilevel security model to classify and restrict data according to various security levels, with users permitted access to only their authorized level. Privacy-sensitive data mining deals with obtaining valid data mining results without learning the underlying data values.

TRENDS IN DATA MINING

- Application exploration: Early data mining applications focused mainly on helping businesses gain a competitive edge.
- Scalable and interactive data mining methods: In contrast with traditional data analysis methods, data mining must be able to handle huge amounts of data efficiently and, if possible, interactively.
- Integration of data mining with database systems, data warehouse systems, and Web database systems: Database systems, data warehouse systems, and the Web have become mainstream information processing systems.
- Standardization of data mining language: A standard data mining language or other standardization efforts will facilitate the systematic development of data mining solutions, improve interoperability among multiple data mining systems and functions, and promote the education and use of data mining systems in industry and society.
- Visual data mining: Visual data mining is an effective way to discover knowledge from huge amounts of data
- Biological data mining: Although biological data mining can be considered under "application exploration" or "mining complex types of data," the unique combination of complexity, richness, size, and importance of biological data warrants special attention in data mining.

- Data mining and software engineering: As software programmes become increasingly bulky in size, sophisticated in complexity, and tend to originate from the integration of multiple components developed by different software teams, it is an increasingly challenging task to ensure software robustness and reliability.
- Web mining
- Distributed data mining: Traditional data mining methods, designed to work at a centralized location, do not work well in many of the distributed computing environments present today (*e.g.*, the Internet, intranets, local area networks, high-speed wireless networks, and sensor networks). Advances in distributed data mining methods are expected.
- Real-time or time-critical data mining: Many applications involving stream data (such as e-commerce, Web mining, stock analysis, intrusion detection, mobile data mining, and data mining for counterterrorism) require dynamic data mining models to be built in real time. Additional development is needed in this area.
- Raph mining, link analysis, and social network analysis: Graph mining, link analysis, and social network analysis are useful for capturing sequential, topological, geometric, and other relational characteristics of many scientific data sets (such as for chemical compounds and biological networks) and social data sets (such as for the analysis of hidden criminal networks)
- Multirelational and multidatabase data mining: Most data mining approaches search for patterns in a single relational table or in a single database. However, most real world data and information are spread across multiple tables and databases.
- New methods for mining complex types of data: mining complex types of data is an important research frontier in data mining. Although progress has been made in mining stream, time-series, sequence, graph, spatiotemporal, multimedia, and text data, there is still a huge gap between the needs for these applications and the available technology.
- Privacy protection and information security in data mining: An abundance of recorded personal information available in electronic forms and on the Web, coupled with increasingly powerful data mining tools, poses a threat to our privacy and data security.

QUANTITATIVE STRUCTURE ACTIVITY RELATIONSHIP

Quantitative structure–activity relationship models (QSAR models) are regression models used in the chemical and biological sciences and engineering. Like other regression models, QSAR models relate measurements on a set of "predictor" variables to the behaviour of the response variable. In QSAR modelling, the predictors consist of properties of chemicals; the QSAR response-variable is a biological activity of the chemicals.

QSAR models first summarize a supposed relationship between chemical structures and biological activity in a data-set of chemicals. Second QSAR models predict the activities of new chemicals. Related terms include *quantitative structure–property relationships* (*QSPR*).

For example, biological activity can be expressed quantitatively as the concentration of a substance required to give a certain biological response. Additionally, when physicochemical properties or structures are expressed by numbers, one can form a mathematical relationship, or quantitative structure-activity relationship, between the two.

The mathematical expression can then be used to predict the biological response of other chemical structures.

A QSAR has the form of a mathematical model:

Activity = *f*(physiochemical properties and/or structural properties) + Error

The error includes model error (bias) and observational variability, that is, the variability in observations even on a correct model.

SAR AND THE SAR PARADOX

The basic assumption for all molecule based hypotheses is that similar molecules have similar activities. This principle is also called Structure–Activity Relationship (SAR). The underlying problem is therefore how to define a *small* difference on a molecular level, since each kind of activity, *e.g.* reaction ability, biotransformation ability, solubility, target activity, and so on, might depend on another difference. A good example was given in the bioisosterism review of Patanie/LaVoie.

In general, one is more interested in finding strong trends. Created hypotheses usually rely on a finite number of chemical data. Thus, the induction principle should be respected to avoid overfitted hypotheses and deriving overfitted and useless interpretations on structural/molecular data.

The SAR paradox refers to the fact that it is not the case that all similar molecules have similar activities.

TYPES

Fragment Based (Group Contribution)

The structure (and hence the activity) of a molecule could be defined as the sum of its individual atoms, but it is better defined for QSAR purposes as the sum of its chemical fragments.

Analogously, the "partition coefficient"—a measurement of differential solubility and itself a component of SAR predictions— can be predicted either by atomic methods (known as "XLogP" or "ALogP") or by chemical fragment methods (known as "CLogP" and other variations). It has been shown that the logP of compound can be determined by the sum of its fragments; fragment-based methods are generally accepted as better predictors than atomic-based methods.

Fragmentary logP values have been determined statistically, based on empirical data for known logP values. This method gives mixed results and is generally not trusted to have accuracy of more than ±0.1 units.

Group or Fragment based QSAR is also known as GQSAR. GQSAR allows flexibility to study various molecular fragments of interest in relation to the variation in biological response. The molecular fragments could be substituents at various substitution sites in congeneric set of molecules or could be on the basis of pre-defined chemical rules in case of non-congeneric set. GQSAR also considers cross-terms fragment descriptors, which could be helpful in identification of key fragment interactions in determining variation of activity. Lead discovery using Fragnomics is an emerging paradigm. In this context FB-QSAR proves to be a promising strategy for fragment library design and in fragment-to-lead identification endeavours.

3D-QSAR

3D-QSAR refers to the application of force field calculations requiring three-dimensional structures, *e.g.* based on protein crystallography or molecule superimposition. It uses computed potentials, *e.g.* the Lennard-Jones potential, rather than experimental constants and is concerned with the overall molecule rather than a single substituent. It examines the steric fields (shape of the molecule), the hydrophobic regions (water-soluble surfaces), and the electrostatic fields.

The created data space is then usually reduced by a following feature extraction. The following learning method can be any of the already mentioned machine learning methods, *e.g.* support vector machines. An alternative approach uses multiple-instance learning by encoding molecules as sets of data instances, each of which represents a possible molecular conformation. A label or response is assigned to each set corresponding to the activity of the molecule, which is assumed to be determined by at least one instance in the set (*i.e.* some conformation of the molecule).

On June 18th 2011 the CoMFA patent has dropped any restriction on the use of GRID and PLS technologies and the RCMD team has opened a 3D QSAR web server based on the 3-D QSAutogrid/R engine. 3-D QSAutogrid/R covers all the main features of CoMFA and GRID/GOLPE with implementation by multiprobe/multiregion variable selection (MPGRS) that improves the simplification of interpretation of the 3-D QSAR map. The methodology is based on the integration of the molecular interaction fields as calculated by AutoGrid and the R statistical environment that can be easily coupled with many free graphical molecular interfaces such as UCSF-Chimera, AutoDock Tools, JMol and others.

Modelling

In the literature it can be often found that chemists have a preference for partial least squares (PLS) methods, since it applies the feature extraction and induction in one step.

DATA MINING APPROACH

Computer SAR models typically calculate a relatively large number of features. Because those lack structural interpretation ability, the preprocessing steps face a feature selection problem (*i.e.,* which structural features should be interpreted to determine the structure-activity relationship). Feature selection can be accomplished by visual inspection (qualitative selection by a human); by data mining; or by molecule mining.

A typical data mining based prediction uses *e.g.* support vector machines, decision trees, neural networks for inducing a predictive learning model.

Molecule mining approaches, a special case of structured data mining approaches, apply a similarity matrix based prediction or an automatic fragmentation scheme into molecular substructures. Furthermore there exist also approaches using maximum common subgraph searches or graph kernels.

EVALUATION OF THE QUALITY OF QSAR MODELS

QSAR modelling produces predictive models derived from application of statistical tools correlating biological activity (including desirable therapeutic effect and undesirable side effects) of chemicals (drugs/toxicants/environmental pollutants) with descriptors representative of molecular structure and/or properties.

QSARs are being applied in many disciplines for example risk assessment, toxicity prediction, and regulatory decisions in addition to drug discovery and lead optimization. Obtaining a good quality QSAR model depends on many factors, such as the quality of biological data, the choice of descriptors and statistical methods. Any QSAR modelling should ultimately lead to statistically robust models capable of making accurate and reliable predictions of biological activities of new compounds.

For validation of QSAR models usually four strategies are adopted:

- Internal validation or cross-validation;
- Validation by dividing the data set into training and test compounds;
- True external validation by application of model on external data and
- Data randomization or Y-scrambling.

The success of any QSAR model depends on accuracy of the input data, selection of appropriate descriptors and statistical tools, and most importantly validation of the developed model. Validation is the process by which the reliability and relevance of a procedure are established for a specific purpose. Leave one-out cross-validation generally leads to an overestimation of predictive capacity, and even with external validation, no one can be sure whether the selection of training and test sets was manipulated to maximize the predictive capacity of the model being published.

Different aspects of validation of QSAR models that need attention includes methods of selection of training set compounds, setting training set size and impact of variable selection for training set models for determining the quality of prediction. Development of novel validation parameters for judging quality of QSAR models is also important.

APPLICATION

Chemical

One of the first historical QSAR applications was to predict boiling points.

It is well known for instance that within a particular family of chemical compounds, especially of organic chemistry, that there are strong correlations between structure and observed properties.

A simple example is the relationship between the number of carbons in alkanes and their boiling points. There is a clear trend in the increase of boiling point with an increase in the number carbons and this serves as a means for predicting the boiling points of higher alkanes.

A still very interesting application is the Hammett equation, Taft equation and pKa prediction methods.

Biological

The biological activity of molecules is usually measured in assays to establish the level of inhibition of particular signal transduction or metabolic pathways. Chemicals can also be biologically active by being toxic. Drug discovery often involves the use of QSAR to identify chemical structures that could have good inhibitory effects on specific targets and have low toxicity (non-specific activity). Of special interest is the prediction of partition coefficient log P, which is an important measure used in identifying "druglikeness" according to Lipinski's Rule of Five.

While many quantitative structure activity relationship analyses involve the interactions of a family of molecules with an enzyme or receptor binding site, QSAR can also be used to study the interactions between the structural domains of proteins. Protein-protein interactions can be quantitatively analysed for structural variations resulted from site-directed mutagenesis.

It is part of the machine learning method to reduce the risk for a SAR paradox, especially taking into account that only a finite amount of data is available. In general all QSAR problems can be divided into a coding and learning.

Other Applications

(Q)SAR models have been used for the risk management of chemicals risk. QSARS are suggested by regulatory authorities; in the European Union, QSARs are suggested by the REACH regulation, where "REACH" abbreviates "[[Registration, Evaluation, Authorisation and Restriction of Chemicals,".

The chemical descriptor space whose convex hull is generated by a particular training set of chemicals is called the training set's applicability domain. Prediction of properties of novel chemicals that are located outside the applicability domain uses extrapolation, and so is less reliable (on average) than prediction within the applicability domain. The assessment of the reliability of QSAR predictions remains a research topic.

6

Introduction to Data Warehouse

Over the last 20 years, $1 trillion has been invested in new computer systems to gain competitive advantage. The vast majority of these systems have automated business processes, to make them faster, cheaper, and more responsive to the customer. Electronic point of sales (EPOS) at supermarkets, itemized billing at telecommunication companies (telcos), and mass market mailing at catalogue companies are some examples of such "Operational Systems". These systems computerized the day-to-day operations of business organizations. Some characteristics of the operational systems are as follows:

- Most organizations have a number of individual *operational systems* (databases, applications)
- On-Line Transaction Processing (OLTP) systems capture the business transactions that occur.
- An Operational System is a system that is used daily (perhaps constantly) to perform routine operations - part of the normal business processes.
- Examples: Order Entry, Purchasing, Stock/Bond trading, bank operations.
- Users make short term, localized business decisions based on operational data. *e.g.*, "Can I fill this order based on the current units in inventory?"

Presently almost all businesses have operational systems and these systems are not giving them any competitive advantage. These systems have gathered a vast amount of "data" over the years. The companies are now realizing the importance of this "hidden treasure" of information. Efforts are now on to tap into this information that will improve the quality of their decision-making. A "data warehouse" is nothing but a repository of data collected from the various operational systems of an organization. This data is then comprehensively analysed to gain competitive advantage. The analysis is basically used in decision making at the top level.

From being just a passing fad, Data Warehousing technology has grown much in scale and reputation in the past few years, as evidenced by the increasing number of products, vendors, organizations, and yes books, even books, devoted to the subject. Enterprises that have successfully implemented data warehouses find it strategic and often wonder how they ever managed to survive without it in the past.

As early as 1995, a Gartner Group survey of Fortune 500 IT managers found that 90% of all organizations had planned to implement Data Warehouses by 1998.

DATA WAREHOUSING SYSTEMS

A data warehousing system can perform advanced analyses of operational data without *impacting* operational systems. OLTP is very fast and efficient at recording the business transactions - not so good at providing answers to high-level strategic questions.

COMPONENT SYSTEMS

Legacy Systems

Any information system currently in use that was built using previous technology generations. Most legacy Systems are operational in nature, largely because the automation of transaction-oriented business process had long been the priority of IT projects.

Source Systems

Any system from which data is taken for a data warehouse. A source system is often called a legacy system in a mainframe environment.

Operational Data Stores (ODS)

An ODS is a collection of integrated databases designed to support the monitoring of operations. Unlike the databases of OLTP applications (that are function oriented), the ODS contains subject oriented, volatile, and current enterprise-wide detailed information. It serves as a system of record that provides comprehensive views of data in operational sources.

Like data warehouses, ODSs are integrated and subject-oriented. However, an ODS is always current and is constantly updated. The ODS is an ideal data source for a data warehouse, since it already contains integrated operational data as of a given point in time.

In short, ODS is an integrated collection of clean data destined for the data warehouse.

Definition

Data Warehouses are mostly populated with periodic migrations of data from operational systems. The second source is made up of external, frequently purchased, databases. Examples of this data would include lists of income and demographic information. This purchased information is linked with internal data about customers to develop a good customer profile.

A Data Warehouse is a

- Subject-oriented
- Integrated
- Time-variant
- Non-volatile.

collection of data in support of management decisions.

SUBJECT ORIENTED

OLTP databases usually hold information about small subsets of the organization. For example, a retailer might have separate order entry systems and databases for retail, catalogue, and outlet sales. Each system will support queries about the information it captures. But if somebody wants to find out details of all sales, then these "separate" systems are not adequate. To address this type of situation, your data warehouse database should be subject-oriented, organized into subject areas like sales, rather than around OLTP data sources.

A data warehouse is organized around major subjects such as customer, products, sales, *etc.* Data are organized according to subject instead of application. For example, an insurance company using a data warehouse would organize their data by customer, premium, and claim instead of by different products (auto, life, property *etc.*).

Integrated

A data warehouse is usually constructed by integrating multiple, heterogeneous sources, such as relational databases, flat files, and OLTP files. When data resides in many separate applications in the operational environment, the encoding of data is often inconsistent. For example, in the above system, the retail system uses a numeric 7-digit code for products, the outlet system code consists of 9 alpha-numerics, and the catalogue system uses 4 alphabets and 4 numerics. To create a useful subject area, the source data must be integrated. There is no need to change the coding in these systems, but there must be some mechanism to modify the data coming into the data warehouse and assign a common coding scheme.

Nonvolatile

Unlike operational databases, warehouses primarily support reporting, not data capture. A data warehouse is always a physically separate store of data. Due to this separation, data warehouses do not require transaction processing, recovery, concurrency control *etc.* The data are not updated or changed in any way once they enter the data warehouse, but are only loaded, refreshed and accessed for queries.

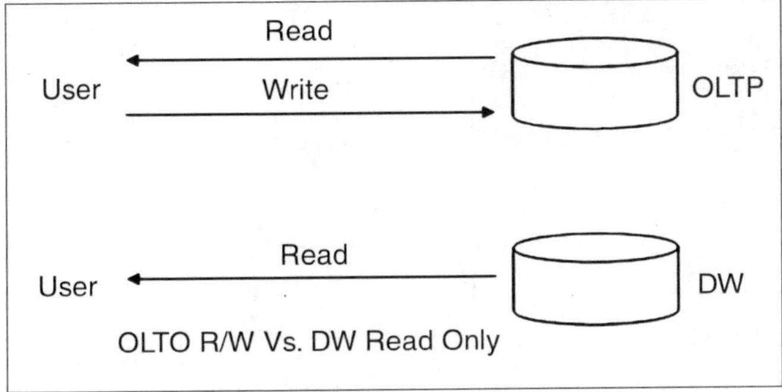

Figure: Time Variant

Data are stored in a data warehouse to provide historical perspective. Every key structure in the data warehouse contains, implicitly or explicitly, an element of time. A data warehouse generally stores data that is 5-10 years old, to be used for comparisons, trends, and forecasting.

Table: Operational Systems vs Data Warehousing Systems

Operational	*Data Warehouse*
Holds current data	Holds historic data
Data is dynamic	Data is largely static
Read/Write accesses	Read only accesses
Repetitive processing	Adhoc complex queries
Transaction driven	Analysis driven
Application oriented	Subject oriented
Used by clerical staff for day-to-day operations	Used by top managers for analysis
Normalized data model (ER model)	Denormalized data model (Dimensional model)
Must be optimized for writes and small queries.	Must be optimized for queries involving a large portion of the warehouse.

Advantages of Data Warehousing:

- Potential high Return on Investment
- Competitive Advantage
- Increased Productivity of Corporate Decision Makers

Problems with Data Warehousing

- Underestimation of resources for data loading
- Hidden problems with source systems
- Required data not captured
- Increased end-user demands
- High maintenance
- Long duration projects
- Complexity of integration

Data Warehouse Architecture*

A typical data warehousing architecture is illustrated below:

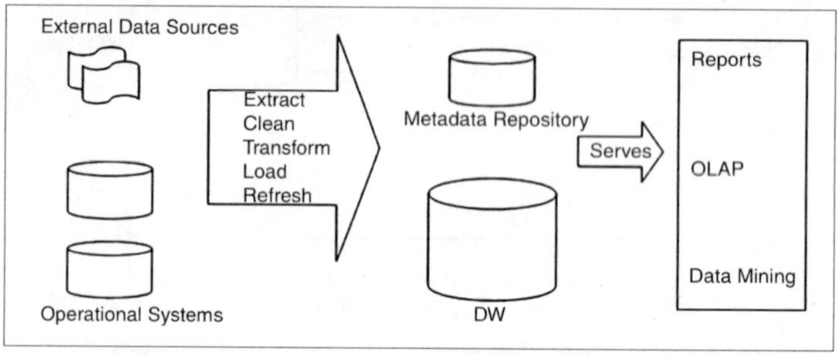

DATA WAREHOUSE COMPONENTS & ARCHITECTURE

The data in a data warehouse comes from operational systems of the organization as well as from other external sources. These are collectively referred to as *source systems*. The data *extracted* from source systems is stored in a area called *data staging area*, where the data is cleaned, transformed, combined, deduplicated to prepare the data for us in the data warehouse. The data staging area is generally a collection of machines where simple activities like sorting and sequential processing takes place. The data staging area does not provide any query or presentation services. As soon as a system provides query or presentation services, it is categorized as a *presentation server*. A presentation server is the target machine on which the data is *loaded* from the data staging area organized and stored for direct querying by end users, report writers and other applications. The three different kinds of systems that are required for a data warehouse are:

- Source Systems
- Data Staging Area
- Presentation servers.

The data travels from source systems to presentation servers via the data staging area. The entire process is popularly known as ETL (extract, transform, and load) or ETT (extract, transform, and transfer). Oracle's ETL tool is called Oracle Warehouse Builder (OWB) and MS SQL Server's ETL tool is called Data Transformation Services (DTS).

Each component and the tasks performed by them are explained below:

OPERATIONAL DATA

The sources of data for the data warehouse is supplied from:

- The data from the mainframe systems in the traditional network and hierarchical format.
- Data can also come from the relational DBMS like Oracle, Informix.
- In addition to these internal data, operational data also includes external data obtained from commercial databases and databases associated with supplier and customers.

Load Manager

The load manager performs all the operations associated with extraction and loading data into the data warehouse. These operations include simple transformations of the data to prepare the data for entry into the warehouse. The size and complexity of this component will vary between data warehouses and may be constructed using a combination of vendor data loading tools and custom built programmes.

WAREHOUSE MANAGER

The warehouse manager performs all the operations associated with the management of data in the warehouse. This component is built using vendor data management tools and custom built programmes. The operations performed by warehouse manager include:

- Analysis of data to ensure consistency
- Transformation and merging the source data from temporary storage into data warehouse tables
- Create indexes and views on the base table.
- Denormalization
- Generation of aggregation
- Backing up and archiving of data

In certain situations, the warehouse manager also generates query profiles to determine which indexes ands aggregations are appropriate.

Query Manager

The query manager performs all operations associated with management of user queries. This component is usually constructed using vendor end-user access tools, data warehousing monitoring tools, database facilities and custom built programmes. The complexity of a query manager is determined by facilities provided by the end-user access tools and database.

Detailed Data

This area of the warehouse stores all the detailed data in the database schema. In most cases detailed data is not stored online but aggregated to the next level of details. However the detailed data is added regularly to the warehouse to supplement the aggregated data.

Lightly and Highly Summerized Data

The area of the data warehouse stores all the predefined lightly and highly summarized (aggregated) data generated by the warehouse manager. This area of the warehouse is transient as it will be subject to change on an ongoing basis in order to respond to the changing query profiles. The purpose of the summarized information is to speed up the query performance. The summarized data is updated continuously as new data is loaded into the warehouse.

Archive and Back up Data

This area of the warehouse stores detailed and summarized data for the purpose of archiving and back up. The data is transferred to storage archives such as magnetic tapes or optical disks.

Meta Data

The data warehouse also stores all the Meta data (data about data) definitions used by all processes in the warehouse. It is used for variety of purposed including:

- The extraction and loading process – Meta data is used to map data sources to a common view of information within the warehouse.
- The warehouse management process – Meta data is used to automate the production of summary tables.
- As part of Query Management process Meta data is used to direct a query to the most appropriate data source.

The structure of Meta data will differ in each process, because the purpose is different.

End-user Access Tools

The principal purpose of data warehouse is to provide information to the business managers for strategic decision-making. These users interact with the warehouse using end user access tools. The examples of some of the end user access tools can be:

- Reporting and Query Tools
- Application Development Tools
- Executive Information Systems Tools
- Online Analytical Processing Tools
- Data Mining Tools.

The ETL (Extract Transformation Load) Process

The 4 major process of the data warehouse. They are extract (data from the operational systems and bring it to the data warehouse), transform (the data into internal format and structure of the data warehouse), cleanse (to make sure it is of sufficient quality to be used for decision making) and load (cleanse data is put into the data warehouse).

The four processes from extraction through loading often referred collectively as Data Staging.

Extract

Some of the data elements in the operational database can be reasonably be expected to be useful in the decision making, but others are of less value for that purpose. For this reason, it is necessary to extract the relevant data from the operational database before bringing into the data warehouse. Many commercial tools are available to help with the extraction process. Data Junction is one of the commercial products. The user of one of these tools typically has an easy-to-use windowed interface by which to specify the following:

- Which files and tables are to be accessed in the source database?
- Which fields are to be extracted from them? This is often done internally by SQL Select statement.
- What are those to be called in the resulting database?
- What is the target machine and database format of the output?
- On what schedule should the extraction process be repeated?

Transform

The operational databases developed can be based on any set of priorities, which keeps changing with the requirements. Therefore those who develop data warehouse based on these databases are typically faced with inconsistency among their data sources. Transformation process deals with rectifying any inconsistency (if any). One of the most common transformation issues is 'Attribute Naming Inconsistency'. It is common for the given data element to be referred to by different data names in different databases. Employee Name may be EMP_NAME in one database, ENAME in the other. Thus one set of Data Names are picked and used consistently in the data warehouse. Once all the data elements have right names, they must be converted to common formats. The conversion may encompass the following:

- Characters must be converted ASCII to EBCDIC or vise versa.
- Mixed Text may be converted to all uppercase for consistency.
- Numerical data must be converted in to a common format.
- Data Format has to be standardized.
- Measurement may have to convert. (Rs/$)
- Coded data (Male/Female, M/F) must be converted into a common format.

All these transformation activities are automated and many commercial products are available to perform the tasks. DataMAPPER from Applied Database Technologies is one such comprehensive tool.

Cleansing

Information quality is the key consideration in determining the value of the information. The developer of the data warehouse is not usually in a position to change the quality of its underlying historic data, though a data warehousing project can put spotlight on the data quality issues and lead to improvements for the future. It is, therefore, usually necessary to go through the data entered into the data warehouse and make it as error free as possible. This process is known as Data Cleansing. Data Cleansing must deal with many types of possible errors. These include missing data and incorrect data at one source; inconsistent data and conflicting data when two or more source are involved.

Loading

Loading often implies physical movement of the data from the computer(s) storing the source database(s) to that which will store the data warehouse database, assuming it is different. This takes place immediately after the extraction phase. The most common channel for data movement is a high-speed communication link. Ex: Oracle Warehouse Builder is the API from Oracle, which provides the features to perform the ETL task on Oracle Data Warehouse.

DATA WAREHOUSE DESIGN

AN INTRODUCTION TO DIMENSIONAL MODELLING

Data Warehouses are not easy to build. Their design requires a way of thinking that is just opposite to manner in which traditional computer systems are developed. Their construction requires radical restructuring of vast amounts of data, often of dubious or inconsistent quality, drawn from numerous heterogeneous sources. Their implementation strains the limits of today's IT. Not surprisingly, a large number of data warehouse projects fail. Successful data warehouses are built for just one reason: to answer business questions. The type of questions to be addressed will vary, but the intention is always the same. Projects that deliver new and relevant information succeed. Projects that do not fail.

To deliver answers to businesspeople, one must understand their questions. The DW design fuses business knowledge and technology know-how. The design of the data warehouse will mean the difference between success and failure.

The design of the data warehouse requires a deep understanding of the business. Yet the task of design is undertaken by IT professionals, but not business decision makers. Is it reasonable to expect the project to succeed? The answer is yes. The key is learning to apply technology towards business objectives.

Most computer systems are designed to capture data, data warehouses are designed to for getting data out. This fundamental difference suggests that the data warehouse should be designed according to a different set of principles.

Dimensional Modelling is the name of a logical design technique often used for data warehouses. It is different from entity-relationship modelling. ER modelling is very useful for transaction capture in OLTP systems.

Dimensional Modelling is the only viable technique for delivering data to the end users in a data warehouse.

COMPARISON BETWEEN ER AND DIMENSIONAL MODELLING

The characteristics of ER Model are well understood; its ability to support operational processes is its underlying characteristic. The conventional ER models are constituted to:

- Remove redundancy in the data model
- Facilitate retrieval of individual records having certain critical identifiers and
- Therefore, optimize online transaction processing (OLTP) performance.

In contrast, the dimensional model is designed to support the reporting and analytical needs of a data warehouse system.

Why ER is not suitable for Data Warehouses?

- End user cannot understand or remember an ER Model. End User cannot navigate an ER Model. There is no graphical user interface or GUI that takes a general ER diagram and makes it usable by end users.
- ER modelling is not optimized for complex, ad-hoc queries. They are optimized for repetitive narrow queries
- Use of ER modelling technique defeats this basic allure of data warehousing, namely intuitive and high performance retrieval of data because it leads to highly normalized relational tables.

DIMENSIONAL MODELLING CONCEPTS

The objective of dimensional modelling is to represent a set of business measurements in a standard framework that is easily understandable by end users. A Dimensional model contains the same information as an ER model but packages the data in a symmetric format whose design goals are

- User understandability
- Query Performance
- Resilience to Change.

The main components of a Dimensional Model are Fact Tables and Dimension Tables. A *fact table* is the primary table in each dimensional model that is meant to contain measurements of the business. The most useful facts are numeric and additive. Every fact table represents a many to many relationship and every fact table contains a set of two or more foreign keys that join to their respective dimension tables.

A fact depends on many factors. For example, sale_amount, a fact, depends on product, location and time. These factors are known as *dimensions*. Dimensions are factors on which a given fact depends. The sale_amount fact can also be thought of as a function of three variables.

sales_amount = f(product, location, time)

Likewise in a sales fact table we may include other facts like sales_unit and cost.

Dimension tables are companion tables to a fact table in a star schema. Each dimension table is defined by it's primary key that serves as the basis for referential integrity with any given fact table to which it is joined. Most dimension tables contain textual information. To understand the concepts of facts, dimension, and star schema, let us consider the following scenario: Imagine standing in the marketplace and watching the products being sold and writing down the quantity sold and the sales amount each day for each product in each store.

Note that a measurement needs to be taken at every intersection of all dimensions (day, product, and store). The information gathered can be stored in the following fact table:

Sales Fact Table
Date Key
Product Key
Store Key
Sale Unite
Sale Amount
Cost

The facts are Sale_Unit, Sale_Amount, and Cost (note that all are numeric and additive), which depend on dimensions Date, Product, and Store. The details of the dimensions are stored in dimension tables.

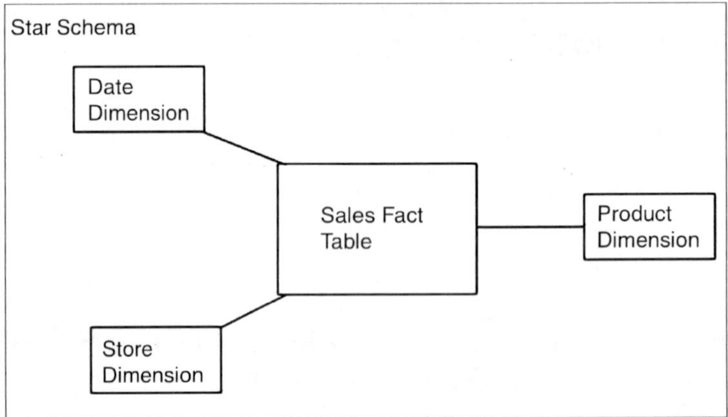

Note the following points about the star schema:

- The most popular schema design for data warehouses is the *Star Schema*
- Each dimension is stored in a *dimension table* and each entry is given its own unique identifier.
- The dimension tables are related to one or more *fact tables.*
- The fact table contains a composite key made up of the identifiers (primary keys) from the dimension tables.
- The fact table also contains facts about the given combination of dimensions. For example a combination of store_key, date_key and product_key giving the amount of a certain product sold on a given day at a given store.
- Fact table has foreign keys to all dimension tables in a star schema. In this example there are three foreign keys (date key, product key, and store key).
- Fact tables are normalized, whereas dimension tables are not
- Fact tables are very large as compared to dimension tables.

The facts in a star schema are of the following three types:

- Fully-additive
- Semi-additive
- Non-additive.

The facts in the above schema are fully-additive.

DESIGNING A DIMENSIONAL MODEL: STEPS INVOLVED

Step 1 - Select the Business Process

The first step in the design is to decide what business process (es) to model by combining an understanding of the business requirements with an understanding of the available data.

Step 2 - Declare the Grain

Once the business process has been identified, the data warehouse team faces a serious decision about the granularity. What level of detail must be made available in the dimensional model? The grain of a fact table represents the level of detail of information in a fact table. Declaring the grain means specifying exactly what an individual fact table record represents. It is recommended that the most atomic information captured by a business process. Atomic data is the most detailed information collected. The more detailed and atomic the fact measurements are, the more we know and we can analyse the data better. In the star schema, the most detailed data would be transaction line item detail in the sale receipt.

(date, time, product code, product name, price/unit, number of units, amount)

18-SEP-2002, 11.02, p1, dettol soap, 15, 2, 30

We provide sales data rolled up by product (all records corresponding to the same product are combined) in a store on a day. A typical fact table record would look like this:

18-SEP-2002, Product1, Store1, 150, 600

This record tells us that on 18th Sept. 150 units of Product1 was sold for Rs. 600 from Store1.

Step 3 – Choose the Dimensions

Once the grain of the fact table has been chosen, the date, product, and store dimensions are readily identified. It is often possible to add more dimensions to the basic grain of the fact table, where these additional dimensions naturally take on only one value under each combination of the primary dimensions. If the additional dimension violates the grain by causing additional fact rows to be generated, then the grain must be revised to accommodate this dimension.

Step 4 – Identify the Facts

The first step in identifying fact tables is where we examine the business, and identify the transaction that may be of interest. In our example the electronic point of sale (EPOS) transactions give us two facts, quantity sold and sale amount.

STRENGTHS OF DIMENSIONAL MODELLING

The dimensional model has a number of important data warehouse advantages that the ER model lacks. Its strengths are:

- The dimensional model is a predictable, standard framework. Report writers, query tools, and end user interfaces canal make strong assumptions to make the user interfaces more understandable and to make processing more efficient
- Star schema can withstand changes in user behaviour. All dimensions can be thought of as symmetrically equal entry points into the fact table. The logical design can be done independent of the expected query patterns.
- It is gracefully extensible to accommodate new data elements and new design decisions.
  (a) All existing tables can be changed by either adding new data rows or by alter table commands. Data should not have to be reloaded.
  (b) No query or reporting tool needs to be reprogrammed to accommodate the change
  (c) Old applications continue to run without yielding different results.

The following graceful can be made to the design after the data warehouse is up and running:

- Adding new facts as long as they are consistent with the grain of the existing fact table
- Adding new dimensions, as long as there is a single value of that dimension defined for each existing fact record
- Adding new, unanticipated dimension attributes
- Standard approaches available for handling common modelling situations in the business world. Each of these situations has well understood set of alternatives that can be easily programmed into report writers, query tools, and other user interfaces. These modelling situations include:
  (a) Slowly changing dimensions, where a dimension such as product or customer evolves slowly. Dimensional modelling provides specific techniques for handling slowly changing dimensions, depending on the business environment and requirements.
  (b) Heterogeneous products, where a business like bank needs to track a number of different lines of business.
  (c) Event handling databases, where the fact table turns out to be "factless"

The modelling situations to be provided in later article.

- Support for aggregates. Aggregates are summary records that are logically redundant with base level data already in the data warehouse, but are used to enhance query performance. If you don't aggregate records then you might be spending lots of money on hardware upgrades to tackle performance problems that could otherwise be addressed by aggregates. All the aggregate management software packages and aggregation navigation utilities depend on very specific single structure of fact and dimension tables that is absolutely dependent on the dimensional approach. If you are not using the dimensional approach, you can't benefit from these tools.

- A dimensional model can be implemented in a relational database, a multi-dimensional database or even an object-oriented database.

SNOWFLAKE AND STARFLAKE SCHEMAS

In dimensional modelling the dimension tables are in denormalized form whereas fact tables are in normalized form.

Snowflaking is removing low cardinality (an attribute not having low distinct values to table cardinality ratio) textual attributes from dimension tables and placing them in secondary dimension tables. For instance, a product category can be treated this way and physically removed from the low-level product dimension table by normalizing the dimension table. This is particularly done on large dimension tables. Snowflaking a dimension means normalizing it and making it more manageable by reducing its size. But this may have an adverse effect on performance, as joins need to be performed.

If all the dimensions in a star schema are normalized, the resulting schema is called a *snowflake schema* and if only a few dimensions are normalized, we call it a starflake schema.

Multidimensional Databases and MOLAP:

- Database Evolution
- Flat files, hierarchical, and network
- Relational
- Distributed relational
- Multidimensional
- Multidimensional Databases
- Result of research at MIT in 1960s
- Database engine of choice for data analysis applications (OLAP)
- OLAP using MDDBs is called MOLAP.

Business process is multidimensional in the sense that mangers ask questions about product sales in different regions over specific time periods.

Dimensions: Product, Region, Time period

Fact or Measure: Sale

An MDDB is a computer software system designed to allow for the efficient and convenient storage and retrieval system of large volumes of data that is

- Intimately related &
- Stored, viewed and analysed form different perspectives.

These perspectives are called Dimensions.

A Motivating Example

An automobile manufacturer wants to increase sale volumes by examining sales data collected throughout the organization. The evaluation would require viewing historical sales volume figures from multiple dimensions such as

- Sales volume by model
- Sales volume by colour
- Sales volume by dealership
- Sales volume over time.

Analysing sales volumes data from any one or more of the above dimensions can give answers to important queries such as: What is the trend in sales volumes over a period of time for a specific model and colour across a specific group of dealerships? Consider the relation given below containing the manufacturer's sales data:

Sales Volumes for Gleason Dealership

Model	*Colour*	*Sales Volume*
Mini Van	Blue	6
Mini Van	Red	5
Mini Van	White	4
Sports Coupe	Blue	3
Sports Coupe	Red	5
Sports Couple	White	5
Sedan	Blue	4
Sedan	Red	3
Sedan	White	2

SALES VOLUMES FOR GLEASON DEALERSHIP

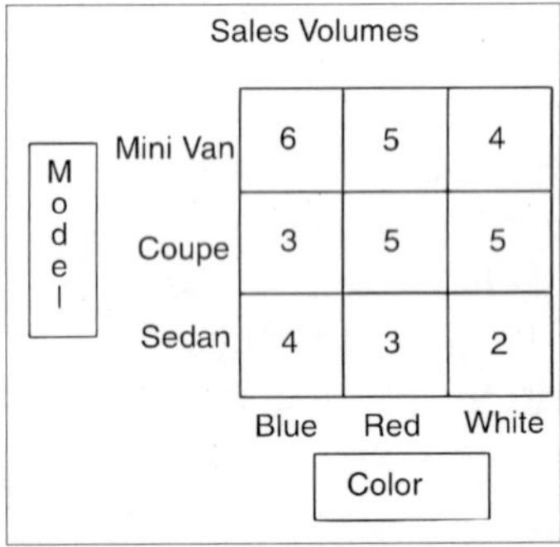

The above matrix is a 2-D array. An array is a fundamental component of MDDBs.

In an array, each axis is called a dimension (MODEL & Colour)

Each element in the dimension is called a position.

For model, 3 positions, van, sedan, and coupe.

For colour, 3 positions, blue, white, and red.

Intersections of dimensions are called cells and are populated with the data of interest or measure or fact (sales).

- Advantages of MDDBs: (a) Direct inspection of an array gives a great deal of information as opposed to relational table; (b) Array conveniently groups "like" information in columns and rows.
  Sedan sales are all "lined up" colour-wise. Total sedan sales can be added very quickly. Similarly sales for each colour are also lined up.
- Represents a higher level of organization than the relational table.

The relational structure tells us nothing about the possible contents of those fields.

Increasingly Complex Relational Tables

If we add a new field, dealers to the relational table, with three possible values, the relational table becomes even more awkward for presenting data to the end user.

Sales Volumes for all Dealerships

Model	*Colour*	*Dealership*	*Volume*
MINI VAN	BLUE	CLYDE	6
MINI VAN	BLUE	GLEASON	6
MINI VAN	BLUE	CARR	2
MINI VAN	RED	CLYDE	3
MINI VAN	RED	GLEASON	5
MINI VAN	RED	CARR	5
MINI VAN	WHITE	CLYDE	2
MINI VAN	WHITE	GLEASON	4
MINI VAN	WHITE	CARR	3
SPORTS COUPE	BLUE	CLYDE	2
SPORTS COUPE	BLUE	GLEASON	3
SPORTS COUPE	BLUE	CARR	2
SPORTS COUPE	RED	CLYDE	7
SPORTS COUPE	RED	GLEASON	5
SPORTS COUPE	RED	CARR	2
SPORTS COUPE	WHITE	CLYDE	4
SPORTS COUPE	WHITE	GLEASON	5
SPORTS COUPE	WHITE	CARR	1
SEDAN	BLUE	CLYDE	6
SEDAN	BLUE	GLEASON	4
SEDAN	BLUE	CARR	2
SEDAN	RED	CLYDE	1
SEDAN	RED	GLEASON	3
SEDAN	RED	CARR	4
SEDAN	WHITE	CLYDE	2
SEDAN	WHITE	GLEASON	2
SEDAN	WHITE	CARR	3

Multidimensional Simplification

We just need to add a third axis or dimension called Dealers. The array now becomes 3-D (3 × 3 × 3 with 27 cells). Earlier it was 2-D (3 × 3 with 9 cells). The array can now be thought of as a cube with 3 faces, with each face having 9 cells. If we have a 10 × 10 × 10 array, with each of the three dimensions having 10 positions. In relational format, we will need 1000 records to represent this array.

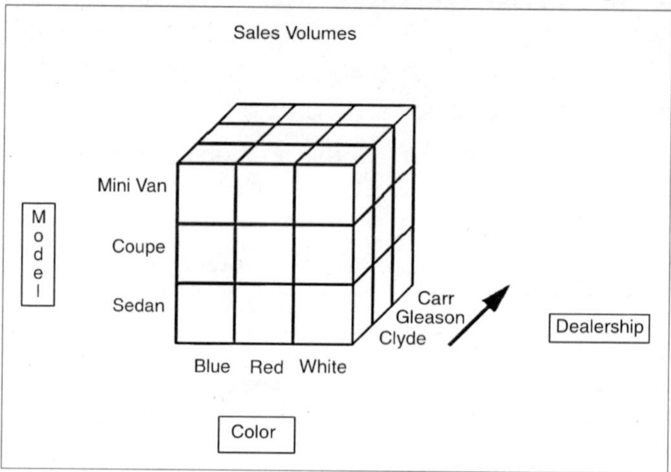

Performance Advantages

Consider a 10 × 10 × 10 array. A user wants to find out the sales figure for blue coloured sedan sold by Gleason dealer. A relational system might have to search through all 1000 records just to find the qualifying records. The multidimensional system has to search only along three dimensions of 10 positions each to find the matching record. This is a maximum of 30 position searches for the array versus 1000 record searches for the table

Adding Dimensions

The 3D model can easily be extended to four dimensions by adding time dimension to indicate the month of the year in which sale was made.

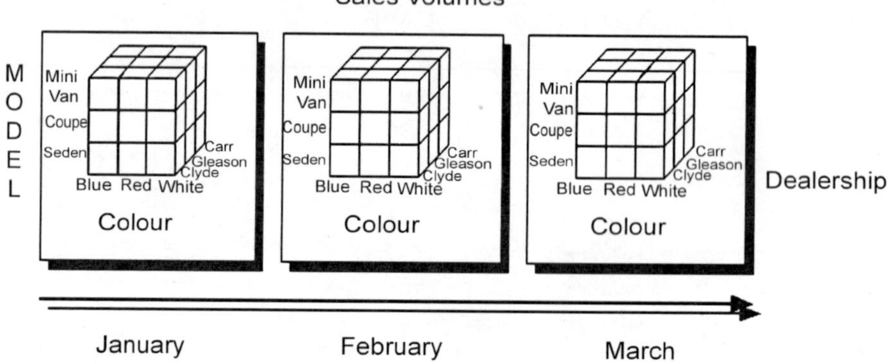

Trade-Offs: MDDB vs. RDBMS.

Consider the following factors when choosing between the multidimensional approaches:

- Size. MDDBS are generally limited by size, although the size limit has been increasing gradually over the years. Today, MDDBs can handle data up to 100GB of data efficiently. Large data warehouses are still served better by relational front-ends running against high-performance and scalable relational databases.
- Volatility of Source Data. Highly volatile data are better handled by relational technology. Multidimensional data in hypercubes generally take long to load and update. Thus, the time required to constantly load and update the multidimensional data structure may prevent the enterprise form loading new data as often as desired.
- Aggregate Strategy. Multidimensional hypercubes (multidimensional arrays) support aggregations better., although this advantage will disappear as RDBMSs improve their support for aggregation navigation.
- Investment Protection. Most organizations have already made significant investments in relational technology and skill sets. The continued use of these tools and skills for another purpose provides additional return on investment and lowers the technical risk for the data warehousing effort. Use of MDDBS will need more investment in buying tools and training people to use these tools.
- Ability to Manage Complexity. MDDB adds a layer to the overall system architecture of the warehouse. Sufficient resources must be allocated to administer and maintain the MDDB layer.
- Type of Users. Power users generally prefer the range of functionality available in MOLAP tools. Users that require broad views of the enterprise data are better served by ROLAP.

Recently, many of the large database vendors have announced plans to integrate their multidimensional and relational database products. In this situation, the end-users make use of the multidimensional front-end tools for all their queries. If the query requires data that are not available in MDDB, the tool will retrieve the required data from the larger relational database. This feature is called as *drill-through*. The following table sums up the comparison between MDDBs and RDBMSs

MDDB	***RDBMS***
Data is stored in multidimensional arrays	Data is stored in relations
Direct inspection of an array gives a great deal of information	Not so
Can handle limited size databases (< 100GB)	Proven track record for handling VLDBs
Takes long to load and update	Highly volatile data are better handled
Support aggregations better	RDBMSs are catching up-Aggregate Navigators

Contd....

New investments need to be made and new skill sets need to be developed	Most enterprises already made significant investments in RDBMS technology and skill sets
Adds complexity to the overall system architecture	No additional complexity
Limited no. of facts an dimensional tables	No such restriction
Examples: • Arbor-Essbase • Brio Query-Enterprise • Dimensional Insight-DI Diver • Oracle-Express Server	Examples: • IBM-DB2 • Microsoft-SQL Server • Oracle-Oracle RDBMS • Red Brick Systems-Red Brick Warehouse

More about aggregation and aggregate navigation later in the course.

Conclusion: Data warehousing and Data Mining are two important components of business intelligence. Data warehousing is necessary to analyse (Analysis) the business needs, integrate (Integration) data from several sources, model (Data Modelling) the data in an appropriate manner to present the business information in the form of dashboards and reports (Reporting).

7

Data Warehousing Tools

As the old Chinese saying goes, "To accomplish a goal, make sure the proper tools are selected." This is especially true when the goal is to achieve business intelligence. Given the complexity of the data warehousing system and the cross-departmental implications of the project, it is easy to see why the proper selection of business intelligence software and personnel is very important.

GENERAL CONSIDERATIONS

When we evaluate which business intelligence tool to use, the first determination is the Buy vs. Build decision. We can use the following table to compare the two approaches.

Category	*Buy*	*Build*
Cost		A
Implementation Time	A	
Documentation	A	
Functionality/Features	A	
Tailored for the exact needs		A
Reliance on third-party		A

Clearly, both approaches have its own advantages and disadvantages, and it is often wise to consider each of the components individually. For example, it is clearly not viable to write a relational database from scratch. Therefore, we may have a case where the hardware and the database are bought, but other tools are built from within. In general, deciding which approach to go is dependent on the following criteria:

- User technical skills
- Requirements
- Available budget
- Time.

Because each tool in the business intelligence arena has different functionalities, the criteria for the "Buy vs. Build" decision is different for each type. Should we decide to purchase an existing third-party business intelligence tool, we must then decide which one to buy. Often, there are a number of choices to pick from, some are well-known, and some others not as well-known, but In addition to tool functionalities, there are several considerations that we should take into account when considering tool vendors in general:

Tool Vendor's Stability: More than anything else, this is probably the most important measure.

In my opinion, this is even more important than the current functionalities that the tool itself provide, for the simple reason that if the company is going to be around for a while, it will be able to make enhancements to its business intelligence tool.

On the other hand, if the company is likely to be out of business in six months, then it doesn't matter that it has the state-of-the-art features, because sooner or later these features will be out-of-date.

Some of the ways to tell about company's stability are:

- What type of office space is it occupying? Is it wasting money by renting the most expensive office space in the area just so that it can be noticed? Or is it plugging all its money back into R&D so that the product can be improved?
- The background of senior management. The company might be new, but if it has seasoned veterans from major companies like IBM, Oracle, and Microsoft, to name a few, it is more likely to be successful because top management has seen how it's done right.

Support: What type of support is offered? It is industry standard for vendors to charge an annual support fee that is 15-20% of the software product license. Will any software issues be handled promptly?

Professional Services: This includes consulting and education. What type of consulting proposal does the vendor give? Is the personnel requirements and consulting rates reasonable?

Is the vendor going to put in someone fresh out of college and charge $200/hr for that person? It might be wise to speak with members of the consulting team before signing on the dotted line. On the education front, what type of training is available? And how much is the consulting team willing to do knowledge transfer? Does the consulting team purposely hold off information so that either 1) you will need to send more people to vendor's education classes, or 2) you will need to hire additional consulting to make any changes to the system.

DATABASE/HARDWARE

In making selection for the database/hardware platform, there are several items that need to be carefully considered:

Scalability: How can the system grow as your data storage needs grow? Which RDBMS and hardware platform can handle large sets of data most efficiently? To get an idea of this, one needs to determine the approximate amount of data that is to be kept in the data warehouse system once it's mature, and base any testing numbers from there.

PARALLEL PROCESSING SUPPORT

The days of multi-million dollar supercomputers with one single CPU are gone, and nowadays the most powerful computers all use multiple CPUs, where each processor can perform a part of the task, all at the same time.

Indeed, parallel computing is gaining popularity now, although a little slower than I had originally thought.

RDBMS/Hardware Combination

Because the RDBMS physically sits on the hardware platform, there are going to be certain parts of the code that is hardware platform-dependent. As a result, bugs and bug fixes are often hardware dependent.

True Case

One of the projects was with a major RDBMS provider paired with a hardware platform that was not so popular (at least not in the data warehousing world).

The DBA constantly complained about the bug not being fixed because the support level for the particular type of hardware that client had chosen was Level 3, which basically meant that no one in the RDBMS support organization will fix any bug particular to that hardware platform.

Popular Relational Databases :

- Oracle
- Microsoft SQL Server
- IBM DB2
- Teradata
- Sybase
- MySQL.

Popular OS Platforms :

- Linux
- FreeBSD
- Microsoft.

OLAP TOOLS

OLAP tools are geared towards slicing and dicing of the data. As such, they require a strong metadata layer, as well as front-end flexibility.

Those are typically difficult features for any home-built systems to achieve. Therefore, my recommendation is that if OLAP analysis is part of your charter for building a data warehouse, it is best to purchase an existing OLAP tool rather than creating one from scratch.

OLAP TOOL FUNCTIONALITIES

Before we speak about OLAP tool selection criterion, we must first distinguish between the two types of OLAP tools, MOLAP (Multidimensional OLAP) and ROLAP (Relational OLAP).

- MOLAP: In this type of OLAP, a cube is aggregated from the relational data source (data warehouse). When user generates a report request, the MOLAP tool can generate the create quickly because all data is already pre-aggregated within the cube.
- ROLAP: In this type of OLAP, instead of pre-aggregating everything into a cube, the ROLAP engine essentially acts as a smart SQL generator. The ROLAP tool typically comes with a 'Designer' piece, where the data warehouse administrator can specify the relationship between the relational tables, as well as how dimensions, attributes, and hierarchies map to the underlying database tables.

Right now, there is a convergence between the traditional ROLAP and MOLAP vendors.

ROLAP vendor recognize that users want their reports fast, so they are implementing MOLAP functionalities in their tools; MOLAP vendors recognize that many times it is necessary to drill down to the most detail level information, levels where the traditional cubes do not get to for performance and size reasons.

So what are the criteria for evaluating OLAP vendors? Here they are:

- Ability to leverage parallelism supplied by RDBMS and hardware: This would greatly increase the tool's performance, and help loading the data into the cubes as quickly as possible.
- Performance: In addition to leveraging parallelism, the tool itself should be quick both in terms of loading the data into the cube and reading the data from the cube.
- Customization efforts: More and more, OLAP tools are used as an advanced reporting tool. This is because in many cases, especially for ROLAP implementations, OLAP tools often *can* be used as a reporting tool. In such cases, the ease of front-end customization becomes an important factor in the tool selection process.
- Security Features: Because OLAP tools are geared towards a number of users, making sure people see only what they are supposed to see is important. By and large, all established OLAP tools have a security layer that can interact with the common corporate login protocols. There are, however, cases where large corporations have developed their own user authentication mechanism and have a "single sign-on" policy. For these cases, having a seamless integration between the tool and the in-house authentication can require some work. I would recommend that you have the tool vendor team come in and make sure that the two are compatible.

- Metadata support: Because OLAP tools aggregates the data into the cube and sometimes serves as the front-end tool, it is essential that it works with the metadata strategy/tool you have selected.

REPORTING TOOLS

There is a wide variety of reporting requirements, and whether to buy or build a reporting tool for your business intelligence needs is also heavily dependent on the type of requirements. Typically, the determination is based on the following:

- Number of reports: The higher the number of reports, the more likely that buying a reporting tool is a good idea. This is not only because reporting tools typically make creating new reports easier (by offering re-usable components), but they also already have report management systems to make maintenance and support functions easier.
- Desired Report Distribution Mode: If the reports will only be distributed in a single mode (for example, email only, or over the browser only), we should then strongly consider the possibility of building the reporting tool from scratch. However, if users will access the reports through a variety of different channels, it would make sense to invest in a third-party reporting tool that already comes packaged with these distribution modes.
- Ad Hoc Report Creation: Will the users be able to create their own ad hoc reports? If so, it is a good idea to purchase a reporting tool. These tool vendors have accumulated extensive experience and know the features that are important to users who are creating ad hoc reports. A second reason is that the ability to allow for ad hoc report creation necessarily relies on a strong metadata layer, and it is simply difficult to come up with a metadata model when building a reporting tool from scratch.

REPORTING TOOL FUNCTIONALITIES

Data is useless if all it does is sit in the data warehouse. As a result, the presentation layer is of very high importance.

Most of the OLAP vendors already have a front-end presentation layer that allows users to call up pre-defined reports or create ad hoc reports. There are also several report tool vendors. Either way, pay attention to the following points when evaluating reporting tools:

Data Source Connection Capabilities

In general there are two types of data sources, one the relationship database, the other is the OLAP multidimensional data source. Nowadays, chances are good that you might want to have both. Many tool vendors will tell you that they offer both options, but upon closer inspection, it is possible that the tool vendor is especially good for one type, but to connect to the other type of data source, it becomes a difficult exercise in programming.

Scheduling and Distribution Capabilities

In a realistic data warehousing usage scenario by senior executives, all they have time for is to come in on Monday morning, look at the most important weekly numbers from the previous week (say the sales numbers), and that's how they satisfy their business intelligence needs. All the fancy ad hoc and drilling capabilities will not interest them, because they do not touch these features.

The reporting tool must have scheduling and distribution capabilities. Weekly reports are scheduled to run on Monday morning, and the resulting reports are distributed to the senior executives either by email or web publishing. There are claims by various vendors that they can distribute reports through various interfaces, but based on my experience, the only ones that really matter are delivery via email and publishing over the intranet.

Security Features: Because reporting tools, similar to OLAP tools, are geared towards a number of users, making sure people see only what they are supposed to see is important. Security can reside at the report level, folder level, column level, row level, or even individual cell level. By and large, all established reporting tools have these capabilities. Furthermore, they have a security layer that can interact with the common corporate login protocols. There are, however, cases where large corporations have developed their own user authentication mechanism and have a "single sign-on" policy. For these cases, having a seamless integration between the tool and the in-house authentication can require some work. I would recommend that you have the tool vendor team come in and make sure that the two are compatible.

Customization

Every one of us has had the frustration over spending an inordinate amount of time tinkering with some office productivity tool only to make the report/ presentation look good. This is definitely a waste of time, but unfortunately it is a necessary evil. In fact, a lot of times, analysts will wish to take a report directly out of the reporting tool and place it in their presentations or reports to their bosses. If the reporting tool offers them an easy way to pre-set the reports to look exactly the way that adheres to the corporate standard, it makes the analysts jobs much easier, and the time savings are tremendous.

Export Capabilities

The most common export needs are to Excel, to a flat file, and to PDF, and a good report tool must be able to export to all three formats. For Excel, if the situation warrants it, you will want to verify that the reporting format, not just the data itself, will be exported out to Excel. This can often be a time-saver.

Integration with the Microsoft Office Environment

Most people are used to work with Microsoft Office products, especially Excel, for manipulating data. Before, people used to export the reports into Excel, and then perform additional formatting/calculation tasks. Some reporting tools now offer a Microsoft Office-like editing environment for users, so all formatting can be done within the reporting tool itself, with no need to export the report into Excel. This is a nice convenience to the users.

METADATA TOOLS

Only in the rarest of cases does it make sense to build a metadata tool from scratch. This is because doing so requires resources that are intimately familiar with the operational, technical, and business aspects of the data warehouse system, and such resources are difficult to come by. Even when such resources are available, there are often other tasks that can provide more value to the organization than to build a metadata tool from scratch.

In fact, the question is often whether any type of metadata tool is needed at all. Although metadata plays an extremely important role in a successful data warehousing implementation, this does not always mean that a tool is needed to keep all the "data about data." It is possible to, say, key such information in the repository of other tools used, in a text documentation, or even in a presentation or a spreadsheet.

Having said the above, though, it is author's believe that having a solid metadata foundation is one of the keys to the success of a data warehousing project. Therefore, even if a metadata tool is not selected at the beginning of the project, it is essential to have a metadata strategy; that is, how metadata in the data warehousing system will be stored.

METADATA TOOL FUNCTIONALITIES

This is the most difficult tool to choose, because there is clearly no standard. In fact, it might be better to call this a selection of the metadata strategy. Traditionally, people have put the data modelling information into a tool such as ERWin and Oracle Designer, but it is difficult to extract information out of such data modelling tools. For example, one of the goals for your metadata selection is to provide information to the end users. Clearly this is a difficult task with a data modelling tool.

So typically what is likely to happen is that additional efforts are spent to create a layer of metadata that is aimed at the end users. While this allows the end users to gain the required insight into what the data and reports they are looking at means, it is clearly inefficient because all that information already resides somewhere in the data warehouse system, whether it be the ETL tool, the data modelling tool, the OLAP tool, or the reporting tool.

There are efforts among data warehousing tool vendors to unify on a metadata model. In June of 2000, the OMG released a metadata standard called CWM (Common Warehouse Metamodel), and some of the vendors such as Oracle have claimed to have implemented it. This standard incorporates the latest technology such as XML, UML, and SOAP, and, if accepted widely, is truly the best thing that can happen to the data warehousing industry. As of right now, though, the author has not really seen that many tools leveraging this standard, so clearly it has not quite caught on yet. So what does this mean about your metadata efforts? In the absence of everything else, I would recommend that whatever tool you choose for your metadata support supports XML, and that whatever other tool that needs to leverage the metadata also supports XML. Then it is a matter of defining your DTD across your data warehousing system. At the same time, there is no need to worry about criteria that typically is important for the other tools such as performance and support for parallelism because the size of the metadata is typically small relative to the size of the data warehouse.

OPEN SOURCE BUSINESS INTELLIGENCE

Open source BI are BI software can be distributed for free and permits users to modify the source code. Open source software is available in all BI tools, from data modelling to reporting to OLAP to ETL. Because open source software is community driven, it relies on the community for improvement. As such, new feature sets typically come from community contribution rather than as a result of dedicated R&D efforts.

ADVANTAGES OF OPEN SOURCE BI TOOLS

Easy to Get Started

With traditional BI software, the business model typically involves a hefty startup cost, and then there is an annual fee for support and maintenance that is calculated as a percentage of the initial purchase price. In this model, a company needs to spend a substantial amount of money before any benefit is realised. With the substantial cost also comes the need to go through a sales cycle, from the RFP process to evaluation to negotiation, and multiple teams within the organization typically get involved. These factors mean that it's not only costly to get started with traditional BI software, but the amount of time it takes is also long. With open source BI, the beginning of the project typically involves a free download of the software. Given this, bureaucracy can be kept to a minimum and it is very easy and inexpensive to get started.

Lower Cost

Because of its low startup cost and the typically lower ongoing maintenance/ support cost, the cost for open source BI software is lower (sometimes much lower) than traditional BI software.

Easy to Customize

By definition, open source software means that users can access and modify the source code directly. That means it is possible for developers to get under the hood of the open source BI tool and add their own features. In contrast, it is much more difficult to do this with traditional BI software because there is no way to access the source code.

DISADVANTAGES OF OPEN SOURCE BI TOOLS

Features are not as Robust

Traditional BI software vendors put in a lot of money and resources into R&D, and the result is that the product has a rich feature set. Open source BI tools, on the other hand, rely on community support, and hence do not have as strong a feature set.

Consulting Help not as Readily Available

Most of the traditional BI software - MicroStrategy, Business Objects, Cognos, Oracle and so on, have been around for a long time. As a result, there are a lot of people with experience with those tools, and finding consulting help to implement these solutions is usually not very difficult. Open source BI tools, on the other hand, are a fairly recent development, and there are relatively few people with implementation experience. So, it is more difficult to find consulting help if you go with open source BI.

DATA WAREHOUSE APPLIANCES

In computing, a data warehouse appliance consists of an integrated set of servers, storage, operating system(s), DBMS and software specifically pre-installed and pre-optimized for data warehousing (DW). Alternatively, the term can also apply to similar software-only systems — purportedly very easy to install on specific recommended hardware configurations or preconfigured as a complete system - a true appliance.

DW appliances provide solutions for the mid-to-large volume data warehouse market, offering low-cost performance most commonly on data volumes in the terabyte to petabyte range.

APPLIANCE TECHNOLOGY

Most DW appliance vendors use massively parallel processing (MPP) architectures to provide high query performance and platform scalability. MPP architectures consist of independent processors or servers executing in parallel. Most MPP architectures implement a "shared-nothing architecture" where each server operates self-sufficiently and controls its own memory and disk. Shared-nothing architectures have a proven record for high scalability and little contention. DW appliances distribute data onto dedicated disk storage units connected to each server in the appliance. This distribution allows DW appliances to resolve a relational query by scanning data on each server in parallel. The divide-and-conquer approach delivers high performance and scales linearly as new servers are added into the architecture. Other DW appliance vendors use specialized hardware and advanced software, instead of MPP architectures. This approach is able to achieve MPP performance in a much smaller form factor. The first vendor to market with a data warehouse appliance featuring specialized SQL hardware was Netezza in 2003 through leveraging FPGA technology as sophisticated projection and restriction filters, minimizing data movement and I/O within the system. Kickfire followed in 2008 with what they deem a dataflow "sql chip".

MPP database architectures have a long pedigree. Teradata, Tandem, Britton Lee, and Sequent offered MPP SQL-based architectures in the 1980s. Open source and commodity components have aided a re-emergence of MPP data warehouses. Advances in technology have reduced costs and improved performance in storage devices, multi-core CPUs and networking components. Open-source RDBMS products, such as Ingres and PostgreSQL, reduce software-license costs and allow DW-appliance vendors to focus on optimization rather than providing basic database functionality. Open-source Linux provides a stable, well-implemented operating system for DW appliances.

HISTORY

Some consider Teradata's initial product as the first DW appliance — or Britton-Lee's. Others disagree, considering appliances as a "disruptive technology" for Teradata. Interest in the data warehouse appliance category is generally dated to the emergence of Netezza in the early 2000s.

As of 2009 a second generation of DW appliances has emerged, marking the move to mainstream vendor integration. IBM integrated its InfoSphere Warehouse (formerly DB2 Warehouse) with its own servers and storage to create the IBM InfoSphere Balanced Warehouse. Netezza introduced its TwinFin platform based on commodity IBM hardware. Other DW appliance vendors have also partnered with major hardware vendors to help bring their appliances to market. DATAllegro, prior to acquisition by Microsoft, partnered with EMC and Dell and implemented open-source Ingres on Linux. Greenplum has a partnership with Sun Microsystems and implements Greenplum Database (based on PostgreSQL) on Solaris using the ZFS file system. HP Neoview has a wholly owned solution and uses HP NonStop SQL. XtremeData offers a FPGA based data-warehousing appliance built on commodity hardware and open-source operating system for "deep analytics" and data mining.

Kognitio offers a row-based "virtual" data warehouse appliance while Vertica, EXASOL and Paraccel offer column-based "virtual" data warehouse appliances. Like Greenplum, ParAccel partners with Sun Microsystems. These solutions provide software-only solutions deployed on clusters of commodity hardware. Kognitio's homegrown WX2 database runs on several blade configurations. Other players in the DW appliance space include Calpont and Kickfire. Kickfire employs a column store storage engine compatible with MySQL for ease of deployment and use, in combination with specialized hardware for proven performance.

The market has also seen the emergence of data-warehouse bundles where vendors combine their hardware and database software together as a data warehouse platform. The Oracle Optimized Warehouse Initiative combines the Oracle Database with hardware from various computer manufacturers (Dell, EMC, HP, IBM, SGI and Sun Microsystems). Oracle's Optimized Warehouses offer pre-validated configurations and the database software comes pre-installed. In 2008 Oracle began offering a more classic appliance offering, the HP Oracle Database Machine, a jointly developed and co-branded platform that Oracle sells and supports and HP builds in configurations specifically for Oracle. In 2009, Oracle released a second-generation Exadata system, based on their newly acquired Sun Microsystems hardware.

In January 2010 HP and Microsoft signed the largest agreement in the IT industry and joined their technology to create a portfolio of appliances and reference architectures called Fast Track and Parallèle Datawarehouse (entreprise Datawarehouse). The code name of this agreement is I2A for Infrastructures To Application. These systems are highly efficient and their performance is guaranteed. The solutions are pre-installed, pre-tuned, assembled and the software layer is already installed. There is also a single point of responsibility for support (HP or MS depending on the system concerned).

BENEFITS

The total cost of ownership (TCO) of a data warehouse consists of initial entry costs, on-going maintenance costs and the cost of changing capacity as the data warehouse grows. DW appliances offer low entry and maintenance costs. Initial costs depend on the size of the appliance installed.

The resource cost for monitoring and tuning the data warehouse makes up a large part of the TCO, often as much as 80%. DW appliances reduce administration for day-to-day operations, setup and integration. Many also offer low costs for expanding processing power and capacity.

With an increased focus on controlling costs combined with tight IT Budgets, data warehouse managers sometimes need to reduce and manage expenses even while leveraging their technology as much as possible, making DW appliances a solution.

PARALLEL PERFORMANCE

Many DW appliances support mixed-workloads where a broad range of *ad hoc* queries and reports run simultaneously with loading. DW appliance vendors use several distribution and partitioning methods to provide parallel performance. Some DW appliances scan data using partitioning and sequential I/O instead of index usage. Other DW appliances use standard database indexing.

With high performance on highly granular data, DW appliances can address analytics that previously could not meet performance requirements.

Reduced Administration

DW appliances provide a single vendor solution and take ownership for optimizing the parts and software within the appliance. This eliminates the customer's costs for integration and regression testing of the DBMS, storage and OS on a terabyte scale and avoids some of the compatibility issues that arise from multi-vendor solutions. A single support-point also provides a single source for problem-resolution and a simplified upgrade-path for software and hardware.

Built-in high Availability

MPP DW appliance vendors provide built-in high availability through redundancy on components within the appliance. Many offer warm-standby servers, dual networks, dual power-supplies, disk mirroring with failover and solutions for server failure.

Scalability

DW appliances scale for both capacity and performance. Many DW appliances implement a modular design that database administrators can add to incrementally, eliminating up-front costs for over-provisioning. In contrast, architectures that do not support incremental expansion result in hours of production downtime, during which database administrators export and re-load terabytes of data. In MPP architectures, adding servers increases performance as well as capacity. This does not always happen with alternate solutions.

Rapid Time-to-value

Companies increasingly expect to use business analytics to improve the current cycle. DW appliances provide fast implementations without the need for regression- and integration-testing. In some cases, reduced tuning, reduced index creation, fast loading and reduced need for aggregation make rapid prototyping possible.

APPLICATION USES

DW appliances provide solutions for many analytic application uses, including:

- Enterprise data warehousing
- Super-sized sandboxes which isolate power users with resource intensive queries
- Pilot projects or projects requiring rapid prototyping and rapid time-to-value

- Off-loading projects from the enterprise data warehouse, such as large analytical query projects that affect the overall workload of the enterprise data warehouse
- Applications with specific performance or loading requirements
- Data marts that have outgrown their present environment
- Turnkey data warehouses or data marts
- Solutions for applications with high data-growth and high-performance requirements
- Applications requiring data warehouse encryption.

Trends

The DW appliance market has started to shift trends in many areas as it evolves:

- Vendors have started moving towards using commodity technologies rather than proprietary assembly of commodity components
- Implemented applications show usage expansion from tactical and data-mart solutions to strategic and enterprise data-warehouse use.
- Mainstream vendor participation has become apparent as of 2009.
- With a lower total cost of ownership, reduced maintenance and high performance to address business analytics on growing data volumes, most analysts believe that DW appliances will gain market share - though TeraData maintain their leadership position.
- Vendors have begun providing the ability to incorporate 'in-database' analytic algortihms to take advantage of their MPP architectures, eliminating the need to extract large datasets into traditional analytic and data mining platforms such as SAS.

POSITIONING THE DATA WAREHOUSE APPLIANCES AND SPECIALTY DBMS

There now are four hardware vendors that each offer or seem about to announce two different tiers of data warehouse appliances: Sun, HP, EMC, and Teradata. Specifically:

- Sun partners with both Greenplum and ParAccel.
- HP sells Neoview, and also is partnered with Vertica.
- EMC (together with Dell in North America and Bull in Europe) sells DATAllegro. Now EMC is also entering a partnership with ParAccel.
- Teradata is pretty far down the road towards releasing a low-end product.

In addition, multiple hardware vendors have "reference architecture" technical arrangements with Oracle, to try to capture some of the benefits of appliances. And IBM is constantly in partnership discussions with data warehouse specialists, notwithstanding having multiple data warehouse offerings of its own. Positioning of these various offerings is confused. Part of the reason is the large vendors' postures "We're big and trustworthy, and those little upstart vendors aren't – until the moment we partner with one of them." Part of the reason is the small vendors' stances of "We can do all things for all people – and by the way, 9 of the 14 customers we've ever had are all doing pretty much the same thing." And part of the reason is just an industry penchant for secrecy.

To a first approximation, I think there are two sensible ways to define the tiers. In each case, we're talking about what kinds of databases the various products are suited for.

- Criterion S (for "Size"). "Bigger than Oracle can handle" vs. "Small enough that Oracle can handle it" (but that depends on what the definition of "handle" is).
- Criterion U (for "Usage"). "Full enterprise data warehouse" vs. "big honking data mart".

But those are very different classification rules – many products that might be upper-tier by Criterion S are lower-tier by Criterion U, and *vice-versa*. For example:

- Teradata's current products are at the upper end by either criterion. Even so, a significant fraction of older Teradata installations are below 5 terabytes or even 1 terabyte in size.
- More generally, Teradata emphasizes Criterion U. Hence any future low-end products will surely be positioned as lower-tier by that criterion. Beyond that, I wouldn't be surprised if release is delayed, with the final version of those products being different than what previously leaked. *E.g.*, they might well be designed to compete with newer vendors that are upper-tier by Criterion S.
- Netezza has clearly made it into the upper tier by the Size criterion. Most of its installations are lower-tier by Criterion U, but it trumpets a few exceptions that it describes as "enterprise data warehouses" in success stories.
- DATAllegro is upper tier by Criterion S — more so than any other vendor except Teradata, in that there are at least two credible stories of DATAllegro warehouses at or above the quarter-petabyte mark. Even so, DATAllegro is still mainly in the lower tier by Criterion U. *I.e.*, the most natural use of DATAllegro technology is to build Very Big data marts.
- Vertica is a purely lower-tier Criterion U player, given its focus on single fact table schemas. But it's well on its way into the upper tier by Criterion S.
- Dataupia straddles the boundary of the tiers by Criterion S. That is, it's meant to offload existing Oracle, SQL Server, or DB2 databases, or in some OEM cases to be a cheaper alternative. That sounds lower-

tier. On the other hand, it has one 120 terabyte reference, which puts it squarely in the upper tier. By Criterion U it's pretty lower-tier.

- ParAccel seems lower-tier by either criterion. And I'm too burned out on ParAccel's secrecy to probe hard for exceptions.
- Oracle, MS SQL Server, *et al.* are – pretty much by definition – lower-tier by Criterion S, but upper-tier by Criterion U.
- HP Neoview is obviously meant to get to the higher end by both criteria. But like most specialty products, right now it's further along by the Size criterion than the Usage one. Even so, it seems no further along by Criterion S than partner HP's partner Vertica is.
- Greenplum has clearly gotten to the upper tier by the Size criterion. But like most of the competition, it still seems to be in the lower tier by Usage.
- Infobright is in the lower tier by either criterion. (They don't even have an MPP offering yet.)
- Kognitio KX2 is in the lower tier by either criterion. However, Kognitio aspires to move up when measured by Usage.

BENEFITS OF DATA WAREHOUSING

Data warehouses are the traditional solution for data integration, and for good reason, but this is becoming increasingly difficult to scale and copy data from multiple data sources in multiple organizations in multiple locations

Data is extracted, transformed from multiple data sources and loaded (ETL) into a separate database, called a data warehouse, which operate as illustrated in the following diagram DW1:

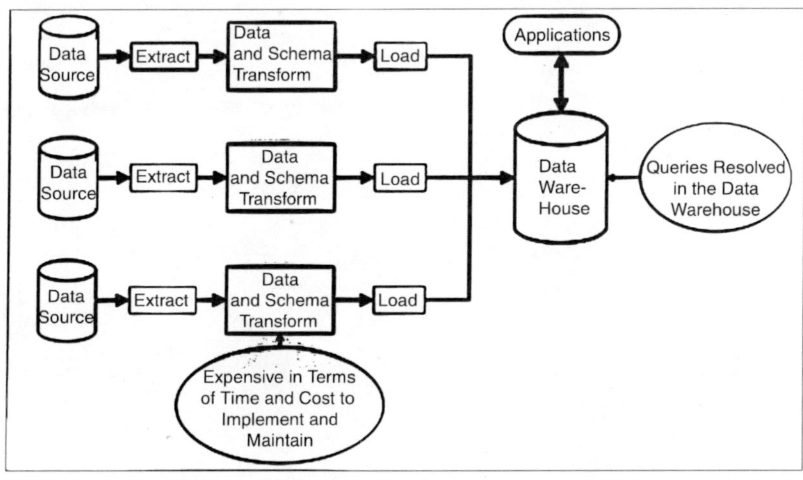

Figure: DW1: Data Warehouse Solution.

Advantages

Data warehouses tend to have a high query success, as they have complete control over the four main areas of data management systems:

- Clean data
- Indexes: multiple types
- Query processing: multiple options
- Security: data and access.

Disadvantages

However, there are considerable disadvantages involved in moving data from multiple, often highly disparate, data sources to one data warehouse that translate into long implementation time, high cost, lack of flexibility, dated information and limited capabilities:

- Major data schema transforms from each of the data sources to one schema in the data warehouse, which can represent more than 50% of the total data warehouse effort
- Data owners lose control over their data, raising ownership (responsibility and accountability), security and privacy issues
- Long initial implementation time and associated high cost
- Adding new data sources takes time and associated high cost
- Limited flexibility of use and types of users - requires multiple separate data marts for multiple uses and types of users
- Typically, data is static and dated
- Typically, no data drill-down capabilities
- Difficult to accommodate changes in data types and ranges, data source schema, indexes and queries
- Typically, cannot actively monitor changes in data.

8

OLAP Technology

INTRODUCTION TO OLAP

OLAP is an acronym for On Line Analytical Processing. OLAP performs multidimensional analysis of business data and provides the capability for complex calculations, trend analysis, and sophisticated data modelling. It is quickly becoming the fundamental foundation for Intelligent Solutions including Business Performance Management, Planning, Budgeting, Forecasting, Financial Reporting, Analysis, Simulation Models, Knowledge Discovery, and Data Warehouse Reporting. OLAP enables end-users to perform ad hoc analysis of data in multiple dimensions, thereby providing the insight and understanding they need for better decision making.

Knowledge is the foundation of all successful decisions. Successful businesses continuously plan, analyse and report on sales and operational activities in order to maximize efficiency, reduce expenditures and gain greater market share. Statisticians will tell you that the more sample data you have, the more likely the resulting statistic will be true. Naturally, the more data a company can access about a specific activity, the more likely that the plan to improve that activity will be effective. All businesses collect data using many different systems, and the challenge remains: how to get all the data together to create accurate, reliable, fast information about the business. A company that can take advantage and turn it into shared knowledge, accurately and quickly, will surely be better positioned to make successful business decisions and rise above the competition.

OLAP—THE MULTIDIMENSIONAL SOLUTION

Business is a multidimensional activity and businesses are run on decisions based on multiple dimensions. Businesses track their activities by considering many variables. When these variables are tracked on a spreadsheet, they are set on axes (x and y) where each axis represents a logical grouping of variables in a category. For example, sales in units or dollars may be tracked over one year's time, by month, where the sales measures might logically be displayed on the y axis and the months might occupy the x axis (*i.e.*, sales measures are rows and months are columns).

	Jan.	*Feb.*	*Mar.*	*Apr.*	*May*	*June*
Revenue	1,050,000.00	945,000.00	787,500.00	1,354,500.00	1,376,000.00	1,311,500.00
Price per Unit	21.00	21.00	21.00	21.50	21.50	21.50
Units Sold	50,000.00	45,000.00	37,500.00	63,000.00	64,000.00	61,000.00

To analyse and report on the health of a business and plan future activity, many variable groups or parameters must be tracked on a continuous basis—which is beyond the scope of any number of linked spreadsheets. These variable groups or parameters are called Dimensions in the On-Line Analytical Processing (OLAP) environment. Nowadays, many spreadsheet users have heard about OLAP technology, but it is not clear to them what OLAP means. Unlike relational databases, OLAP tools do not store individual transaction records in two-dimensional, row-by-column format, like a worksheet, but instead use multidimensional database structures—known as Cubes in OLAP terminology—to store arrays of consolidated information. The data and formulas are stored in an optimized multidimensional database, while views of the data are created on demand. Analysts can take any view, or Slice, of a Cube to produce a worksheet-like view of points of interest.

Rather than simply working with three dimensions, companies have many dimensions to track—for example, a business that distributes goods from more than a single facility will have at least the following Dimensions to consider: Accounts, Locations, Periods, Salespeople and Products. These Dimensions comprise a base for the company's planning, analysis and reporting activities. Together they represent the "whole" business picture, providing the foundation for all business planning, analysis and reporting activities.

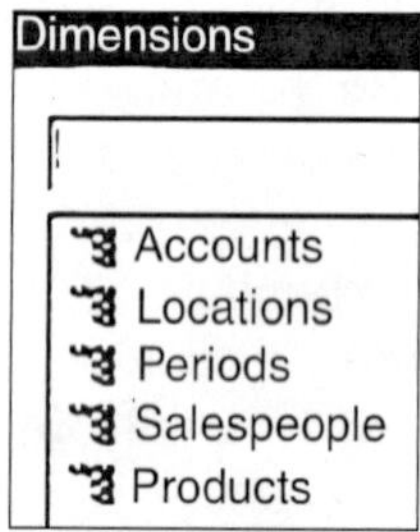

The capability to perform the most sophisticated analyses—specifically, the multidimensional analysis provided by OLAP technology—is an organizational imperative. Analysts need to view and manipulate data along the multiple dimensions that define an enterprise—essentially, the dimensions necessary for the creation of an effective business model.

OLAP IMPLEMENTATION

OLAP implementation depends not only from technological basis software that is going to be used – but more from the business models and data sources.

Each industry sector or business area is specific and required detailed modelling to create multidimensional cubes for easy data load and reporting building. For instance, approach for OLAP technology based system for medical institutions activities analysis or OLAP based data warehouse model development for police relevant activities analysis. OLAP model could also be build when information sources are common and not in a company landscape, but analysis of such kind of public, for instance economic, data is much valuable. In this case approach for web-services provided information analysis by use of OLAP technologies could be used.

EMPOWERING THE OLAP TECHNOLOGY TO SUPPORT COMPLEX DIMENSION HIERARCHIES

Data warehouse technology introduced in the early 90s to support data analysis in business environments has recently reached out to non-business domains such as medicine, education, research, government, *etc.* End-users interact with data using advanced visual interfaces that enable intuitive navigation to the desired data subset and granularity and provide a visually enhanced presentation using a variety of visualization techniques.

Data warehouse systems adopt a *multidimensional data model* tackling the challenges of the online analytical processing (OLAP) via efficient execution of queries that aggregate over large amount of detailed data. The analysis is preceded by a highly complex ETL (extract, transform, load) process of integrating the data from multiple systems and bringing it into a consistent state.

In relational OLAP systems, multidimensional views of data, or *data cubes*, are structured using a *star* or a *snowflake* schema consisting of fact tables and dimension hierarchies. *Fact tables* contain data records (*facts*) such as transactions or events, which represent the focus of the analysis. Facts are composed of two types of attributes: (1) *measures* (*i.e.*, the actual elements of the analysis), and 2) *dimensions,* which uniquely determine the measures and serve as exploration axes for aggregation. Members of a dimension are typically organized in a containment type hierarchy to support multiple granularities.

In the dimension table, the attributes that form the hierarchy are called *dimension levels*, or *categories*. Other descriptive attributes belonging to a particular category are known as *property* attributes. Dimension levels along with parent/ child relationships between them are referred to as the dimension's *intension*, or *schema*, whereas the hierarchy of its members forms its *extension*.

The star schema view of a data cube storing the administrative expenditures of a university: the facts in the fact table ORDER are determined by five dimensions. In the star schema, the whole dimension hierarchy is placed into a single table, whereas the snowflake schema enforces the hierarchy to be decomposed into separate tables, one table per dimension level. The star schema produces a single table period with all dimension levels and property attributes.

Obviously, in such de-normalized view it is impossible to explicitly recognize the hierarchical relationships. In the snowflake schema, however, each dimension category with its property attributes is placed into a separate table referencing its parent. The arrows correspond to the foreign keys (*i.e.*, the roll-up relationships between the levels).

The resulting schema is rather complex, but it offers the advantage of automatic extraction of the hierarchy schema with all valid aggregation paths from the foreign key constraints. Notice that reoccurring intervals such as weeks, months, quarters, *etc.* are presented by a two-category lattice (*e.g.*, months ! month) in order to be able to roll-up single instances to the instance's type. For example, months instances *"January 1997"* and *"January 1998"* rollup to month instance *"January."*

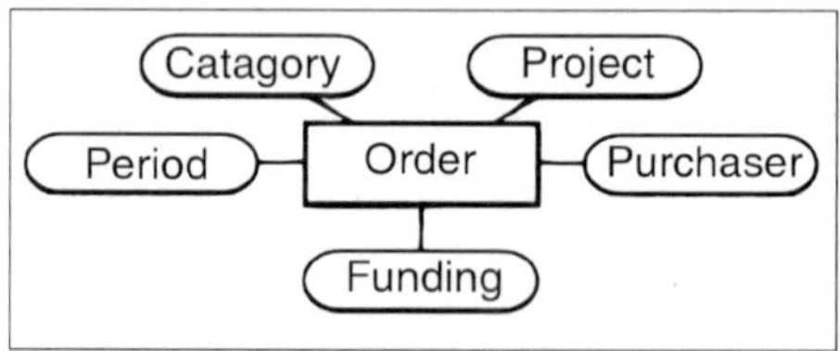

SUMMARIZABILITY AND HOMOGENEITY

The rigidness of the standard OLAP technology is caused primarily by the enforcement of summarizability for all dimensional hierarchies. The concept of summarizability, coined by Rafanelli and Shoshani, and further explored by other authors, requires distributive aggregate functions and dimension hierarchy values, or informally, that (1) facts map directly to the lowest-level dimension values and to only one value per dimension, and (2) dimensional hierarchies are balanced trees.

In practice, summarizability guarantees correct aggregation and optimized performance, as any aggregate view is obtainable from a set of pre-computed views defined at lower aggregation levels.

However, the hierarchies in many real-world applications are not summarizable and, therefore, cannot be used as dimensions in their original form. In case of small irregularities, the tree can be balanced by filling the "gaps" with artificial nodes. In highly unbalanced hierarchies, such transformations may be very confusing and undesirable. Yet in other scenarios, it is crucial to preserve the original state of the hierarchy.

At the level of visual analysis, summarizability is also imperative for generating a proper navigation hierarchy. Data browsers present hierarchical dimensions as recursively nested folders of their levels allowing users to browse either directly in the dimension's data or to access its schema.

In the former approach, henceforth denoted *"extension-based,"* the navigation tree of a dimension is a straightforward mapping of the dimension's data tree: each hierarchical value is a node that can be expanded to access the child values nested therein. Popular commercial and open-source OLAP tools, such as Cognos PowerPlay and Mondrian OLAP Server provide only this simple navigation. Alternatively, the navigation hierarchy can explicitly display the schema of the dimension, with each category as a child node of its parent category. This so called *"intension-based"* approach is especially suitable for power analysis and employment of advanced visualization techniques.

Sophisticated OLAP solutions, such as Tableau Software and SAP NetWeaver BI, combine schema navigation with data display.

Figure shows the difference between instance-based and schema-based browsing for a hierarchical dimension Period.

Another restriction of the traditional approach to dimension modelling is that of *homogeneity*.

Even though it is admissible to define multiple hierarchies within the same dimension (*e.g.*, date in Figure can be rolled-up to weekday, weeks, or months), each of those hierarchies must be homogeneous (*i.e.*, each level of the tree corresponds to a single dimension category and all members of a given category have ancestors in the same set of categories). The necessity of dropping this restriction has been recognized by the researchers who proposed respective extensions in the form of multidimensional normal forms, dimension constraints, transformation techniques, and mapping algorithms.

Analysts are frequently confronted with non-summarizable data that cannot be adequately supported by standard models and systems. In a survey on open issues in multidimensional modelling, Hümmer, Lehner, Bauer, & Schlesinger identified unbalanced and irregular hierarchies as one of the major modelling challenges for both researchers and practitioners.

To overcome the restrictions of summarizability and homogeneity and thus increase the capacity of the OLAP technology to handle a broader spectrum of practical situations, analysis tools have to be extended at virtually all levels of the system architecture:

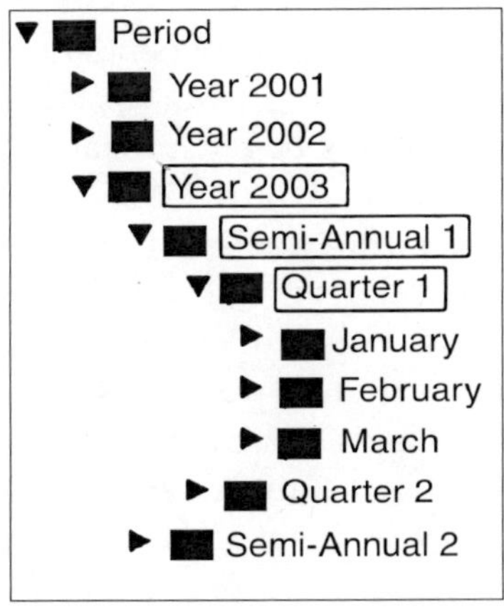

(a) Dimension Instances

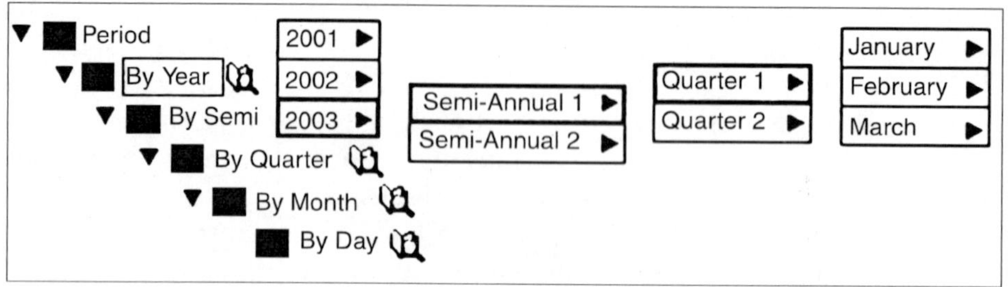

(b) Dimension Levels with on-demand Data Display

Figure: Browsing in Dimensional Hierarchies: Extension vs. Intension Navigation

- Recognition and classification of complex hierarchies,
- Conceptual and logical model extensions,
- Data and schema normalization techniques,
- Enhanced metadata model to ensure correct querying and aggregation,
- Lossless mapping of dimension schema to a visual navigation,
- Adequate visualization techniques for presenting complex query results.

Related Work

Limitations and deficiencies of the classical multidimensional data model have become a fundamental issue in the data warehousing research in the last decade. The necessity to develop novel concepts has been recognized (Zurek & Sinnwell) and a series of extensions have been proposed in the recent past. As state-of-the-art solutions are far from being ultimate and overall satisfactory, the problem will continue to attract interest and encourage new contributions in the years to come.

A powerful approach to modelling dimension hierarchies along with SQL query language extensions called SQL was presented by Jagadish, Lakshmanan, and Srivastava. SQL does not require data hierarchies to be balanced or homogeneous. Niemi, Nummenmaa, and Thanisch analysed unbalanced and ragged data trees and demonstrated how dependency information can assist in designing summarizable hierarchies. Lehner *et al.* relaxed the condition of summarizability to enable modelling of generalization hierarchies by defining a generalized multidimensional normal form (GMNF) as a yardstick for the quality of multidimensional schemata. Lechtenbörger *et al.* pointed out the methodological deficiency in deriving multidimensional schema from the relational one and extended the framework of normal forms proposed by Lehner *et al.* to provide more guidance in data warehouse design.

Other works focus on formalizing the dimension hierarchies and summarizability related constraints. Hurtado *et al.* proposed integrity constraints for inferring summarizability in heterogeneous dimensions and defined a comprehensive formal framework for constraint-conform hierarchy modelling in a follow-up work in 2005. Another remarkable contribution to the conceptual design was made by Malinowski *et al.* who presented a classification of dimensional hierarchies, including those not addressed by current OLAP systems in 2004 and formalized their conceptual model and its mapping to the relational schema in 2006.

Pedersen *et al.* have made manifold contributions in the area of multidimensional modelling. In 2001, they formulated the major requirements an extended multidimensional data model should satisfy and examined 14 state-of-the-art models from both the research community and commercial systems. Since none of the models was even close to meeting most of the defined requirements, the authors proposed an extended model for capturing and querying complex multidimensional data. This model, supporting non-summarizable hierarchies, many-to-many relationships between facts and dimensions, handling temporal changes and imprecision, is by far one of the most powerful multidimensional data models of the state of the art.

Support for complex hierarchies in the existing OLAP systems falls far behind the respective abilities of the formal models: to our best knowledge, most of the extensions proposed in the above contributions have not been incorporated into any analysis software.

In a previous work (Vinnik & Mansmann), we presented some insights into visual querying of a subset of irregular dimensions.

A more recent work (Mansmann & Scholl) analyses the limitations of the standard OLAP systems and the underlying data model in handling complex dimensional hierarchies and proposes the extensions at the conceptual level, which are then propagated to an advanced visual interface. The current work builds upon the proposals of the latter work, however, with the focus on providing a more formal and comprehensive categorization of dimensional hierarchies and proposing the approaches to their modelling and transformation at the conceptual and logical level. As a proof of concept, an approach to visual querying and analysis of complex hierarchies via a schema based navigation is presented.

Contributions and Outline

This work is an attempt to further reduce the gap between powerful concepts and deficient practices in providing data warehouse support for complex data. In the context of our research, complex data is used as a generic term referring to all types of dimension hierarchies not supported by traditional systems. The techniques we present evolved from the practical experiences with data warehouse design and challenges encountered in the real-world applications.

The related proposals to handling complex hierarchies found in the literature tend to focus on the formal aspects of the multidimensional data modelling and provide no solution for implementing the proposed extensions in a visual interface. However, since the analysis is performed predominantly via visual tools, we consider the practicability a crucial aspect for judging about the value of the modelling proposals. Therefore, we also identify the potential problems of supporting complex data at the level of user interfaces and present an approach to adequately mapping the extended data model to a navigation structure of a prototypical OLAP tool.

Our approach to extending the capabilities of OLAP systems is meant as a comprehensive framework that includes the conceptual and the logical design, transformation techniques, metadata management, and mapping algorithms for presenting data cubes as navigation hierarchies and translating user interactions into valid queries.

The advantage of the presented solution is its ability to handle a wide spectrum of hierarchy patterns in a uniform and intuitive manner. At the conceptual level, we propose a systematic categorization of dimension hierarchies, with formal definitions, examples from a real-world scenario, and a description of relationships between various dimension types.

We also see a two-phase data transformation approach aimed at bringing complex hierarchies into a navigable state. The awareness of the supported hierarchy types is propagated to the analysis tools by enriching the metadata that describes the schema of the data warehouse.

Consequently, the analysis tools need to implement the necessary "database-to-navigation," "navigation-to-query," and "query-to-visualization" mappings to support querying of the newly added types of dimensions.

The process of generating a powerful navigation framework from the data schema and examples of using the latter for visual exploration of complex data are presented in the next section.

TERMINOLOGY AND BASIC CONCEPTS

We rely on the terminology and formalization introduced by Pedersen *et al.* since their model is the most powerful of the state of the art in part of handling complex hierarchies. We also adopt some elements of SQL model to account for heterogeneous hierarchies.

Hierarchy Schema and Instance

Intuitively, data hierarchy is a tree with each node being a tuple over a set of attributes. A dimension hierarchy is based on a hierarchical attribute, also referred to as the *analysis criterion*, propagated to all levels of the tree. It is possible to impose different hierarchies within the same dimension by defining multiple criteria, for instance, the projects can be analysed along the hierarchy of geographic locations or along that of supervising institutions.

DATA WAREHOUSING AND OLAP

Although sometimes used interchangeably, the terms *data warehousing* and *online analytical processing* (OLAP) apply to different components of systems often referred to as decision support systems or business intelligence systems. Components of these types of systems include databases and applications that provide the tools analysts need to support organizational decision-making.

A data warehouse is a database containing data that usually represents the business history of an organization. This historical data is used for analysis that supports business decisions at many levels, from strategic planning to performance evaluation of a discrete organizational unit. Data in a data warehouse is organized to support analysis rather than to process real-time transactions as in online transaction processing systems (OLTP).

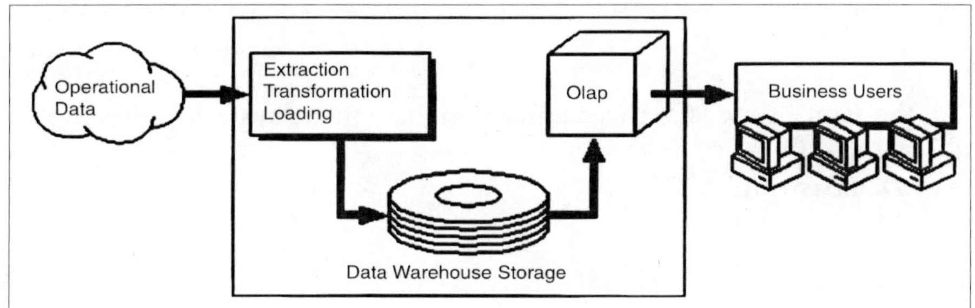

OLAP technology enables data warehouses to be used effectively for online analysis, providing rapid responses to iterative complex analytical queries. OLAP's multidimensional data model and data aggregation techniques organize and summarize large amounts of data so it can be evaluated quickly using online analysis and graphical tools. The answer to a query into historical data often leads to subsequent queries as the analyst searches for answers or explores possibilities. OLAP systems provide the speed and flexibility to support the analyst in real time.

9

DBMS

As the name suggests, the database management system consists of two parts. They are:

- Database and
- Management System.

INTRODUCTION TO DATABASE

To find out what database is, we have to start from data, which is the basic building block of any DBMS.

Data: Facts, figures, statistics *etc.* having no particular meaning.

Record: Collection of related data items, *e.g.* in the above example the three data items had no meaning.

But if we organize them in the following way, then they collectively represent meaningful information.

Roll	Name	Age
1	ABC	19

Table or Relation: Collection of related records.

Roll	Name	Age
1	ABC	19
2	DEF	22
3	XYZ	28

The columns of this relation are called Fields, Attributes or Domains. The rows are called Tuples or Records.

Database: Collection of related relations. Consider the following collection of tables:

T1

Roll	Name	Age
1	ABC	19
2	DEF	22
3	XYZ	28

T2

Roll	Address
1	KOL
2	DEL
3	MUM

T3

Roll	Year
1	I
2	II
3	I

T4

Year	Hostel
I	H1
II	H2

We now have a collection of 4 tables. They can be called a "related collection" because we can clearly find out that there are some common attributes existing in a selected pair of tables. Because of these common attributes we may combine the data of two or more tables together to find out the complete details of a student. Questions like "Which hostel does the youngest student live in?" can be answered now, although *Age* and *Hostel* attributes are in different tables.

In a database, data is organized strictly in row and column format. The rows are called Tuple or Record. The data items within one row may belong to different data types. On the other hand, the columns are often called Domain or Attribute. All the data items within a single attribute are of the same data type.

The term *database system* implies that the data is managed to some level of quality (measured in terms of accuracy, availability, usability, and resilience) and this in turn often implies the use of a general-purpose database management system (DBMS). A general-purpose DBMS is typically a complex software system that meets many usage requirements, and the databases that it maintains are often large and complex.

The utilization of databases is now so widespread that virtually every technology and product relies on databases and DBMSs for its development and commercialization, or even may have such software embedded in it. Also, organizations and companies, from small to large, depend heavily on databases for their operations.

Well known DBMSs include Oracle, IBM DB2, Microsoft SQL Server, Microsoft Access, PostgreSQL, MySQL, and SQLite. A database is not generally portable across different DBMS, but different DBMSs can inter-operate to some degree by using standards like SQL and ODBC together to support a single application. A DBMS also needs to provide effective run-time execution to properly support (*e.g.*, in terms of performance, availability, and security) as many end-users as needed.

A way to classify databases involves the type of their contents, for example: bibliographic, document-text, statistical, or multimedia objects. Another way is by their application area, for example: accounting, music compositions, movies, banking, manufacturing, or insurance.

The term *database* may be narrowed to specify particular aspects of organized collection of data and may refer to the logical database, to the physical database as data content in computer data storage or to many other database sub-definitions.

DATABASE CONCEPT

The Database concept has evolved since the 1960s to ease increasing difficulties in designing, building, and maintaining complex information systems (typically with many concurrent end-users, and with a large amount of diverse data). It has evolved together with database management systems which enable the effective handling of databases.

Though the terms database and DBMS define different entities, they are inseparable: a database's properties are determined by its supporting DBMS and *vice-versa*.

The Oxford English dictionary cites a 1962 technical report as the first to use the term "data-base." With the progress in technology in the areas of processors, computer memory, computer storage and computer networks, the sizes, capabilities, and performance of databases and their respective DBMSs have grown in orders of magnitudes. For decades it has been unlikely that a complex information system can be built effectively without a proper database supported by a DBMS. The utilization of databases is now spread to such a wide degree that virtually every technology and product relies on databases and DBMSs for its development and commercialization, or even may have such embedded in it. Also, organizations and companies, from small to large, heavily depend on databases for their operations.

No widely accepted exact definition exists for DBMS. However, a system needs to provide considerable functionality to qualify as a DBMS. Accordingly its supported data collection needs to meet respective usability requirements to qualify as a database. Thus, a database and its supporting DBMS are defined here by a set of general requirements. Virtually all existing mature DBMS products meet these requirements to a great extent, while less mature either meet them or converge to meet them.

EVOLUTION OF DATABASE AND DBMS TECHNOLOGY

The introduction of the term *database* coincided with the availability of direct-access storage (disks and drums) from the mid-1960s onwards. The term represented a contrast with the tape-based systems of the past, allowing shared interactive use rather than daily batch processing.

In the earliest database systems, efficiency was perhaps the primary concern, but it was already recognized that there were other important objectives. One of the key aims was to make the data independent of the logic of application programmes, so that the same data could be made available to different applications.

The first generation of database systems were *navigational,* applications typically accessed data by following pointers from one record to another. The two main data models at this time were the hierarchical model, epitomized by IBM's IMS system, and the Codasyl model (Network model), implemented in a number of products such as IDMS.

The Relational model, first proposed in 1970 by Edgar F. Codd, departed from this tradition by insisting that applications should search for data by content, rather than by following links. This was considered necessary to allow the content of the database to evolve without constant rewriting of applications. Relational systems placed heavy demands on processing resources, and it was not until the mid 1980s that computing hardware became powerful enough to allow them to be widely deployed. By the early 1990s, however, relational systems were dominant for all large-scale data processing applications, and they remain dominant today (2012) except in niche areas. The dominant database language is the standard SQL for the Relational model, which has influenced database languages also for other data models.

Because the relational model emphasizes search rather than navigation, it does not make relationships between different entities explicit in the form of pointers, but represents them rather using *primary keys* and *foreign keys.* While this is a good basis for a query language, it is less well suited as a modelling language. For this reason a different model, the Entity-relationship model which emerged shortly later, gained popularity for database design.

In the period since the 1970s database technology has kept pace with the increasing resources becoming available from the computing platform: notably the rapid increase in the capacity and speed (and reduction in price) of disk storage, and the increasing capacity of main memory. This has enabled ever larger databases and higher throughputs to be achieved.

The rigidity of the relational model, in which all data is held in tables with a fixed structure of rows and columns, has increasingly been seen as a limitation when handling information that is richer or more varied in structure than the traditional 'ledger-book' data of corporate information systems: for example, document databases, engineering databases, multimedia databases, or databases used in the molecular sciences. Various attempts have been made to address this problem, many of them gathering under banners such as *post-relational* or NoSQL. Two developments of note are the Object database and the XML database. The vendors of relational databases have fought off competition from these newer models by extending the capabilities of their own products to support a wider variety of data types.

GENERAL-PURPOSE DBMS

A DBMS has evolved into a complex software system and its development typically requires thousands of person-years of development effort. Some general-purpose DBMSs, like Oracle, Microsoft SQL Server, and IBM DB2, have been undergoing upgrades for thirty years or more. General-purpose DBMSs aim to satisfy as many applications as possible, which typically makes them even more complex than special-purpose databases. However, the fact that they can be used "off the shelf", as well as their amortized cost over many applications and instances, makes them an attractive alternative (Vs. one-time development) whenever they meet an application's requirements.

Though attractive in many cases, a general-purpose DBMS is not always the optimal solution: When certain applications are pervasive with many operating instances, each with many users, a general-purpose DBMS may introduce unnecessary overhead and too large "footprint" (too large amount of unnecessary, unutilized software code). Such applications usually justify dedicated development. Typical examples are email systems, though they need to possess certain DBMS properties: email systems are built in a way that optimizes email messages handling and managing, and do not need significant portions of a general-purpose DBMS functionality.

Types of People Involved

Three types of people are involved with a general-purpose DBMS:

- *DBMS developers* - These are the people that design and build the DBMS product, and the only ones who touch its code. They are typically the employees of a DBMS vendor (*e.g.*, Oracle, IBM, Microsoft, Sybase), or, in the case of Open source DBMSs (*e.g.*, MySQL), volunteers or people supported by interested companies and organizations. They are typically skilled systems programmers. DBMS development is a complicated task, and some of the popular DBMSs have been under development and enhancement (also to follow progress in technology) for decades.
- *Application developers and Database administrators* - These are the people that design and build a database-based application that uses the DBMS. The latter group members design the needed database and maintain it. The first group members write the needed application programmes which the application comprises. Both are well familiar with the DBMS product and use its user interfaces (as well as usually other tools) for their work. Sometimes the application itself is packaged and sold as a separate product, which may include the DBMS inside, or sold separately as an add-on to the DBMS.
- *Application's end-users (e.g., accountants, insurance people, medical doctors, etc.)* - These people know the application and its end-user interfaces, but need not know nor understand the underlying DBMS. Thus,

though they are the intended and main beneficiaries of a DBMS, they are only indirectly involved with it.

DATABASE MACHINES AND APPLIANCES

In the 1970s and 1980s attempts were made to build database systems with integrated hardware and software. The underlying philosophy was that such integration would provide higher performance at lower cost. Examples were IBM System/38, the early offering of Teradata, and the Britton Lee, Inc. database machine.

Another approach to hardware support for database management was ICL's CAFS accelerator, a hardware disk controller with programmable search capabilities. In the long term these efforts were generally unsuccessful because specialized database machines could not keep pace with the rapid development and progress of general-purpose computers. Thus most database systems nowadays are software systems running on general-purpose hardware, using general-purpose computer data storage. However this idea is still pursued for certain applications by some companies like Netezza and Oracle (Exadata).

Database Research

Database research has been an active and diverse area, with many specializations, carried out since the early days of dealing with the database concept in the 1960s. It has strong ties with database technology and DBMS products. Database research has taken place at research and development groups of companies (*e.g.*, notably at IBM Research, who contributed technologies and ideas virtually to any DBMS existing today), research institutes, and Academia. Research has been done both through Theory and Prototypes. The interaction between research and database related product development has been very productive to the database area, and many related key concepts and technologies emerged from it. Notable are the Relational and the Entity-relationship models, the Atomic transaction concept and related Concurrency control techniques, Query languages and Query optimization methods, RAID, and more. Research has provided deep insight to virtually all aspects of databases, though not always has been pragmatic, effective (and cannot and should not always be: research is exploratory in nature, and not always leads to accepted or useful ideas). Ultimately market forces and real needs determine the selection of problem solutions and related technologies, also among those proposed by research. However, occasionally, not the best and most elegant solution wins (*e.g.*, SQL). Along their history DBMSs and respective databases, to a great extent, have been the outcome of such research, while real product requirements and challenges triggered database research directions and sub-areas.

The database research area has several notable dedicated academic journals (*e.g.*, ACM Transactions on Database Systems-TODS, Data and Knowledge Engineering-DKE, and more) and annual conferences (*e.g.*, ACM SIGMOD, ACM

PODS, VLDB, IEEE ICDE, and more), as well as an active and quite heterogeneous (subject-wise) research community all over the world.

DATABASE TYPE EXAMPLES

The following are examples of various database types. Some of them are not main-stream types, but most of them have received special attention (*e.g.*, in research) due to end-user requirements. Some exist as specialized DBMS products, and some have their functionality types incorporated in existing general-purpose DBMSs.

Active Database

An *active database* is a database that includes an event-driven architecture which can respond to conditions both inside and outside the database. Possible uses include security monitoring, alerting, statistics gathering and authorization. Most modern relational databases include active database features in the form of database trigger.

Cloud Database

A *Cloud database* is a database that relies on cloud technology. Both the database and most of its DBMS reside remotely, "in the cloud," while its applications are both developed by programmers and later maintained and utilized by (application's) end-users through a Web browser and Open APIs. More and more such database products are emerging, both of new vendors and by virtually all established database vendors.

Data Warehouse

Data warehouses archive data from operational databases and often from external sources such as market research firms. Often operational data undergoes transformation on its way into the warehouse, getting summarized, anonymized, reclassified, *etc.* The warehouse becomes the central source of data for use by managers and other end-users who may not have access to operational data. For example, sales data might be aggregated to weekly totals and converted from internal product codes to use UPCs so that it can be compared with ACNielsen data. Some basic and essential components of data warehousing include retrieving, analysing, and mining data, transforming, loading and managing data so as to make it available for further use. Operations in a data warehouse are typically concerned with bulk data manipulation, and as such, it is unusual and inefficient to target individual rows for update, insert or delete. Bulk native loaders for input data and bulk SQL passes for aggregation are the norm.

Distributed Database

The definition of a *distributed database* is broad, and may be utilized in different meanings. In general it typically refers to a modular DBMS architecture that allows distinct DBMS instances to cooperate as a single DBMS over processes, computers, and sites, while managing a single database distributed itself over multiple computers, and different sites.

Examples are databases of local work-groups and departments at regional offices, branch offices, manufacturing plants and other work sites. These databases can include both segments shared by multiple sites, and segments specific to one site and used only locally in that site.

Document-oriented Database

A document-oriented database is a computer programme designed for storing, retrieving, and managing document-oriented, or semi structured data, information. Document-oriented databases are one of the main categories of so-called NoSQL databases and the popularity of the term "document-oriented database" (or "document store") has grown with the use of the term NoSQL itself.

Utilized to conveniently store, manage, edit and retrieve documents.

Embedded Database

An *embedded database* system is a DBMS which is tightly integrated with an application software that requires access to stored data in a way that the DBMS is "hidden" from the application's end-user and requires little or no ongoing maintenance. It is actually a broad technology category that includes DBMSs with differing properties and target markets. The term "embedded database" can be confusing because only a small subset of embedded database products is used in real-time embedded systems such as telecommunications switches and consumer electronics devices.

End-user Database

These databases consist of data developed by individual end-users. Examples of these are collections of documents, spreadsheets, presentations, multimedia, and other files. Several products exist to support such databases. Some of them are much simpler than full fledged DBMSs, with more elementary DBMS functionality (*e.g.*, not supporting multiple concurrent end-users on a same database), with basic programming interfaces, and a relatively small "foot-print" (not much code to run as in "regular" general-purpose databases). However, also available general-purpose DBMSs can often be used for such purpose, if they provide basic user-interfaces for straightforward database applications (limited query and data display; no real programming needed), while still enjoying the database qualities and protections that these DBMSs can provide.

Federated Database and Multi-database

A *federated database* is an integrated database that comprises several distinct databases, each with its own DBMS. It is handled as a single database by a federated database management system (FDBMS), which transparently integrates multiple autonomous DBMSs, possibly of different types (which makes it a heterogeneous database), and provides them with an integrated conceptual view. The constituent databases are interconnected via computer network, and may be geographically decentralized. Sometime the term *multi-database* is used as a synonym to federated database, though it may refer to a less integrated (*e.g.*, without an FDBMS and a managed integrated schema) group of databases that cooperate in a single application. In this case typically middleware for distribution is used which typically includes an atomic commit protocol (ACP), *e.g.*, the two-phase commit protocol, to allow distributed (global) transactions across the participating databases.

Graph Database

A *graph database* is a kind of NoSQL database that uses graph structures with nodes, edges, and properties to represent and store information. General graph databases that can store any graph are distinct from specialized graph databases such as triplestores and network databases.

Hypermedia Databases

The World Wide Web can be thought of as a database, albeit one spread across millions of independent computing systems. Web browsers "process" this data one page at a time, while Web crawlers and other software provide the equivalent of database indexes to support search and other activities.

Hypertext Database

In a *Hypertext database*, any word or a piece of text representing an object, *e.g.*, another piece of text, an article, a picture, or a film, can be linked to that object. Hypertext databases are particularly useful for organizing large amounts of disparate information. For example they are useful for organizing online encyclopedias, where users can conveniently jump in the texts, in a controlled way, by using hyperlinks.

In-memory Database

An *in-memory database* (IMDB; also *main memory database* or MMDB) is a database that primarily resides in main memory, but typically backed-up by non-volatile computer data storage. Main memory databases are faster than disk databases. Accessing data in memory reduces the I/O reading activity when, for example, querying the data. In applications where response time is critical, such as telecommunications network equipment, main memory databases are often used.

Knowledge Base

A knowledge base (abbreviated KB, kb or Δ) is a special kind of database for knowledge management, providing the means for the computerized collection, organization, and retrieval of knowledge. Also a collection of data representing problems with their solutions and related experiences.

Operational Database

These databases store detailed data about the operations of an organization. They are typically organized by subject matter, process relatively high volumes of updates using transactions. Essentially every major organization on earth uses such databases. Examples include customer databases that record contact, credit, and demographic information about a business' customers, personnel databases that hold information such as salary, benefits, skills data about employees, Enterprise resource planning that record details about product components, parts inventory, and financial databases that keep track of the organization's money, accounting and financial dealings.

Parallel Database

A parallel database, run by a parallel DBMS, seeks to improve performance through parallelization for tasks such as loading data, building indexes and evaluating queries. Parallel databases improve processing and input/output speeds by using multiple central processing units (CPUs) (including multi-core processors) and storage in parallel. In parallel processing, many operations are performed simultaneously, as opposed to serial, sequential processing, where operations are performed with no time overlap.

The major parallel DBMS architectures (which are induced by the underlying hardware architecture are:

- Shared memory architecture, where multiple processors share the main memory space, as well as other data storage.
- Shared disk architecture, where each processing unit (typically consisting of multiple processors) has its own main memory, but all units share the other storage.
- Shared nothing architecture, where each processing unit has its own main memory and other storage.
- Real-time database.

If a DBMS system responses users' request in a given time period, it can be regarded as a real time database.

Spatial Database

A spatial database can store the data with multidimensional features. The queries on such data include location based queries, like "where is the closest hotel in my area".

Temporal Database

A temporal database is a database with built-in time aspects, for example a temporal data model and a temporal version of Structured Query Language

(SQL). More specifically the temporal aspects usually include valid-time and transaction-time.

Unstructured-data Database

An unstructured-data database is intended to store in a manageable and protected way diverse objects that do not fit naturally and conveniently in common databases. It may include email messages, documents, journals, multimedia objects *etc.* The name may be misleading since some objects can be highly structured. However, the entire possible object collection does not fit into a predefined structured framework. Most established DBMSs now support unstructured data in various ways, and new dedicated DBMSs are emerging.

MAJOR DATABASE USAGE REQUIREMENTS

The major purpose of a database is to provide the information system (in its broadest sense) that utilizes it with the information the system needs according to its own requirements. A certain broad set of requirements refines this general goal. These database requirements translate to requirements for the respective DBMS, to allow conveniently building a proper database for the given application. If this goal is met by a DBMS, then the designers and builders of the specific database can concentrate on the application's aspects, and not deal with building and maintaining the underlying DBMS. Also, since a DBMS is complex and expensive to build and maintain, it is not economical to build such a new tool (DBMS) for every application. Rather it is desired to provide a flexible tool for handling databases for as many as possible given applications, *i.e.*, a general-purpose DBMS.

Functional Requirements

Certain general functional requirements need to be met in conjunction with a database. They describe what is needed to be defined in a database for any specific application.

Defining the Structure of Data: Data Modelling and Data Definition Languages

The database needs to be based on a data model that is sufficiently rich to describe in the database all the needed respective application's aspects. A data definition language exists to describe the databases within the data model. Such language is typically data model specific.

Manipulating the Data: Data Manipulation Languages and Query Languages

A database data model needs support by a sufficiently rich data manipulation language to allow all database manipulations and information generation (from the data) as needed by the respective application. Such language is typically data model specific.

Protecting the Data: Setting Database Security Types and Levels

The DB needs built-in security means to protect its content (and users) from dangers of unauthorized users (either humans or programmes). Protection is also provided from types of unintentional breach. Security types and levels should be defined by the database owners.

Describing Processes that use the Data: Workflow and Business Process Modelling

Manipulating database data often involves processes of several interdependent steps, at different times (*e.g.*, when different people's interactions are involved; *e.g.*, generating an insurance policy). Data manipulation languages are typically intended to describe what is needed in a single such step.

Dealing with multiple steps typically requires writing quite complex programmes.

Most applications are programmed using common programming languages and software development tools. However the area of process description has evolved in the frameworks of *workflow* and *business processes* with supporting languages and software packages which considerably simplify the tasks. Traditionally these frameworks have been out of the scope of common DBMSs, but utilization of them has become common-place, and often they are provided as add-on's to DBMSs.

Operational Requirements

Operational requirements are needed to be met by a database in order to effectively support an application when operational.

Though it typically may be expected that operational requirements are automatically met by a DBMS, in fact it is not so in most of the cases: To be met substantial work of design and tuning is typically needed by database administrators.

This is typically done by specific instructions/operations through special database user interfaces and tools, and thus may be viewed as secondary functional requirements (which are not less important than the primary).

Availability

A DB should maintain needed levels of availability, *i.e.*, the DB needs to be available in a way that a user's action does not need to wait beyond a certain time range before starting executing upon the DB. Availability also relates to failure and recovery from it: Upon failure and during recovery normal availability changes, and special measures are needed to satisfy availability requirements.

Performance

Users' actions upon the DB should be executed within needed time ranges.

Isolation between Users

When multiple users access the database concurrently the actions of a user should be uninterrupted and unaffected by actions of other users. These concurrent actions should maintain the DB's consistency (*i.e.*, keep the DB from corruption).

Recovery from Failure and Disaster

All computer systems, including DBMSs, are prone to failures for many reasons (both software and hardware related). Failures typically corrupt the DB, typically to the extent that it is impossible to repair it without special measures. The DBMS should provide automatic recovery from failure procedures that repair the DB and return it to a well defined state.

Backup and Restore

Sometimes it is desired to bring a database back to a previous state (for many reasons, *e.g.*, cases when the database is found corrupted due to a software error, or if it has been updated with erroneous data). To achieve this a backup operation is done occasionally or continuously, where each desired database state (*i.e.*, the values of its data and their embedding in database's data structures) is kept within dedicated backup files (many techniques exist to do this effectively). When this state is needed, *i.e.*, when it is decided by a database administrator to bring the database back to this state (*e.g.*, by specifying this state by a desired point in time when the database was in this state), these files are utilized to restore that state.

Data Independence

Data independence pertains to a database's life cycle. It strongly impacts the convenience and cost of maintaining an application and its database, and has been the major motivation for the emergence and success of the Relational model, as well as the convergence to a common database architecture. In general the term "data independence" means that changes in the database's structure do not require changes in its application's computer programmes, and that changes in the database at a certain architectural level do not affect the database's levels above.

Data independence is achieved to a great extent in contemporary DBMS, but it is not completely attainable, and achieved at different degrees for different types of database structural changes.

MAJOR DATABASE FUNCTIONAL AREAS

The functional areas are domains and subjects that have evolved in order to provide proper answers and solutions to the functional requirements above.

DATA MODELS

A data model is an abstract structure that provides the means to effectively describe specific data structures needed to model an application. As such a data model needs sufficient expressive power to capture the needed aspects of applications. These applications are often typical to commercial companies and other organizations (like manufacturing, human-resources, stock, banking, *etc.*). For effective utilization and handling it is desired that a data model is relatively simple and intuitive. This may be in conflict with high expressive power needed to deal with certain complex applications. Thus any popular general-purpose data model usually well balances between being intuitive and relatively simple, and very complex with high expressive power. The application's semantics is usually not explicitly expressed in the model, but rather implicit (and detailed by documentation external to the model) and hinted to by data item types' names (*e.g.*, "part-number") and their connections (as expressed by generic data structure types provided by each specific model).

Early Data Models

These models were popular in the 1960s, 1970s, but nowadays can be found primarily in old legacy systems. They are characterized primarily by being navigational with strong connections between their logical and physical representations, and deficiencies in data independence.

Hierarchical Model

In the Hierarchical model different record types (representing real-world entities) are embedded in a predefined hierarchical (tree-like) structure. This hierarchy is used as the physical order of records in storage. Record access is done by navigating through the data structure using pointers combined with sequential accessing.

This model has been supported primarily by the IBM IMS DBMS, one of the earliest DBMSs. Various limitations of the model have been compensated at later IMS versions by additional logical hierarchies imposed on the base physical hierarchy.

Network Model

In this model a hierarchical relationship between two record types (representing real-world entities) is established by the *set* construct. A set consists of circular linked lists where one record type, the set owner or parent, appears once in each circle, and a second record type, the subordinate or child, may appear multiple times in each circle. In this way a hierarchy may be established between any two record types, *e.g.*, type A is the owner of B. At the same time another set may be defined where B is the owner of A. Thus all the sets comprise a general directed graph (ownership defines a direction), or *network* construct. Access to records is either sequential (usually in each record type) or by navigation in the circular linked lists. This model is more general and powerful than the hierarchical, and has been the most popular before being replaced by the Relational model. It has been standardized by CODASYL. Popular DBMS products that utilized it were Cincom Systems' Total and Cullinet's IDMS.

Inverted File Model

An *inverted file* or *inverted index* of a first file, by a field in this file (the inversion field), is a second file in which this field is the key. A record in the second file includes a key and pointers to records in the first file where the inversion field has the value of the key. This is also the logical structure of contemporary database indexes. The related *Inverted file data model* utilizes inverted files of primary database files to efficiently directly access needed records in these files.

Notable for using this data model is the ADABAS DBMS of Software AG, introduced in 1970. ADABAS has gained considerable customer base and exists and supported until today. In the 1980s it has adopted the Relational model and SQL in addition to its original tools and languages.

Relational Model

The relational model is a simple model that provides flexibility. It organizes data based on two-dimensional arrays known as relations, or tables as related to databases. These relations consist of a heading and a set of zero or more tuples in arbitrary order. The heading is an unordered set of zero or more attributes, or columns of the table. The tuples are a set of unique attributes mapped to values, or the rows of data in the table. Data can be associated across multiple tables with a key. A key is a single, or set of multiple, attribute(s) that is common to both tables. The most common language associated with the relational model is the Structured Query Language (SQL), though it differs in some places.

Object Model

In recent years, the object-oriented paradigm has been applied in areas such as engineering and spatial databases, telecommunications and in various scientific domains. The conglomeration of object oriented programming and database technology led to this new kind of database. These databases attempt to bring the database world and the application-programming world closer together, in particular by ensuring that the database uses the same type system as the application programme. This aims to avoid the overhead of converting information between its representation in the database and its representation in the application programme (typically as objects). At the same time, object databases attempt to introduce key ideas of object programming, such as encapsulation and polymorphism, into the world of databases.

A variety of these ways have been tried for storing objects in a database. Some products have approached the problem from the application-programming side, by making the objects manipulated by the programme persistent. This also typically requires the addition of some kind of query language, since conventional programming languages do not provide language-level functionality for finding objects based on their information content. Others have attacked the problem from the database end, by defining an object-oriented data model for the database, and defining a database programming language that allows full programming capabilities as well as traditional query facilities.

OTHER DATABASE MODELS

Products offering a more general data model than the relational model are sometimes classified as post-relational. Alternate terms include "hybrid database", "Object-enhanced RDBMS" and others. The data model in such products incorporates relations but is not constrained by E.F. Codd's Information Principle, which requires that all information in the database must be cast explicitly in terms of values in relations and in no other way

Some of these extensions to the relational model integrate concepts from technologies that pre-date the relational model. For example, they allow representation of a directed graph with trees on the nodes. The German company *sones* implements this concept in its GraphDB.

Some post-relational products extend relational systems with non-relational features. Others arrived in much the same place by adding relational features to pre-relational systems. Paradoxically, this allows products that are historically pre-relational, such as PICK and MUMPS, to make a plausible claim to be post-relational.

The resource space model (RSM) is a non-relational data model based on multi-dimensional classification.

Database Languages

Database languages are dedicated programming languages, tailored and utilized to:

- Define a database (*i.e.*, its specific data types and the relationships among them),
- Manipulate its content (*e.g.*, insert new data occurrences, and update or delete existing ones), and
- Query it (*i.e.*, request information: compute and retrieve any information based on its data).

Database languages are data-model-specific, *i.e.*, each language assumes and is based on a certain structure of the data (which typically differs among different data models). They typically have commands to instruct execution of the desired operations in the database. Each such command is equivalent to a complex expression (programme) in a regular programming language, and thus programming in dedicated (database) languages simplifies the task of handling databases considerably. An expressions in a database language is automatically transformed (by a compiler or interpreter, as regular programming languages) to a proper computer programme that runs while accessing the database and providing the needed results. The following are notable examples:

SQL for the Relational Model

A major Relational model language supported by all the relational DBMSs and a standard. SQL was one of the first commercial languages for the relational model. Despite not adhering to the relational model as described by Codd, it has become the most widely used database language. Though often described as, and to a great extent is a declarative language, SQL also includes procedural elements. SQL became a standard of the American National Standards Institute (ANSI) in 1986, and of the International Organization for Standards (ISO) in 1987. Since then the standard has been enhanced several times with added features. However, issues of SQL code portability between major RDBMS products still exist due to lack of full compliance with, or different interpretations of the standard. Among the reasons mentioned are the large size, and incomplete specification of the standard, as well as vendor lock-in.

OQL for the Object Model

An Object model language standard (by the Object Data Management Group) that has influenced the design of some of the newer query languages like JDOQL and EJB QL, though they cannot be considered as different flavours of OQL.

XQuery for the XML Model

XQuery is an XML based database language (also named XQL). SQL/XML combines XQuery and XML with SQL.

Database Architecture

Database architecture may be viewed, to some extent, as an extension of Data modelling. It is used to conveniently answer requirements of different end-users from a same database, as well as for other benefits. For example, a financial department of a company needs the payment details of all employees as part of the company's expenses, but not other many details about employees, that are the interest of the human resources department. Thus different departments need different *views* of the company's database, that both include the employees' payments, possibly in a different level of detail (and presented in different visual forms). To meet such requirement effectively database architecture consists of three levels: *external*, *conceptual* and *internal*. Clearly separating the three levels was a major feature of the relational database model implementations that dominate 21st century databases.

- The external level defines how each end-user type understands the organization of its respective relevant data in the database, *i.e.*, the different needed end-user views. A single database can have any number of views at the external level.

- The conceptual level unifies the various external views into a coherent whole, global view. It provides the common-denominator of all the external views. It comprises all the end-user needed generic data, *i.e.*, all the data from which any view may be derived/computed. It is provided in the simplest possible way of such generic data, and comprises the back-bone of the database. It is out of the scope of the various database end-users, and serves database application developers and defined by database administrators that build the database.
- The Internal level (or *Physical level*) is as a matter of fact part of the database implementation inside a DBMS. It is concerned with cost, performance, scalability and other operational matters. It deals with storage layout of the conceptual level, provides supporting storage-structures like indexes, to enhance performance, and occasionally stores data of individual views (materialized views), computed from generic data, if performance justification exists for such redundancy. It balances all the external views' performance requirements, possibly conflicting, in attempt to optimize the overall database usage by all its end-uses according to the database goals and priorities.

All the three levels are maintained and updated according to changing needs by database administrators who often also participate in the database design.

The above three-level database architecture also relates to and being motivated by the concept of *data independence* which has been described for long time as a desired database property and was one of the major initial driving forces of the Relational model.

In the context of the above architecture it means that changes made at a certain level do not affect definitions and software developed with higher level interfaces, and are being incorporated at the higher level automatically. For example, changes in the internal level do not affect application programmes written using conceptual level interfaces, which saves substantial change work that would be needed otherwise.

In summary, the conceptual is a level of indirection between internal and external. On one hand it provides a common view of the database, independent of different external view structures, and on the other hand it is uncomplicated by details of how the data is stored or managed (internal level). In principle every level, and even every external view, can be presented by a different data model. In practice usually a given DBMS uses the same data model for both the external and the conceptual levels (*e.g.*, relational model). The internal level, which is hidden inside the DBMS and depends on its implementation, requires a different level of detail and uses its own data structure types, typically different in nature from the structures of the external and conceptual levels which are exposed to DBMS users: While the external and conceptual levels are focused on and serve DBMS users, the concern of the internal level is effective implementation details.

Database Security

Database security deals with all various aspects of protecting the database content, its owners, and its users. It ranges from protection from intentional unauthorized database uses to unintentional database accesses by unauthorized entities (*e.g.*, a person or a computer programme).

The following are major areas of database security (among many others).

Access Control

Database access control deals with controlling who (a person or a certain computer programme) is allowed to access what information in the database. The information may comprise specific database objects (*e.g.*, record types, specific records, data structures), certain computations over certain objects (*e.g.*, query types, or specific queries), or utilizing specific access paths to the former (*e.g.*, using specific indexes or other data structures to access information).

Database access controls are set by special authorized (by the database owner) personnel that uses dedicated protected security DBMS interfaces.

Data Security

The definition of data security varies and may overlap with other database security aspects. Broadly it deals with protecting specific chunks of data, both physically, or the interpretation of them, or parts of them to meaningful information (*e.g.*, by looking at the strings of bits that they comprise, concluding specific valid credit-card numbers).

Database Audit

Database audit primarily involves monitoring that no security breach, in all aspects, has happened. If security breach is discovered then all possible corrective actions are taken.

DATABASE DESIGN

Database design is done before building it to meet needs of end-users within a given application/information-system that the database is intended to support. The database design defines the needed data and data structures that such a database comprises. A design is typically carried out according to the common three architectural levels of a database. First, the conceptual level is designed, which defines the over-all picture/view of the database, and reflects all the real-world elements (entities) the database intends to model, as well as the relationships among them. On top of it the external level, various views of the database, are designed according to (possibly completely different) needs of specific end-user types. More external views can be added later. External views requirements may modify the design of the conceptual level (*i.e.*, add/remove entities and relationships), but usually a well designed conceptual level for an application well supports most of the needed external views. The conceptual view also determines the internal level (which primarily deals with data layout in storage) to a great extent. External views requirement may add supporting storage structures, like materialized views and indexes, for enhanced performance. Typically the internal layer is optimized for top performance, in an average way that takes into account performance requirements (possibly conflicting) of different external views according to their relative importance. While the conceptual and external levels design can usually be done independently of any DBMS (DBMS-independent design software packages exist, possibly with interfaces to some specific popular DBMSs), the internal level design highly relies on the capabilities and internal data structure of the specific DBMS utilized.

A common way to carry out conceptual level design is to use the Entity-relationship model (ERM) (both the basic one, and with possible enhancement that it has gone over), since it provides a straightforward, intuitive perception of an application's elements and semantics. An alternative approach, which preceded the ERM, is using the Relational model and dependencies (mathematical relationships) among data to normalize the database, *i.e.*, to define the ("optimal") relations (data record or tupple types) in the database. Though a large body of research exists for this method it is more complex, less intuitive, and not more effective than the ERM method. Thus normalization is less utilized in practice than the ERM method.

The ERM may be less subtle than normalization in several aspects, but it captures the main needed dependencies which are induced by keys/identifiers of entities and relationships. Also the ERM inherently includes the important inclusion dependencies (*i.e.*, an entity instance that does not exist (has not been explicitly inserted) cannot appear in a relationship with other entities) which usually have been ignored in normalization. In addition the ERM allows entity type generalization (the Is-a relationship) and implied property (attribute) inheritance (similarly to the that found in the Object model).

Another aspect of database design is its security. It involves both defining access control to database objects (*e.g.*, Entities, Views) as well as defining security levels and methods for the data itself.

Entities and Relationships

The most common database design methods are based on the Entity relationship model (ERM, or ER model). This model views the world in a simplistic but very powerful way: It consists of "Entities" and the "Relationships" among them. Accordingly a database consists of *entity* and *relationship* types, each with defined *attributes* (field types) that model concrete entities and relationships. Modelling a database in this way typically yields an effective one with desired properties. Such models can be translated to any other data model required by any specific DBMS for building an effective database.

Database Normalization

In the design of a relational database, the process of organizing database relations to minimize redundancy is called *normalization*. The goal is to produce well-structured relations so that additions, deletions, and modifications of a field can be made in just one relation (table) without worrying about appearance and update of the same field in other relations. The process is algorithmic and based on dependencies (mathematical relations) that exist among relations' field types. The process result is bringing the database relations into a certain "normal form". Several normal forms exist with different properties.

DATABASE BUILDING, MAINTAINING AND TUNING

After designing a database for an application arrives the stage of building the database. Typically an appropriate general-purpose DBMS can be selected to be utilized for this purpose. A DBMS provides the needed user interfaces to be utilized by database administrators to define the needed application's data structures within the DBMS's respective data model. Other user interfaces are used to select needed DBMS parameters (like security related, storage allocation parameters, *etc.*).

When the database is ready (all its data structures and other needed components are defined) it is typically populated with initial application's data (database initialization, which is typically a distinct project; in many cases using specialized DBMS interfaces that support bulk insertion) before making it operational.

In some cases the database becomes operational while empty from application's data, and data are accumulated along its operation.

After completing building the database and making it operational arrives the database maintenance stage: Various database parameters may need changes and tuning for better performance, application's data structures may be changed or added, new related application programmes may be written to add to the application's functionality, *etc.*

MISCELLANEOUS AREAS

Database Migration between DBMSs

A database built with one DBMS is not portable to another DBMS (*i.e.*, the other DBMS cannot run it). However, in some situations it is desirable to move, migrate a database from one DBMS to another. The reasons are primarily economical (different DBMSs may have different total costs of ownership-TCO), functional, and operational (different DBMSs may have different capabilities). The migration involves the database's transformation from one DBMS type to another. The transformation should maintain (if possible) the database related application (*i.e.*, all related application programmes) intact. Thus, the database's conceptual and external architectural levels should be maintained in the transformation.

It may be desired that also some aspects of the architecture internal level are maintained. A complex or large database migration may be a complicated and costly (one-time) project by itself, which should be factored into the decision to migrate. This in spite of the fact that tools may exist to help migration between specific DBMS. Typically a DBMS vendor provides tools to help importing databases from other popular DBMSs.

IMPLEMENTATION: DATABASE MANAGEMENT SYSTEMS

A *database management system* (DBMS) is a system that allows to build and maintain databases, as well as to utilize their data and retrieve information from it. A DBMS defines the database type that it supports, as well as its functionality and operational capabilities.

A DBMS provides the internal processes for external applications built on them. The end-users of some such specific application are usually exposed only to that application and do not directly interact with the DBMS. Thus end-users enjoy the effects of the underlying DBMS, but its internals are completely invisible to end-users.

Database designers and database administrators interact with the DBMS through dedicated interfaces to build and maintain the applications' databases, and thus need some more knowledge and understanding about how DBMSs operate and the DBMSs' external interfaces and tuning parameters. A DBMS consists of software that operates databases, providing storage, access, security, backup and other facilities to meet needed requirements. DBMSs can be categorized according to the database model(s) that they support, such as relational or XML, the type(s) of computer they support, such as a server cluster or a mobile phone, the query language(s) that access the database, such as SQL or XQuery, performance trade-offs, such as maximum scale or maximum speed or others. Some DBMSs cover more than one entry in these categories, *e.g.*, supporting multiple query languages. Database software typically support the Open Database Connectivity (ODBC) standard which allows the database to integrate (to some extent) with other databases.

The development of a mature general-purpose DBMS typically takes several years and many man-years. Developers of DBMS typically update their product to follow and take advantage of progress in computer and storage technologies. Several DBMS products like Oracle and IBM DB2 have been in on-going development since the 1970s-1980s. Since DBMSs comprise a significant economical market, computer and storage vendors often take into account DBMS requirements in their own development plans.

DBMS ARCHITECTURE: MAJOR DBMS COMPONENTS

DBMS architecture specifies its components (including descriptions of their functions) and their interfaces. DBMS architecture is distinct from database architecture. The following are major DBMS components:

- *DBMS external interfaces* - They are the means to communicate with the DBMS (both ways, to and from the DBMS) to perform all the operations needed for the DBMS. These can be operations on a database, or operations to operate and manage the DBMS. For example:
  (a) Direct database operations: defining data types, assigning security levels, updating data, querying the database, *etc.*
  (b) Operations related to DBMS operation and management: backup and restore, database recovery, security monitoring, database storage allocation and database layout configuration monitoring, performance monitoring and tuning, *etc.*

An external interface can be either a *user interface* (*e.g.*, typically for a database administrator), or an *application programming interface* (API) used for communication between an application programme and the DBMS.

- Database language engines (or processors) - Most operations upon databases are performed through expression in Database languages. Languages exist for data definition, data manipulation and queries (*e.g.*, SQL), as well as for specifying various aspects of security, and more. Language expressions are fed into a DBMS through proper interfaces. A language engine processes the language expressions (by a compiler or language interpreter) to extract the intended database operations from the expression in a way that they can be executed by the DBMS.
- Query optimizer - Performs query optimization on every query to choose for it the most efficient *query plan* (a partial order (tree) of operations) to be executed to compute the query result.
- Database engine - Performs the received database operations on the database objects, typically at their higher-level representation.
- Storage engine - translates the operations to low-level operations on the storage bits. In some references the Storage engine is viewed as part of the Database engine.
- Transaction engine - for correctness and reliability purposes most DBMS internal operations are performed encapsulated in transactions. Transactions can also be specified externally to the DBMS to encapsulate a group of operations. The transaction engine tracks all the transactions and manages their execution according to the transaction rules (*e.g.*, proper concurrency control, and proper *commit* or *abort* for each).
- DBMS management and operation component - Comprises many components that deal with all the DBMS management and operational aspects like performance monitoring and tuning, backup and restore,

recovery from failure, security management and monitoring, database storage allocation and database storage layout monitoring, *etc.*

DATABASE STORAGE

Database storage is the container of the physical materialization of a database. It comprises the *Internal* (physical) *level* in the database architecture. It also contains all the information needed (*e.g.*, metadata, "data about the data", and internal data structures) to reconstruct the *Conceptual level* and *External level* from the Internal level when needed. It is not part of the DBMS but rather manipulated by the DBMS to manage the database that resides in it. Though typically accessed by a DBMS through the underlying Operating system (and often utilizing the operating systems' File systems as intermediates for storage layout), storage properties and configuration setting are extremely important for the efficient operation of the DBMS, and thus are closely maintained by database administrators.

A DBMS, while in operation, always has its database residing in several types of storage (*e.g.*, memory and external storage). The database data and the additional needed information, possibly in very large amounts, are coded into bits. Data typically reside in the storage in structures that look completely different from the way the data look in the conceptual and external levels, but in ways that attempt to optimize (the best possible) these levels' reconstruction when needed by users and programmes, as well as for computing additional types of needed information from the data (*e.g.*, when querying the database).

In principle the database storage can be viewed as a linear address space, where every bit of data has its unique address in this address space. Practically only a very small percentage of addresses is kept as initial reference points (which also requires storage), and most of the database data is accessed by indirection using displacement calculations (distance in bits from the reference points) and data structures which define access paths (using pointers) to all needed data in effective manner, optimized for the needed data access operations.

Coding the Data and Error-correcting Codes

- Data is encoded by assigning a bit pattern to each language alphabet character, digit, other numerical patterns, and multimedia object. Many standards exist for encoding (*e.g.*, ASCII, JPEG, MPEG-4).
- By adding bits to each encoded unit, the redundancy allows both to detect errors in coded data and to correct them based on mathematical algorithms. Errors occur regularly in low probabilities due to random bit value flipping, or "physical bit fatigue," loss of the physical bit in storage its ability to maintain distinguishable value (0 or 1), or due to errors in inter or intra-computer communication. A random bit flip (*e.g.*, due to random radiation) is typically corrected upon detection.

A bit, or a group of malfunctioning physical bits (not always the specific defective bit is known; group definition depends on specific storage device) is typically automatically fenced-out, taken out of use by the device, and replaced with another functioning equivalent group in the device, where the corrected bit values are restored (if possible). The Cyclic redundancy check (CRC) method is typically used in storage for error detection.

Data Compression

Data compression methods allow in many cases to represent a string of bits by a shorter bit string ("compress") and reconstruct the original string ("decompress") when needed. This allows to utilize substantially less storage (tens of percents) for many types of data at the cost of more computation (compress and decompress when needed). Analysis of trade-off between storage cost saving and costs of related computations and possible delays in data availability is done before deciding whether to keep certain data in a database compressed or not.

Data compression is typically controlled through the DBMS's data definition interface, but in some cases may be a default and automatic.

Data Encryption

For security reasons certain types of data (*e.g.*, credit-card information) may be kept encrypted in storage to prevent the possibility of unauthorized information reconstruction from chunks of storage snapshots (taken either via unforeseen vulnerabilities in a DBMS, or more likely, by bypassing it).

Data encryption is typically controlled through the DBMS's data definition interface, but in some cases may be a default and automatic.

DATA STORAGE TYPES

This collection of bits describes both the contained database data and its related metadata (*i.e.*, data that describes the contained data and allows computer programmes to manipulate the database data correctly).

The size of a database can nowadays be tens of Terabytes, where a byte is eight bits.

The physical materialization of a bit can employ various existing technologies, while new and improved technologies are constantly under development. Common examples are:

- *Magnetic medium* (*e.g.*, in Magnetic disk) - Orientation of magnetic field in magnetic regions on a surface of material (two orientation directions, for 0 and 1).
- *Dynamic random-access memory* (DRAM) - State of a miniature electronic circuit consisting of few transistors (among millions nowadays) in an integrated circuit (two states for 0 and 1).

These two examples are respectively for two major storage types:

- *Nonvolatile storage* can maintain its bit states (0s and 1s) without electrical power supply, or when power supply is interrupted;
- *Volatile storage* loses its bit values when power supply is interrupted (*i.e.*, its content is erased).

Sophisticated storage units, which can, in fact, be effective dedicated parallel computers that support a large amount of nonvolatile storage, typically must include also components with volatile storage. Some such units employ batteries that can provide power for several hours in case of external power interruption and thus maintain the content of the volatile storage parts intact. Just before such a device's batteries lose their power the device typically automatically backs-up its volatile content portion (into nonvolatile) and shuts off to protect its data.

Databases are usually too expensive (in terms of importance and needed investment in resources, *e.g.*, time, money, to build them) to be lost by a power interruption. Thus at any point in time most of their content resides in nonvolatile storage. Even if for operational reason very large portions of them reside in volatile storage (*e.g.*, tens of Gigabytes in volatile memory, for in-memory databases), most of this is backed-up in nonvolatile storage. A relatively small portion of this, which temporarily may not have nonvolatile backup, can be reconstructed by proper automatic database recovery procedures after volatile storage content loss.

More examples of storage types:

- Volatile storage can be found in processors, computer memory (*e.g.*, DRAM), *etc.*
- Non-volatile storage types include ROM, EPROM, Hard disk drives, Flash memory and drives, Storage arrays, *etc.*

Storage Metrics

Databases always use several types of storage when operational (and implied several when idle). Different types may significantly differ in their properties, and the optimal mix of storage types is determined by the types and quantities of operations that each storage type needs to perform, as well as considerations like physical space and energy consumption and dissipation (which may become critical for a large database). Storage types can be categorized by the following attributes:

- Volatile/Nonvolatile.
- Cost of the medium (*e.g.*, per Megabyte), Cost to operate (cost of energy consumed per unit time).
- Access speed (*e.g.*, bytes per second).
- Granularity — from fine to coarse (*e.g.*, size in bytes of access operation).
- Reliability (the probability of spontaneous bit value change under various conditions).

- Maximal possible number of writes (of any specific bit or specific group of bits; could be constrained by the technology used (*e.g.*, "write once" or "write twice"), or due to "physical bit fatigue," loss of ability to distinguish between the 0, 1 states due to many state changes (*e.g.*, in Flash memory)).
- Power needed to operate (Energy per time; energy per byte accessed), Energy efficiency, Heat to dissipate.
- Packaging density (*e.g.*, realistic number of bytes per volume unit).

PROTECTING STORAGE DEVICE CONTENT: DEVICE MIRRORING (REPLICATION) AND RAID

While a group of bits malfunction may be resolved by error detection and correction mechanisms, storage device malfunction requires different solutions. The following solutions are commonly used and valid for most storage devices:

- Device mirroring (replication) - A common solution to the problem is constantly maintaining an identical copy of device content on another device (typically of a same type). The downside is that this doubles the storage, and both devices (copies) need to be updated simultaneously with some overhead and possibly some delays. The upside is possible concurrent read of a same data group by two independent processes, which increases performance. When one of the replicated devices is detected to be defective, the other copy is still operational, and is being utilized to generate a new copy on another device (usually available operational in a pool of stand-by devices for this purpose).
- Redundant array of independent disks (RAID) - This method generalizes the device mirroring above by allowing one device in a group of N devices to fail and be replaced with content restored (Device mirroring is RAID with N=2). RAID groups of N=5 or N=6 are common. N>2 saves storage, when comparing with N=2, at the cost of more processing during both regular operation (with often reduced performance) and defective device replacement.

Device mirroring and typical RAID are designed to handle a single device failure in the RAID group of devices. However, if a second failure occurs before the RAID group is completely repaired from the first failure, then data can be lost. The probability of a single failure is typically small. Thus the probability of two failures in a same RAID group in time proximity is much smaller (approximately the probability squared, *i.e.*, multiplied by itself). If a database cannot tolerate even such smaller probability of data loss, then the RAID group itself is replicated (mirrored). In many cases such mirroring is done geographically remotely, in a different storage array, to handle also recovery from disasters.

Database Storage Layout

Database bits are laid-out in storage in data-structures and grouping that can take advantage of both known effective algorithms to retrieve and manipulate them and the storage own properties. Typically the storage itself is design to meet requirements of various areas that extensively utilize storage, including databases. A DBMS in operation always simultaneously utilizes several storage types (*e.g.*, memory, and external storage), with respective layout methods.

Database Storage Hierarchy

A database, while in operation, resides simultaneously in several types of storage. By the nature of contemporary computers most of the database part inside a computer that hosts the DBMS resides (partially replicated) in volatile storage. Data (pieces of the database) that are being processed/manipulated reside inside a processor, possibly in processor's caches. These data are being read from/ written to memory, typically through a computer bus (so far typically volatile storage components). Computer memory is communicating data (transferred to/ from) external storage, typically through standard storage interfaces or networks (*e.g.*, fibre channel, iSCSI). A storage array, a common external storage unit, typically has storage hierarchy of it own, from a fast cache, typically consisting of (volatile and fast) DRAM, which is connected (again via standard interfaces) to drives, possibly with different speeds, like flash drives and magnetic disk drives (non-volatile). The drives may be connected to magnetic tapes, on which typically the least active parts of a large database may reside, or database backup generations.

Typically a correlation exists currently between storage speed and price, while the faster storage is typically volatile.

Data Structures

A data structure is an abstract construct that embeds data in a well defined manner. An efficient data structure allows to manipulate the data in efficient ways. The data manipulation may include data insertion, deletion, updating and retrieval in various modes. A certain data structure type may be very effective in certain operations, and very ineffective in others. A data structure type is selected upon DBMS development to best meet the operations needed for the types of data it contains. Type of data structure selected for a certain task typically also takes into consideration the type of storage it resides in (*e.g.*, speed of access, minimal size of storage chunk accessed, *etc.*). In some DBMSs database administrators have the flexibility to select among options of data structures to contain user data for performance reasons. Sometimes the data structures have selectable parameters to tune the database performance.

Databases may store data in many data structure types. Common examples are the following:

- ordered/unordered flat files

- hash tables
- B+ trees
- ISAM
- heaps.

Application Data and DBMS Data

A typical DBMS cannot store the data of the application it serves alone. In order to handle the application data the DBMS need to store this data in data structures that comprise specific data by themselves. In addition the DBMS needs its own data structures and many types of bookkeeping data like indexes and logs. The DBMS data is an integral part of the database and may comprise a substantial portion of it.

Database Indexing

Indexing is a technique for improving database performance. The many types of indexes share the common property that they reduce the need to examine every entry when running a query. In large databases, this can reduce query time/cost by orders of magnitude. The simplest form of index is a sorted list of values that can be searched using a binary search with an adjacent reference to the location of the entry, analogous to the index in the back of a book. The same data can have multiple indexes (an employee database could be indexed by last name and hire date.) Indexes affect performance, but not results. Database designers can add or remove indexes without changing application logic, reducing maintenance costs as the database grows and database usage evolves.

Given a particular query, the DBMS' query optimizer is responsible for devising the most efficient strategy for finding matching data.

Indexes can speed up data access, but they consume space in the database, and must be updated each time the data is altered. Indexes therefore can speed data access but slow data maintenance. These two properties determine whether a given index is worth the cost.

Database Data Clustering

In many cases substantial performance improvement is gained if different types of database objects that are usually utilized together are laid in storage in proximity, being *clustered*. This usually allows to retrieve needed related objects from storage in minimum number of input operations (each sometimes substantially time consuming). Even for in-memory databases clustering provides performance advantage due to common utilization of large caches for input-output operations in memory, with similar resulting behaviour.

For example it may be beneficial to cluster a record of an *item* in stock with all its respective *order* records. The decision of whether to cluster certain objects or not depends on the objects' utilization statistics, object sizes, caches sizes, storage types, *etc.* In a relational database clustering the two respective relations

"Items" and "Orders" results in saving the expensive execution of a Join operation between the two relations whenever such a join is needed in a query (the join result is already ready in storage by the clustering, available to be utilized).

Database Materialized Views

Often storage redundancy is employed to increase performance. A common example is storing *materialized views*, which are frequently needed *External views*. Storing such external views saves expensive computing of them each time they are needed.

Database and Database Object Replication

Occasionally a database employs storage redundancy by database objects replication (with one or more copies) to increase data availability (both to improve performance of simultaneous multiple end-user accesses to a same database object, and to provide resiliency in a case of partial failure of a distributed database). Updates of a replicated object need to be synchronized across the object copies. In many cases the entire database is replicated.

DATABASE TRANSACTIONS

As with every software system, a DBMS that operates in a faulty computing environment is prone to failures of many kinds. A failure can corrupt the respective database unless special measures are taken to prevent this. A DBMS achieves certain levels of fault tolerance by encapsulating operations within transactions. The concept of a *database transaction* (or *atomic transaction*) has evolved in order to enable both a well understood database system behaviour in a faulty environment where crashes can happen any time, and *recovery* from a crash to a well understood database state. A database transaction is a unit of work, typically encapsulating a number of operations over a database (*e.g.*, reading a database object, writing, acquiring lock, *etc.*), an abstraction supported in database and also other systems. Each transaction has well defined boundaries in terms of which programme/code executions are included in that transaction (determined by the transaction's programmer via special transaction commands).

ACID RULES

Every database transaction obeys the following rules:

- Atomicity - Either the effects of all or none of its operations remain ("all or nothing" semantics) when a transaction is completed (*committed* or *aborted* respectively). In other words, to the outside world a committed transaction appears (by its effects on the database) to be indivisible, atomic, and an aborted transaction does not leave effects on the database at all, as if never existed.

- Consistency - Every transaction must leave the database in a consistent (correct) state, *i.e.,* maintain the predetermined integrity rules of the database (constraints upon and among the database's objects). A transaction must transform a database from one consistent state to another consistent state (however, it is the responsibility of the transaction's programmer to make sure that the transaction itself is correct, *i.e.,* performs correctly what it intends to perform (from the application's point of view) while the predefined integrity rules are enforced by the DBMS). Thus since a database can be normally changed only by transactions, all the database's states are consistent. An aborted transaction does not change the database state it has started from, as if it never existed.
- Isolation - Transactions cannot interfere with each other (as an end result of their executions). Moreover, usually (depending on concurrency control method) the effects of an incomplete transaction are not even visible to another transaction. Providing isolation is the main goal of concurrency control.
- Durability - Effects of successful (committed) transactions must persist through crashes (typically by recording the transaction's effects and its commit event in a non-volatile memory).

Isolation, Concurrency Control and Locking

Isolation provides the ability for multiple users to operate on the database at the same time without corrupting the data.

- Concurrency control comprises the underlying mechanisms in a DBMS which handle isolation and guarantee related correctness. It is heavily utilized by the Database and Storage engines both to guarantee the correct execution of concurrent transactions, and (different mechanisms) the correctness of other DBMS processes. The transaction-related mechanisms typically constrain the database data access operations' timing (transaction schedules) to certain orders characterized as the Serializability and Recoverabiliry schedule properties. Constraining database access operation execution typically means reduced performance (rates of execution), and thus concurrency control mechanisms are typically designed to provide the best performance possible under the constraints. Often, when possible without harming correctness, the serializability property is compromised for better performance. However, recoverability cannot be compromised, since such typically results in a quick database integrity violation.
- Locking is the most common transaction concurrency control method in DBMSs, used to provide both serializability and recoverability for correctness. In order to access a database object a transaction first needs

to acquire a lock for this object. Depending on the access operation type (*e.g.*, reading or writing an object) and on the lock type, acquiring the lock may be blocked and postponed, if another transaction is holding a lock for that object.

Query Optimization

A query is a request for information from a database. It can be as simple as "finding the address of a person with SS# 123-45-6789," or more complex like "finding the average salary of all the employed married men in California between the ages 30 to 39, that earn less than their wives." Queries results are generated by accessing relevant database data and manipulating it in a way that yields the requested information. Since database structures are complex, in most cases, and especially for not-very-simple queries, the needed data for a query can be collected from a database by accessing it in different ways, through different data-structures, and in different orders. Each different way typically requires different processing time. Processing times of a same query may have large variance, from a fraction of a second to hours, depending on the way selected. The purpose of query optimization, which is an automated process, is to find the way to process a given query in minimum time. The large possible variance in time justifies performing query optimization, though finding the exact optimal way to execute a query, among all possibilities, is typically very complex, time consuming by itself, may be too costly, and often practically impossible. Thus query optimization typically tries to approximate the optimum by comparing several common-sense alternatives to provide in a reasonable time a "good enough" plan which typically does not deviate much from the best possible result.

DBMS Support for the Development and Maintenance of a Database and its Application

A DBMS typically intends to provide convenient environment to develop and later maintain an application built around its respective database type. A DBMS either provides such tools, or allows integration with such external tools. Examples for tools relate to database design, application programming, application programme maintenance, database performance analysis and monitoring, database configuration monitoring, DBMS hardware configuration (a DBMS and related database may span computers, networks, and storage units) and related database mapping (especially for a distributed DBMS), storage allocation and database layout monitoring, storage migration, *etc.*

DATABASE MANAGEMENT SYSTEM

A management system is a set of rules and procedures which help us to create organize and manipulate the database. It also helps us to add, modify delete data items in the database. The management system can be either manual or computerized.

The management system is important because without the existence of some kind of rules and regulations it is not possible to maintain the database. We have to select the particular attributes which should be included in a particular table; the common attributes to create relationship between two tables; if a new record has to be inserted or deleted then which tables should have to be handled *etc.* These issues must be resolved by having some kind of rules to follow in order to maintain the integrity of the database.

THREE VIEWS OF DATA

We know that the same thing, if viewed from different angles produces difference sights. Likewise, the database that we have created already can have different aspects to reveal if seen from different levels of abstraction. The term Abstraction is very important here. Generally it means the amount of detail you want to hide. Any entity can be seen from different perspectives and levels of complexity to make it a reveal its current amount of abstraction. Let us illustrate by a simple example.

A computer reveals the minimum of its internal details, when seen from outside.

We do not know what parts it is built with. This is the highest level of abstraction, meaning very few details are visible. If we open the computer case and look inside at the hard disc, motherboard, CD drive, CPU and RAM, we are in middle level of abstraction. If we move on to open the hard disc and examine its tracks, sectors and read-write heads, we are at the lowest level of abstraction, where no details are invisible.

In the same manner, the database can also be viewed from different levels of abstraction to reveal different levels of details. From a bottom-up manner, we may find that there are three levels of abstraction or views in the database.

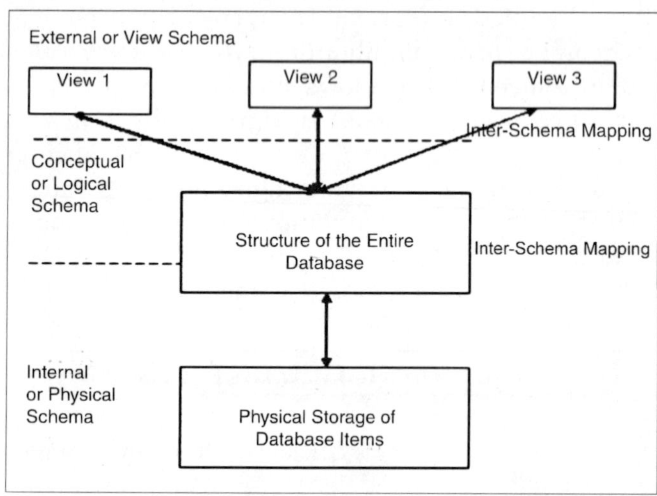

The word schema means arrangement – how we want to arrange things that we have to store. The three different schemas used in DBMS, seen from different levels of abstraction.

The lowest level, called the Internal or Physical schema, deals with the description of how raw data items (like 1, ABC, KOL, H2 *etc.*) are stored in the physical storage (Hard Disc, CD, Tape Drive *etc.*). It also describes the data type of these data items, the size of the items in the storage media, the location (physical address) of the items in the storage device and so on. This schema is useful for database application developers and database administrator.

The middle level is known as the Conceptual or Logical Schema, and deals with the structure of the entire database. Please note that at this level we are not interested with the raw data items anymore, we are interested with the structure of the database. This means we want to know the information about the attributes of each table, the common attributes in different tables that help them to be combined, what kind of data can be input into these attributes, and so on. Conceptual or Logical schema is very useful for database administrators whose responsibility is to maintain the entire database.

The highest level of abstraction is the External or View Schema. This is targeted for the end users. Now, an end user does not need to know everything about the structure of the entire database, rather than the amount of details he/she needs to work with. We may not want the end user to become confused with astounding amount of details by allowing him/her to have a look at the entire database, or we may also not allow this for the purpose of security, where sensitive information must remain hidden from unwanted persons. The database administrator may want to create custom made tables, keeping in mind the specific kind of need for each user. These tables are also known as virtual tables, because they have no separate physical existence. They are crated dynamically for the users at runtime. Say for example, in our sample database we have created earlier, we have a special officer whose responsibility is to keep in touch with the parents of any under aged student living in the hostels. That officer does not need to know every detail except the *Roll, Name, Address* and *Age*. The database administrator may create a virtual table with only these four attributes, only for the use of this officer.

DATA INDEPENDENCE

This brings us to our next topic: data independence. It is the property of the database which tries to ensure that if we make any change in any level of schema of the database, the schema immediately above it would require minimal or no need of change.

What does this mean? We know that in a building, each floor stands on the floor below it. If we change the design of any one floor, *e.g.* extending the width of a room by demolishing the western wall of that room, it is likely that the design in the above floors will have to be changed also. As a result, one change needed in one particular floor would mean continuing to change the design of each floor until we reach the top floor, with an increase in the time, cost and labour. Would not life be easy if the change could be contained in one floor only? Data independence is the answer for this.

It removes the need for additional amount of work needed in adopting the single change into all the levels above.

Data independence can be classified into the following two types:

- Physical Data Independence: This means that for any change made in the physical schema, the need to change the logical schema is minimal. This is practically easier to achieve. Let us explain with an example. Say, you have bought an Audio CD of a recently released film and one of your friends has bought an Audio Cassette of the same film. If we consider the physical schema, they are entirely different. The first is digital recording on an optical media, where random access is possible. The second one is magnetic recording on a magnetic media, strictly sequential access. However, how this change is reflected in the logical schema is very interesting. For music tracks, the logical schema for both the CD and the Cassette is the title card imprinted on their back. We have information like Track no, Name of the Song, Name of the Artist and Duration of the Track, things which are identical for both the CD and the Cassette. We can clearly say that we have achieved the physical data independence here.
- Logical Data Independence: This means that for any change made in the logical schema, the need to change the external schema is minimal. Let us explain with an example. Suppose the CD you have bought contains 6 songs, and some of your friends are interested in copying some of those songs (which they like in the film) into their favourite collection. One friend wants the songs 1, 2, 4, 5, 6, another wants 1, 3, 4, 5 and another wants 1, 2, 3, 6. Each of these collections can be compared to a view schema for that friend. Now by some mistake, a scratch has appeared in the CD and you cannot extract the song 3. Obviously, you will have to ask the friends who have song 3 in their proposed collection to alter their view by deleting song 3 from their proposed collection as well.

DATABASE ADMINISTRATOR

The Database Administrator, better known as DBA, is the person (or a group of persons) responsible for the well being of the database management system. S/he has the flowing functions and responsibilities regarding database management:

- Definition of the schema, the architecture of the three levels of the data abstraction, data independence.
- Modification of the defined schema as and when required.

- Definition of the storage structure *i.e.* and access method of the data stored *i.e.* sequential, indexed or direct.
- Creating new used-id, password *etc.*, and also creating the access permissions that each user can or cannot enjoy. DBA is responsible to create user roles, which are collection of the permissions (like read, write *etc.*) granted and restricted for a class of users. S/he can also grant additional permissions to and/or revoke existing permissions from a user if need be.
- Defining the integrity constraints for the database to ensure that the data entered conform to some rules, thereby increasing the reliability of data.
- Creating a security mechanism to prevent unauthorized access, accidental or intentional handling of data that can cause security threat.
- Creating backup and recovery policy. This is essential because in case of a failure the database must be able to revive itself to its complete functionality with no loss of data, as if the failure has never occurred. It is essential to keep regular backup of the data so that if the system fails then all data up to the point of failure will be available from a stable storage. Only those amount of data gathered during the failure would have to be fed to the database to recover it to a healthy status.

ADVANTAGES AND DISADVANTAGES OF DATABASE MANAGEMENT SYSTEM

We must evaluate whether there is any gain in using a DBMS over a situation where we do not use it. Let us summarize the advantages.

- Reduction of Redundancy: This is perhaps the most significant advantage of using DBMS. Redundancy is the problem of storing the same data item in more one place. Redundancy creates several problems like requiring extra storage space, entering same data more than once during data insertion, and deleting data from more than one place during deletion. Anomalies may occur in the database if insertion, deletion etc. are not done properly.
- Sharing of Data: In a paper-based record keeping, data cannot be shared among many users. But in computerized DBMS, many users can share the same database if they are connected via a network.
- Data Integrity: We can maintain data integrity by specifying integrity constrains, which are rules and restrictions about what kind of data may be entered or manipulated within the database. This increases the reliability of the database as it can be guaranteed that no wrong data can exist within the database at any point of time.
- Data security: We can restrict certain people from accessing the database or allow them to see certain portion of the database while

blocking sensitive information. This is not possible very easily in a paper-based record keeping.

However, there could be a few disadvantages of using DBMS. They can be as following:

- As DBMS needs computers, we have to invest a good amount in acquiring the hardware, software, installation facilities and training of users.
- We have to keep regular backups because a failure can occur any time. Taking backup is a lengthy process and the computer system cannot perform any other job at this time.
- While data security system is a boon for using DBMS, it must be very robust. If someone can bypass the security system then the database would become open to any kind of mishandling.

THE HIERARCHICAL STRUCTURE

The *hierarchical structure* was used in early mainframe DBMS. Records' relationships form a treelike model. This structure is simple but nonflexible because the relationship is confined to a one-to-many relationship. IBM's IMS system and the RDM Mobile are examples of a hierarchical database system with multiple hierarchies over the same data. RDM Mobile is a newly designed embedded database for a mobile computer system. The hierarchical structure is used primarily today for storing geographic information and file systems.

A hierarchical database model is a data model in which the data is organized into a tree-like structure. The structure allows representing information using parent/child relationships: each parent can have many children, but each child has only one parent (also known as a 1-to-many relationship). All attributes of a specific record are listed under an entity type.

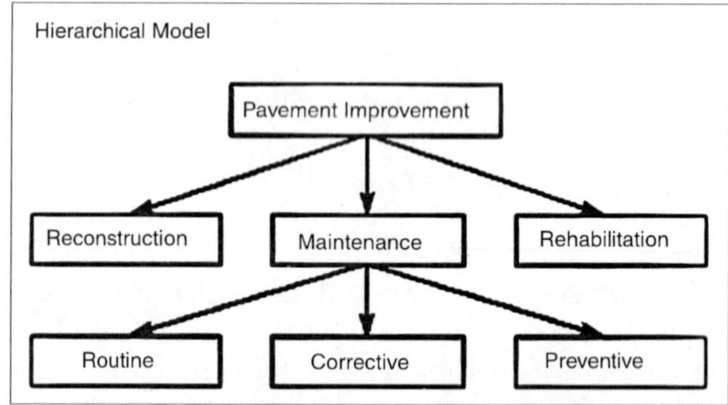

Figure: Example of a Hierarchical Model

In a database an entity type is the equivalent of a table. Each individual record is represented as a row, and each attribute as a column. Entity types are related to each other using *1:N* mappings, also known as one-to-many relationships. This model is recognized as the first database model created by IBM in the 1960s.

Currently the most widely used hierarchical databases are IMS developed by IBM and Windows Registry by Microsoft.

THE NETWORK STRUCTURE

The *network structure* consists of more complex relationships. Unlike the hierarchical structure, it can relate to many records and accesses them by following one of several paths. In other words, this structure allows for many-to-many relationships.

The network model is a database model conceived as a flexible way of representing objects and their relationships. Its distinguishing feature is that the schema, viewed as a graph in which object types are nodes and relationship types are arcs, is not restricted to being a hierarchy or lattice.

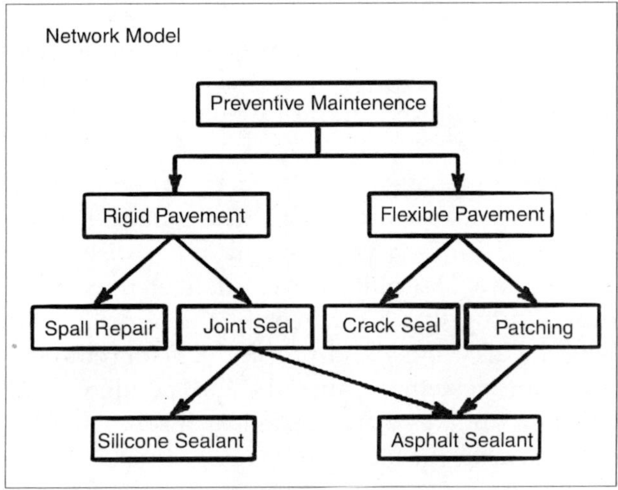

Figure: Example of a Network Model

The network model's original inventor was Charles Bachman, and it was developed into a standard specification published in 1969 by the CODASYL Consortium.

THE RELATIONAL STRUCTURE

The *relational structure* is the most commonly used today. It is used by mainframe, midrange and microcomputer systems. It uses two-dimensional rows and columns to store data. The tables of records can be connected by common key values. While working for IBM, E.F. Codd designed this structure in 1970. The model is not easy for the end user to run queries with because it may require a complex combination of many tables.

THE MULTIDIMENSIONAL STRUCTURE

The *multidimensional structure* is similar to the relational model. The dimensions of the cube-like model have data relating to elements in each cell. This structure gives a spreadsheet-like view of data. This structure is easy to maintain because records are stored as fundamental attributes—in the same way they are viewed—and the structure is easy to understand. Its high performance has made it the most popular database structure when it comes to enabling online analytical processing (OLAP).

THE OBJECT-ORIENTED STRUCTURE

The *object-oriented structure* has the ability to handle graphics, pictures, voice and text, types of data, without difficulty unlike the other database structures. This structure is popular for multimedia Web-based applications. It was designed to work with object-oriented programming languages such as Java.

The dominant model in use today is the ad hoc one embedded in SQL, despite the objections of purists who believe this model is a corruption of the relational model since it violates several fundamental principles for the sake of practicality and performance. Many DBMSs also support the Open Database Connectivity API that supports a standard way for programmers to access the DBMS.

Before the database management approach, organizations relied on file processing systems to organize, store, and process data files. End users criticized file processing because the data is stored in many different files and each organized in a different way. Each file was specialized to be used with a specific application. File processing was bulky, costly and inflexible when it came to supplying needed data accurately and promptly. Data redundancy is an issue with the file processing system because the independent data files produce duplicate data so when updates were needed each separate file would need to be updated. Another issue is the lack of data integration. The data is dependent on other data to organize and store it. Lastly, there was not any consistency or standardization of the data in a file processing system which makes maintenance difficult. For these reasons, the database management approach was produced.

DATA STRUCTURE

Data structures (fields, records, files and objects) optimized to deal with very large amounts of data stored on a permanent data storage device (which implies relatively slow access compared to volatile main memory).

Database Query Language

A database query language and report object allows users to interactively interrogate the database, analyse its data and update it according to the users privileges on data. It also controls the security of the database. Data security prevents unauthorized users from viewing or updating the database. Using passwords, users are allowed access to the entire database or subsets of it called *subschemas*. For example, an employee database can contain all the data about an individual employee, but one group of users may be authorized to view only payroll data, while others are allowed access to only work history and medical data.

If the DBMS provides a way to interactively enter and update the database, as well as interrogate it, this capability allows for managing personal databases. However, it may not leave an audit trail of actions or provide the kinds of controls necessary in a multi-user organization. These controls are only available when a set of application programmes are customised for each data entry and updating function.

Transaction Mechanism

A database transaction mechanism ideally guarantees ACID properties in order to ensure data integrity despite concurrent user accesses (concurrency control), and faults (fault tolerance). It also maintains the integrity of the data in the database. The DBMS can maintain the integrity of the database by not allowing more than one user to update the same record at the same time. The DBMS can help prevent duplicate records via unique index constraints; for example, no two customers with the same customer numbers (key fields) can be entered into the database.

Topics

External, Logical and Internal View

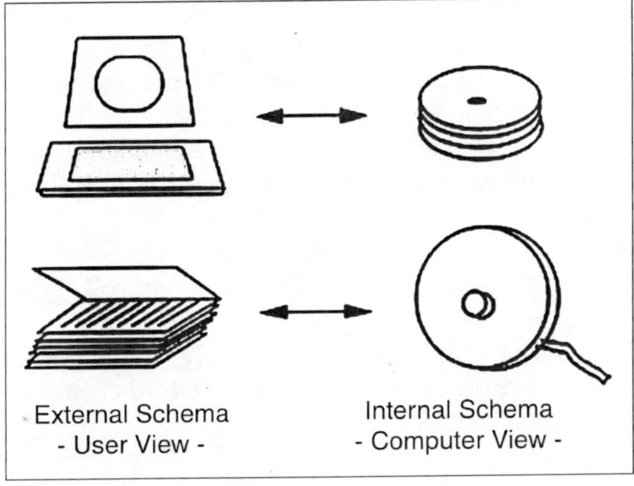

Figure: Traditional View of Data

A DBMS Provides the ability for many different users to share data and process resources. As there can be many different users, there are many different database needs. The question is: How can a single, unified database meet varying requirements of so many users?

A DBMS minimizes these problems by providing three views of the database data: an external view (or user view), logical view (or conceptual view) and physical (or internal) view. The user's view of a database programme represents data in a format that is meaningful to a user and to the software programmes that process those data. One strength of a DBMS is that while there is typically only one conceptual (or logical) and physical (or internal) view of the data, there can be an endless number of different external views. This feature allows users to see database information in a more business-related way rather than from a technical, processing viewpoint. Thus the logical view refers to the way the user views the data, and the physical view refers to the way the data are physically stored and processed.

Features and Capabilities

Alternatively, and especially in connection with the relational model of database management, the relation between attributes drawn from a specified set of domains can be seen as being primary. For instance, the database might indicate that a car that was originally "red" might fade to "pink" in time, provided it was of some particular "make" with an inferior paint job. Such higher arity relationships provide information on all of the underlying domains at the same time, with none of them being privileged above the others.

Simple Definition

A database management system is the system in which related data is stored in an efficient or compact manner. "Efficient" means that the data which is stored in the DBMS can be accessed quickly and "compact" means that the data takes up very little space in the computer's memory. The phrase "related data" means that the data stored pertains to a particular topic.

Specialized databases have existed for scientific, imaging, document storage and like uses. Functionality drawn from such applications has begun appearing in mainstream DBMS's as well. However, the main focus, at least when aimed at the commercial data processing market, is still on descriptive attributes on repetitive record structures. Thus, the DBMS of today roll together frequently needed services and features of attribute management. By externalizing such functionality to the DBMS, applications effectively share code with each other and are relieved of much internal complexity. Features commonly offered by database management systems include:

Query Ability

Querying is the process of requesting attribute information from various perspectives and combination of factors. Example: "How many 2-door cars in Texas are green?" A database query language and report writer allow users to interactively interrogate the database, analyse its data and update it according to the users privileges on data.

Backup and Replication

Copies of attributes need to be made regularly in case primary disks or other equipment fails. A periodic copy of attributes may also be created for a distant organization that cannot readily access the original. DBMS usually provide utilities to facilitate the process of extracting and disseminating attribute sets. When data is replicated between database servers, so that the information remains consistent throughout the database system and users cannot tell or even know which server in the DBMS they are using, the system is said to exhibit replication transparency.

Rule Enforcement

Often one wants to apply rules to attributes so that the attributes are clean and reliable. For example, we may have a rule that says each car can have only one engine associated with it (identified by Engine Number). If somebody tries to associate a second engine with a given car, we want the DBMS to deny such a request and display an error message. However, with changes in the model specification such as, in this example, hybrid gas-electric cars, rules may need to change. Ideally such rules should be able to be added and removed as needed without significant data layout redesign.

Security

For security reasons, it is desirable to limit who can see or change specific attributes or groups of attributes. This may be managed directly on an individual basis, or by the assignment of individuals and privileges to groups, or (in the most elaborate models) through the assignment of individuals and groups to roles which are then granted entitlements.

Computation

Common computations requested on attributes are counting, summing, averaging, sorting, grouping, cross-referencing, and so on. Rather than have each computer application implement these from scratch, they can rely on the DBMS to supply such calculations.

Change and Access Logging

This describes who accessed which attributes, what was changed, and when it was changed. Logging services allow this by keeping a record of access occurrences and changes.

Automated Optimization

For frequently occurring usage patterns or requests, some DBMS can adjust themselves to improve the speed of those interactions. In some cases the DBMS will merely provide tools to monitor performance, allowing a human expert to make the necessary adjustments after reviewing the statistics collected.

Meta-data Repository

Metadata is data describing data. For example, a listing that describes what attributes are allowed to be in data sets is called "meta-information".

Advanced DBMS

An example of an advanced DBMS is Distributed Data Base Management System (DDBMS), a collection of data which logically belong to the same system but are spread out over the sites of the computer network. The two aspects of a distributed database are distribution and logical correlation:

- Distribution: The fact that the data are not resident at the same site, so that we can distinguish a distributed database from a single, centralized database.
- Logical Correlation: The fact that the data have some properties which tie them together, so that we can distinguish a distributed database from a set of local databases or files which are resident at different sites of a computer network.

DIFFERENCE BETWEEN DBMS AND RDBMS

The software application that enables the users to store the data is known as a database. In database architecture, there are different implementations and theories in order to store physical data. The database which stores data in the tables that have relationships with other tables in the database is called RDBMS or Relational Database Management System. However, in DBMS or Database Management System, there are no relationships among tables.

DBMS

DBMS is defined as the software programme that is used to manage all the databases that are stored on the network or system hard disk. There are different types of database management systems and some of them are configured for specific purposes.

DBMS is available in different forms as a tool that is used to manage databases. Some popular DBMS solutions include DB2, Oracle, FileMaker and Microsoft Access. Using these products, privileges or rights can be created that can be specific to particular users. It means that the administrators of the database can grant specific rights to some users or assign different levels of administration.

Every DBMS has some fundamental elements. First is the implementation of the modelling language which defines the language used for each database. Second, DBMS also administers the data structures. Data query language is the third element of a DBMS. Data structures work with data query language in order to make sure that irrelevant data cannot be entered into the database used in the system.

RDBMS

The database system in which the relationships among different tables are maintained is called Relational Database Management System. Both RDBMS and DBMS are used to store information in physical database.

RDBMS solution is required when large amounts of data are to be stored as well as maintained. A relational data model consists of indexes, keys, foreign keys, tables and their relationships with other tables. Relational DBMS enforces the rules even though foreign keys are support by both RDBMS and DBMS.

In 1970s, Edgar Frank Codd introduced the theory of relational database. Thirteen rules were defined by Codd for this relational theory or model. Relationships among different types of data Is the main requirement of the relational model.

RDMS can be termed as the next generation of database management system. DBMS is used as a base model in order to store data in a relational database system. However, complex business applications use RDBMS rather than DBMS.

DBMS vs. RDBMS

- Relationship among tables is maintained in a RDBMS whereas this not the case DBMS as it is used to manage the database.
- DBMS accepts the 'flat file' data that means there is no relation among different data whereas RDBMS does not accepts this type of design.
- DBMS is used for simpler business applications whereas RDBMS is used for more complex applications.
- Although the foreign key concept is supported by both DBMS and RDBMS but its only RDBMS that enforces the rules.
- RDBMS solution is required by large sets of data whereas small sets of data can be managed by DBMS.

10

Introduction to MATLAB

MATLAB, which stands for MATrix LABoratory, is a state-of-the-art mathematical software package, which is used extensively in both academia and industry. It is an interactive programme for *numerical* computation and data visualization, which along with its programming capabilities provides a very useful tool for almost all areas of science and engineering. Unlike other mathematical packages, such as MAPLE or MATHEMATICA, MATLAB cannot perform symbolic manipulations without the use of additional Toolboxes. It remains however, one of the leading software packages for *numerical* computation.

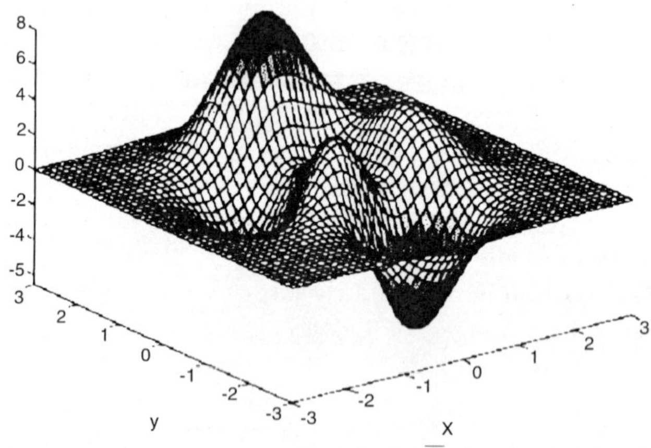

In the 1960s and 1970s before the appearance of personal computers, complex and large scale calculations were done on large mainframes using code primarily developed with FORTRAN. As a number of related large subroutines were developed for specific computational purposes, they were organized into public domain packages and distributed for free. Matlab was originally created as a front end for one of these, the LINPACK package — a group of routines for working with matrices and linear algebra.

The primary developer, Professor Cleve Moler at the University of New Mexico, eventually founded Mathworks, Inc., to further develop and market the product in a commercial setting. From the original Matlab, a high powered suite of applications has evolved.

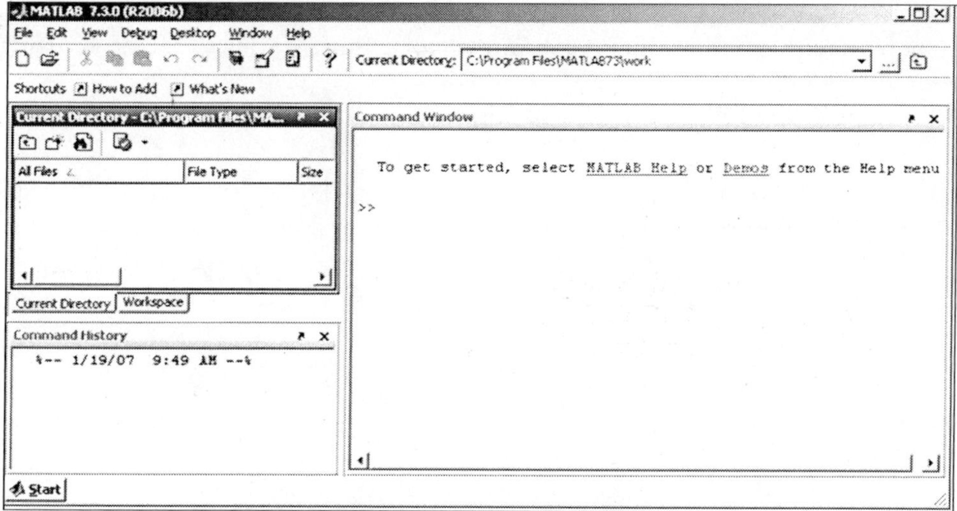

Figure : Matlab GUI.

DEFINITION OF VARIABLES

Variables are assigned numerical values by typing the expression directly, for example, typing

a = 1 + 2 yields: a = 3

The answer will not be displayed when a semicolon is put at the end of an expression, for example type a = 1+2;.

MATLAB utilizes the following arithmetic operators:

+ addition
- subtraction
* multiplication
/ division
^ power operator
' transpose

Let us define a row vector with components the numbers 1, 2, 3, 4, 5 and assigning it a variable name, say *x*.

» x = [1 2 3 4 5]

x = 1 2 3 4 5

Note that we used the equal sign for assigning the variable name *x* to the vector, brackets to enclose its entries and spaces to separate them. (Just like you would using the linear algebra notation). We could have used commas (,) instead of spaces to separate the entries, or even a combination of the two. The use of either spaces or commas is essential!

To create a column vector (MATLAB distinguishes between row and column vectors, as it should) we can either use semicolons (;) to separate the entries, or first define a row vector and take its *transpose* to obtain a column vector. Let us demonstrate this by defining a column vector *y* with entries 6, 7, 8, 9, 10 using both techniques.

```
» y = [6;7;8;9;10]
y =
6
7
8
9
10
» y = [6,7,8,9,10]
y =
6 7 8 9 10
» y'
ans =
6
7
8
9
10
```

The command whos gives all sorts of information on what variables are active.

```
» whos
Name Size Elements Bytes Density Complex
ans 5 by 1 5 40 Full No
x 1 by 5 5 40 Full No
y 1 by 5 5 40 Full No
```

A similar command, called who, only provides the names of the variables that are active.

```
» who
Your variables are:
ans x y
```

The command clear used by itself, "erases" all the variables from the memory.

MATLAB is started by clicking the mouse on the appropriate icon and is ended by typing exit or by using the menu option. After each MATLAB command, the "return" or "enter" key must be depressed.

DEFINITION OF MATRICES

MATLAB is based on matrix and vector algebra; even scalars are treated as 1×1 matrices. Therefore, vector and matrix operations are as simple as common calculator operations. Vectors can be defined in two ways. The first method is used for arbitrary elements:

v = [1 3 5 7];

creates a 1 × 4 vector with elements 1, 3, 5 and 7. Note that commas could have been used in place of

spaces to separate the elements. Additional elements can be added to the vector:

v(5) = 8;

yields the vector v = [1 3 5 7 8].

Built-in Functions

There are numerous built-in functions (*i.e.* commands) in MATLAB.

Scalar Functions

Certain MATLAB functions are essentially used on scalars, but operate element-wise when applied to a matrix (or vector). They are summarized in the table below.

sin trigonometric sine
cos trigonometric cosine
tan trigonometric tangent
asin trigonometric inverse sine (arcsine)
acos trigonometric inverse cosine (arccosine)
atan trigonometric inverse tangent (arctangent)
exp exponential
log natural logarithm
abs absolute value
sqrt square root
rem remainder
round round towards nearest integer
floor round towards negative infinity
ceil round towards positive infinity

Vector Functions

Other MATLAB functions operate essentially on vectors returning a scalar value. Some of these functions are given in the table below.

max largest component
min smallest component
length length of a vector
sort sort in ascending order
sum sum of elements
prod product of elements
median median value
mean mean value
std standard deviation.

Matrix Functions

Much of MATLAB's power comes from its matrix functions.
eye identity matrix
zeros matrix of zeros
ones matrix of ones
diag extract diagonal of a matrix or create diagonal matrices
triu upper triangular part of a matrix
tril lower triangular part of a matrix
rand randomly generated matrix
size size of a matrix
det determinant of a square matrix
inv inverse of a matrix
rank rank of a matrix
rref reduced row echelon form
eig eigenvalues and eigenvectors
poly characteristic polynomial
norm norm of matrix (1-norm, 2-norm, ∞ -norm)
cond condition number in the 2-norm
lu LU factorization
qr QR factorization
chol Cholesky decomposition
svd singular value decomposition.

Plotting

By typing help plot you can see the various capabilities of this main command for two-dimensional plotting.

If x and y are two vectors of the same length then plot(x, y) plots x versus y.

For example, to obtain the graph of $y = \cos(x)$ from $-\pi$ to π, we can first define the vector x with components equally spaced numbers between $-\pi$ and π, with increment, say 0.01.

» x = –pi:0.01:pi;

We placed a semicolon at the end of the input line to avoid seeing the (long) output.

Note that the smallest the increment, the "smoother" the curve will be.

1 – 2

Next, we define the vector y

» y = cos(x);

(using a semicolon again) and we ask for the plot

» plot(x, y)

At this point a new window will open on our desktop in which the graph will appear.

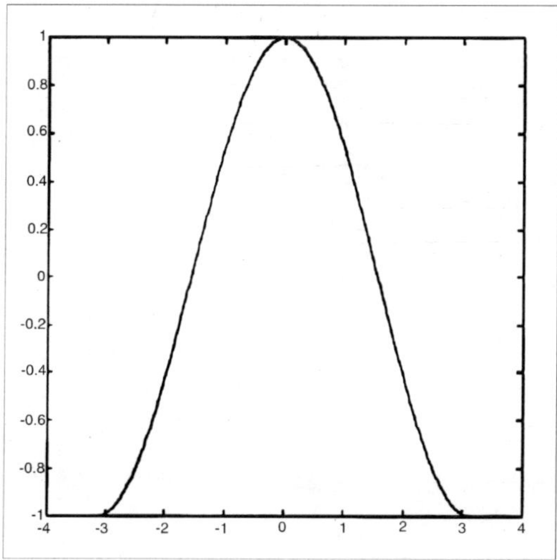

Figure : Sample Plot Generated in Matlab.

subplot create an array of (tiled) plots in the same window
loglog plot using log-log scales
semilogx plot using log scale on the x-axis
semilogy plot using log scale on the y-axis
surf 3-D shaded surface graph
surfl 3-D shaded surface graph with lighting
mesh 3-D mesh surface

PROGRAMMING IN MATLAB

M-files: Scripts and Functions

To take advantage of MATLAB's full capabilities, we need to know how to construct long (and sometimes complex) sequences of statements. This can be done by writing the commands in a file and calling it from within MATLAB. Such files are called "m-files" because they must have the filename extension ".m". This extension is required in order for these files to be interpreted by MATLAB.

There are two types of m-files: *script files* and *function files*. Script files contain a sequence of usual MATLAB commands, that are executed (in order) once the script is called within MATLAB. For example, if such a file has the name compute. m, then typing the command compute at the MATLAB prompt will cause the statements in that file to be executed. Script files can be very useful when entering data into a matrix.

Every MATLAB function begins with a header, which consists of the following :

- The word function,
- The output(s) in brackets, (the variable a in the above example)

- The equal sign,
- The name of the function, which must match the function filename (log3 in the above example) and
- The input(s) (the variable x in the above example).

Loading and Saving Data

When using MATLAB, you may wish to leave the programme but save the vectors and matrices you have defined. To save the file to the working directory, type

save filename

where "filename" is a name of your choice. To retrieve the data later, type

load filename

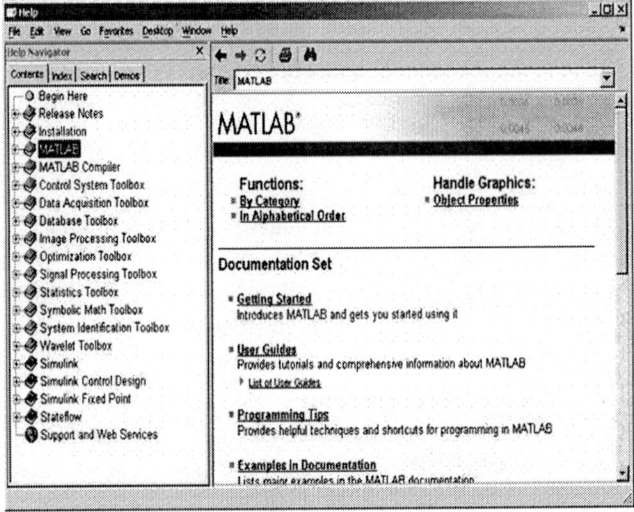

Figure : Help Section in Matlab

MATLAB IMAGE PROCESSING

Do you have a keen interest in Image Processing? Do you want to know how you can easily implement Image Processing tools and techniques using MATLAB and explore the limitless possibilities it has to offer? If yes, then read on..

- MATLAB Installation
- Your first run
- MATLAB Help
- Function Browser: a quick search tool
- Your journey begins
  (a) Sample Code 1: Scaling an image to 50% of original size
  (b0 Sample Code 2: Comparing two images pixel by pixel

- Get started with these..

Installation:

Installation is easy; just run the CD and follow the steps that the installation wizard shows you.

Your First Run

This is what you would generally see when you successfully install MATLAB and run it. The interface basically consists of 5 sections:

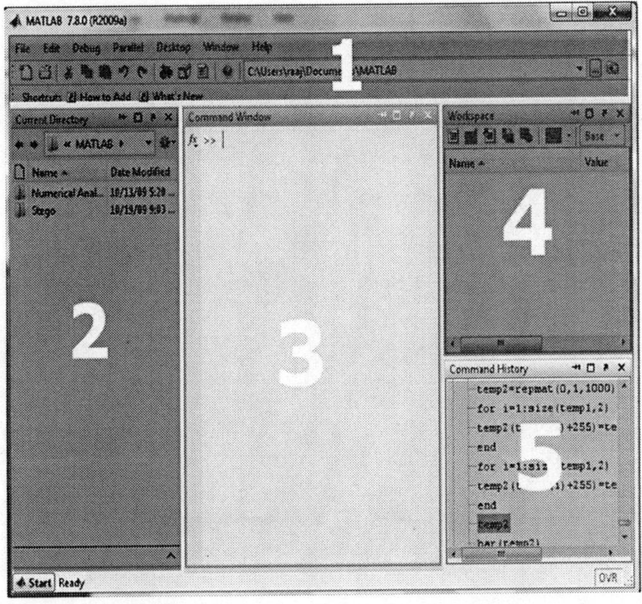

- The toolbar is where you can access the various features, tools and options regarding your code, debugging process, formatting, etc
- The file-manager shows your current directory and the files in it. You can change the directory by double clicking any folder or using the drop-down menu at the top.

Note: If you are in the directory 'Matlab Codes' and it has the MATLAB files 'code1.m', 'code2.m' and 'code3.m', then you can run them by simply typing code1, code2 or code3 in the command window!

The command window is the place from where you tell MATLAB what is to be done! You have the option of either writing commands directly or running a 'MATLAB' file (with the extension .m) which would consist of commands, functions or programmes.

> Note: If You are in the Directory 'Motlab Codes' and It has the Matlab Files ' Codel.m', 'Code2.m' and 'Code3.m', then you Can Run them By Simply Typing Codel, Code2 or Code3 in the Command Window!

- When you write a new programme or type in some commands, you would almost always, use variables to store the values obtained. The workspace shows you all your current variables and their values and allows you to edit, copy or duplicate them.
- The command history window saves your recent commands and helps you in keeping a track of what you have been up to! It comes out quite handy when you have to use long commands repeatedly: *Simply double click on that command in the command history window and it will start running!*

MATLAB Help

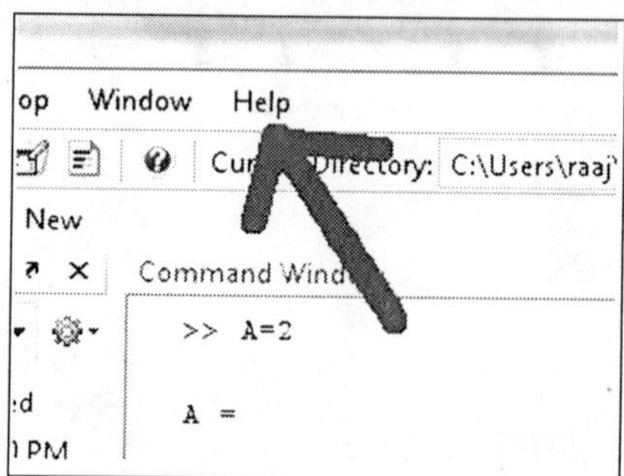

MATLAB provides an excellent documentation of all its toolboxes and their respective commands. It also includes sample codes and examples! Go to the Help option and MATLAB and click on 'Product Help' *(or simply press F1)*.

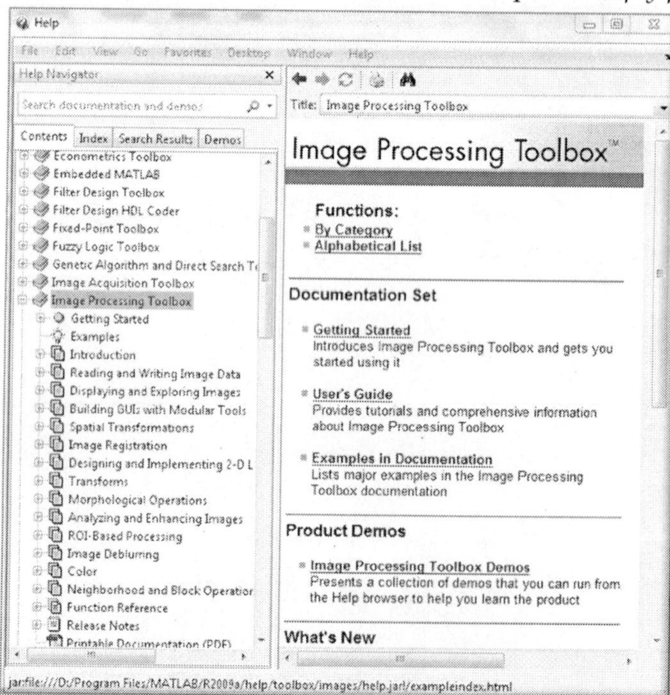

Explore the Help contents and you would find loads of useful things. Here is a snapshot of the first example in Image Processing toolbox. It teaches how to read and display an image.

Title: Example 1 - Reading and Writing Images :: Getting Started (Image Processing Toolbox™)

Back to Top

Step 1: Read and Display an Image

First, clear the MATLAB workspace of any variables and close open figure windows.

```
close all
```

To read an image, use the `imread` command. The example reads one of the sample images included with the toolbox, `pout.tif`, and stores it in an array named `I`.

```
I = imread('pout.tif');
```

`imread` infers from the file that the graphics file format is Tagged Image File Format (TIFF). For the list of supported graphics file formats, see the `imread` function reference documentation.

Now display the image. The toolbox includes two image display functions: `imshow` and `imtool`. `imshow` is the toolbox's fundamental image display function. `imtool` starts the Image Tool which presents an integrated environment for displaying images and performing some common image processing tasks. The Image Tool provides all the image display capabilities of `imshow` but also provides access to several other tools for navigating and exploring images, such as scroll bars, the Pixel Region tool, Image Information tool, and the Contrast Adjustment tool. For more information, see Displaying and Exploring Images. You can use either function to display an image. This example uses `imshow`.

```
imshow(I)
```

Grayscale Image pout.tif

oolbox/images/help.jar!/f10-22542.html

Following this, there are nearly a hundred examples and sample codes of various commands and tools required in image processing. The following sections have been covered for the Image Processing toolbox:

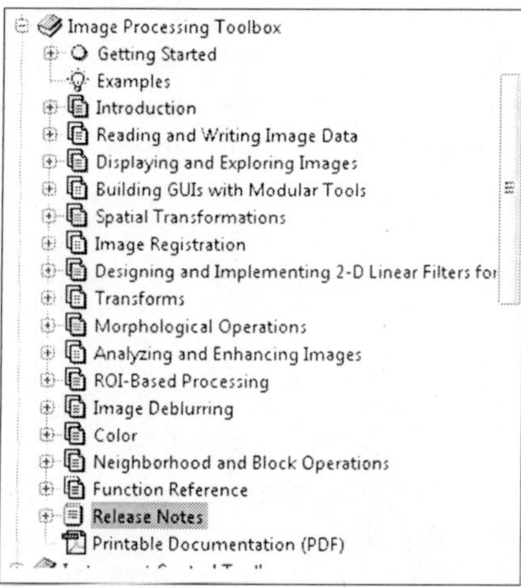

Function Browser: a quick search tool!

Click on 'Help' on the toolbar and go to 'Function Browser' (or press Shift+F1). This is what will pop up:

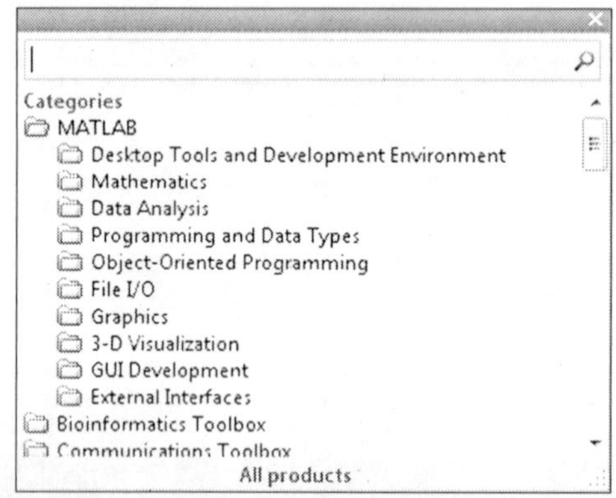

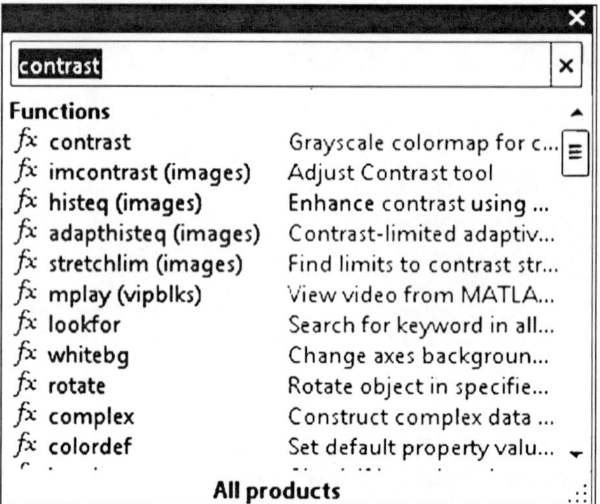

The 'Function Browser', as the name suggests, is a quick search tool for description and synopsis of commands and functions of MATLAB. In the figure towards the right, I have searched for 'contrast' and it lists all the functions and commands related to that keyword. It gives concise information about the function you are looking for. (For details and examples, you can always go to the 'Help and Documentation' by pressing F1!). It serves as a useful tool when you are stuck in the middle of a programme and you want to quickly refer the syntax of a particular function.

Your journey begins..

So, now that you have a basic idea of working with MATLAB and its Image Processing toolbox, you are ready for the rich programming experience that MATLAB has to offer you! As beginners, make sure you refer to the 'Help' section (F1) and 'Function Browser' (Shift+F1) frequently as this will fasten your progress. A basic Image Processing programme that you can start off with:

Sample code 1: Scaling an image to 50% of original size

```
% Reading the image
img=imread(img.bmp','bmp');
% Removing alternate columns
img1 = img(:,1:2:size(img,2),:);
% Removing alternate rows
img2 = img1(1:2:size(img1,1),:,:);
% Viewing the new scaled down image
figure, imshow(img2);
```

Here is a very simple MATLAB code that scales down an image called 'img.jpg' to 50% of its original size.

Figure: Original Image

Figure: Final Image

Understanding the code:

Tip!!: Go to the function browser and search for the functions 'imread()' and 'imshow()'. You will find the descriptions of the functions as well as the various arguments and parameters they require.

img=imread ('img.bmp','bmp'); is used to read the image. The imread() function takes two arguments: the name of the image and the type of the image. The variable 'img' would basically be NXMX3 matrix where N is the height of the image and M is the width. The three layers correspond to the Red, Blue and Green components.

- img1 = img(:,1:2:size(img,2),:); copies all the rows to the new matrix img1. But for columns, it copies only the alternate ones. This is done for all the three components: Red, Blue and Green. Note that size(img,2) returns the horizontal size of the image (length) whereas size(img,1) would have returned the vertical size (height) which is used in the next command.
- img2 = img1(1:2:size(img1,1),:,:); copies all the columns to the new matrix img2. But for rows, it copies only the alternate ones. This is done for all the three components: Red, Blue and Green.

Tip!!: Go to the Function Browser and Search for the Functions 'Imread0' and 'Imshow0'. You Will Find the Descriptions of the Function as Well As the Various Agruments and Parameters they Require.

- Now, that we have removed the alternate rows and alternate columns from the image, we view the image using the command figure, imshow(img2);

Running the code:

- Open an empty MATLAB file from the toolbar menu (or press Ctrl+N)
- Type in the code given in the textbox above
- Save the file with some name, say code1.m (note the .m extension)
- Click once on the command window, type code1 and press 'enter'.

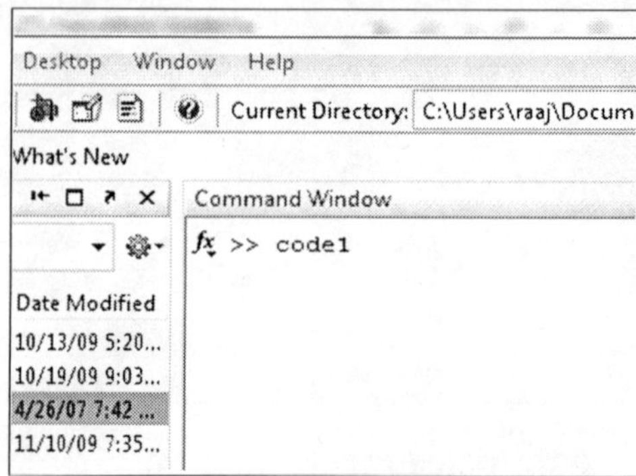

Sample code 2: Comparing two images pixel by pixel

```
img1 = imread('img1.bmp','bmp');      % Read image 1
img2 = imread('img2.bmp','bmp');      % Read image 2
if size(img1)~=size(img2)
     disp('Images not same: Different sizes!');
    return;
end

for i=1:size(img1,1)
    for j=1:size(img1,2)
  for k=1:3
         if img1(i,j,k)~=img2(i,j,k)
            disp('Images not same: Different pixel values');
           return;
end
        end
  end
end
disp('Same Images !!');
```

- This code first checks whether the sizes of the two images is the same or not. If it is not the same, it displays 'Images not same: Different sizes!'

SCRATCH YOUR HEAD!! : A further enhancement to this code could be specifying a threshold to the comparison, meaning that the RGB values to be matched in img2 could lie in a range around the value in img1. For example, if the value of a particular pixel in img1 is 133, 'threshold=2' would imply that all the corresponding value in img2 could have a value of 131, 132, 133, 134 or 135 for a successful match (*i.e.* $(133 - 2) <= x <= (133 + 2)$). Thus, threshold would define the 'degree' of similarity I want in the two images.

If the sizes of the two images are the same, then the images are compared pixel by pixel. If there is any difference, in the pixels, it would display: ''Images not same: Different pixel values '

- If the sizes are the same and every pixel in img1 is correspondingly equal to every pixel in img2, then the code displays: 'Same images!!'.

11

Extract, Transform, Load (ETL)

You need to load your data warehouse regularly so that it can serve its purpose of facilitating business analysis. To do this, data from one or more operational systems needs to be extracted and copied into the data warehouse. The challenge in data warehouse environments is to integrate, rearrange and consolidate large volumes of data over many systems, thereby providing a new unified information base for business intelligence.

The process of extracting data from source systems and bringing it into the data warehouse is commonly called ETL, which stands for extraction, transformation, and loading. Note that ETL refers to a broad process, and not three well-defined steps. The acronym ETL is perhaps too simplistic, because it omits the transportation phase and implies that each of the other phases of the process is distinct. Nevertheless, the entire process is known as ETL.

The methodology and tasks of ETL have been well known for many years, and are not necessarily unique to data warehouse environments: a wide variety of proprietary applications and database systems are the IT backbone of any enterprise. Data has to be shared between applications or systems, trying to integrate them, giving at least two applications the same picture of the world. This data sharing was mostly addressed by mechanisms similar to what we now call ETL.

ETL BASICS IN DATA WAREHOUSING

What happens during the ETL process? The following tasks are the main actions in the process.

EXTRACTION OF DATA

During extraction, the desired data is identified and extracted from many different sources, including database systems and applications. Very often, it is not possible to identify the specific subset of interests, therefore more data than necessary has to be extracted, so the identification of the relevant data will be done at a later point in time. Depending on the source system's capabilities (for example, operating system resources), some transformations may take place during this extraction process. The size of the extracted data varies from hundreds of kilobytes up to gigabytes, depending on the source system and the business situation. The same is true for the time delta between two (logically) identical extractions: the time span may vary between days/hours and minutes to near real-time. Web server log files, for example, can easily grow to hundreds of megabytes in a very short period of time.

TRANSPORTATION OF DATA

After data is extracted, it has to be physically transported to the target system or to an intermediate system for further processing. Depending on the chosen way of transportation, some transformations can be done during this process, too. For example, a SQL statement which directly accesses a remote target through a gateway can concatenate two columns as part of the SELECT statement.

The emphasis in many of the examples in this section is scalability. Many long-time users of Oracle Database are experts in programming complex data transformation logic using PL/SQL. These chapters suggest alternatives for many such data manipulation operations, with a particular emphasis on implementations that take advantage of Oracle's new SQL functionality, especially for ETL and the parallel query infrastructure.

ETL TOOLS FOR DATA WAREHOUSES

Designing and maintaining the ETL process is often considered one of the most difficult and resource-intensive portions of a data warehouse project. Many data warehousing projects use ETL tools to manage this process. Oracle Warehouse Builder (OWB), for example, provides ETL capabilities and takes advantage of inherent database abilities. Other data warehouse builders create their own ETL tools and processes, either inside or outside the database.

Besides the support of extraction, transformation, and loading, there are some other tasks that are important for a successful ETL implementation as part of the daily operations of the data warehouse and its support for further enhancements. Besides the support for designing a data warehouse and the data flow, these tasks are typically addressed by ETL tools such as OWB.

Oracle is not an ETL tool and does not provide a complete solution for ETL. However, Oracle does provide a rich set of capabilities that can be used by both ETL tools and customized ETL solutions. Oracle offers techniques for transporting data between Oracle databases, for transforming large volumes of data, and for quickly loading new data into a data warehouse.

Daily Operations in Data Warehouses

The successive loads and transformations must be scheduled and processed in a specific order. Depending on the success or failure of the operation or parts of it, the result must be tracked and subsequent, alternative processes might be started. The control of the progress as well as the definition of a business workflow of the operations are typically addressed by ETL tools such as Oracle Warehouse Builder.

EVOLUTION OF THE DATA WAREHOUSE

As the data warehouse is a living IT system, sources and targets might change. Those changes must be maintained and tracked through the lifespan of the system without overwriting or deleting the old ETL process flow information. To build and keep a level of trust about the information in the warehouse, the process flow of each individual record in the warehouse can be reconstructed at any point in time in the future in an ideal case. ETL, or Extract, Transform and Load, eases the combination of heterogeneous sources into a unified central repository. Usually this repository is a data warehouse or mart which will support enterprise business intelligence. Extract – read data from multiple source systems into a single format. This process extracts the data from each native system and saves it to one target location. That source data may be any number of database formats, flat files, or document repositories. Usually, the goal is to extract the entire unmodified source system data, though certain checks and filters may be performed here to ensure the data meets an expected layout or to selectively remove data (e.g. potentially confidential information).

Transform – in this step, the data from the various systems is made consistent and linked. Some of the key operations here are:

- Standardization – data is mapped to a consistent set of lookup values (e.g. US, USA, United States and blank/null – all mapped to the standard ISO country code)
- Cleansing – perform validity checks and either remove or modify problem data
- Surrogate keys – new key values applied to similar data from different source systems prevent key collisions in the future and provide a cross reference across these systems
- Transposing – organizes data to optimize reporting. Many source systems are optimized for transactional performance but the warehouse will be primarily used for reporting. Often this involves denormalizing and re-organizing into a dimensional model.

Load – the transformed data is now written out to a warehouse/mart. The load process will usually preserve prior data. In some instances existing warehouse data is never removed, just marked as inactive. This provides full auditing and supports historical reporting.

ANALYSIS

ETL Tools

There are a number of commercial and open source ETL tools available to assist in any ETL process. Some of the prominent ones are:

- Business Objects Data Integrator
- Informatica PowerCenter
- IBM InfoSphere DataStage
- Oracle Warehouse Builder / Data Integrator
- Microsoft SQL Server Integration Services
- Pentaho Data Integration (Open Source)
- Jasper ETL (Open Source).

These tools provide a number of functions to facilitate the ETL workflow. The variety of source data types are handled automatically. A transformation engine makes it easy to create reusable scripts to handle the data mapping. Scheduling and error handling are also built in. It is particularly advantageous to use an ETL tool in the following situations:

- When there are many source systems to be integrated
- When source systems are in different formats
- When this process needs to be run repeatedly
- To take advantage of pre-built warehouses/marts. Many of these exist for popular platforms such as PeopleSoft, SAP, JD Edwards.

There are also times where the overhead and cost of setting up an ETL tool might not make sense. In these situations some combination of stored procedures, custom coding and off the shelf packages may make more sense. Scenarios of this type include:

- One time conversion of data
- A limited number of source systems that share key identifiers .

REAL-LIFE ETL CYCLE

The typical real-life ETL cycle consists of the following execution steps:

- Cycle initiation
- Build reference data
- Extract (from sources)
- Validate
- Transform (clean, apply business rules, check for data integrity, create aggregates or disaggregates)
- Stage (load into staging tables, if used)
- Audit reports (for example, on compliance with business rules. Also, in case of failure, helps to diagnose/repair)
- Publish (to target tables)
- Archive
- Clean up.

CHALLENGES

ETL processes can involve considerable complexity, and significant operational problems can occur with improperly designed ETL systems.

The range of data values or data quality in an operational system may exceed the expectations of designers at the time validation and transformation rules are specified. Data profiling of a source during data analysis can identify the data conditions that will need to be managed by transform rules specifications. This will lead to an amendment of validation rules explicitly and implicitly implemented in the ETL process.

Data warehouses are typically assembled from a variety of data sources with different formats and purposes. As such, ETL is a key process to bring all the data together in a standard, homogeneous environment.

Design analysts should establish the scalability of an ETL system across the lifetime of its usage. This includes understanding the volumes of data that will have to be processed within service level agreements. The time available to extract from source systems may change, which may mean the same amount of data may have to be processed in less time. Some ETL systems have to scale to process terabytes of data to update data warehouses with tens of terabytes of data. Increasing volumes of data may require designs that can scale from daily batch to multiple-day microbatch to integration with message queues or real-time change-data capture for continuous transformation and update.

PERFORMANCE

ETL vendors benchmark their record-systems at multiple TB (terabytes) per hour (or ~1 GB per second) using powerful servers with multiple CPUs, multiple hard drives, multiple gigabit-network connections, and lots of memory. The fastest ETL record is currently held by Syncsort, Vertica and HP at 5.4TB in under an hour which is more than twice as fast as the earlier record held by Microsoft and Unisys. In real life, the slowest part of an ETL process usually occurs in the database load phase. Databases may perform slowly because they have to take care of concurrency, integrity maintenance, and indices. Thus, for better performance, it may make sense to employ:

- Direct Path Extract method or bulk unload whenever is possible (instead of querying the database) to reduce the load on source system while getting high speed extract
- Most of the transformation processing outside of the database
- Bulk load operations whenever possible.

Still, even using bulk operations, database access is usually the bottleneck in the ETL process. Some common methods used to increase performance are:

- Partition tables (and indices). Try to keep partitions similar in size (watch for null values which can skew the partitioning).
- Do all validation in the ETL layer before the load. Disable integrity checking (disable constraint ...) in the target database tables during the load.
- Disable triggers (disable trigger ...) in the target database tables during the load. Simulate their effect as a separate step.

- Generate IDs in the ETL layer (not in the database).
- Drop the indices (on a table or partition) before the load - and recreate them after the load (SQL: drop index ...; create index ...).
- Use parallel bulk load when possible — works well when the table is partitioned or there are no indices. Note: attempt to do parallel loads into the same table (partition) usually causes locks — if not on the data rows, then on indices.
- If a requirement exists to do insertions, updates, or deletions, find out which rows should be processed in which way in the ETL layer, and then process these three operations in the database separately. You often can do bulk load for inserts, but updates and deletes commonly go through an API (using SQL).

Whether to do certain operations in the database or outside may involve a trade-off. For example, removing duplicates using distinct may be slow in the database; thus, it makes sense to do it outside. On the other side, if using distinct will significantly (x100) decrease the number of rows to be extracted, then it makes sense to remove duplications as early as possible in the database before unloading data.

A common source of problems in ETL is a big number of dependencies among ETL jobs. For example, job "B" cannot start while job "A" is not finished. You can usually achieve better performance by visualizing all processes on a graph, and trying to reduce the graph making maximum use of parallelism, and making "chains" of consecutive processing as short as possible. Again, partitioning of big tables and of their indices can really help.

Another common issue occurs when the data is spread between several databases, and processing is done in those databases sequentially. Sometimes database replication may be involved as a method of copying data between databases - and this can significantly slow down the whole process. The common solution is to reduce the processing graph to only three layers:

- Sources
- Central ETL layer
- Targets.

This allows processing to take maximum advantage of parallel processing. For example, if you need to load data into two databases, you can run the loads in parallel (instead of loading into 1st - and then replicating into the 2nd).

Of course, sometimes processing must take place sequentially. For example, you usually need to get dimensional (reference) data before you can get and validate the rows for main "fact" tables.

PARALLEL PROCESSING

A recent development in ETL software is the implementation of parallel processing. This has enabled a number of methods to improve overall performance of ETL processes when dealing with large volumes of data.

ETL applications implement three main types of parallelism:

- Data: By splitting a single sequential file into smaller data files to provide parallel access.
- Pipeline: Allowing the simultaneous running of several components on the same data stream. For example: looking up a value on record 1 at the same time as adding two fields on record 2.
- Component: The simultaneous running of multiple processes on different data streams in the same job, for example, sorting one input file while removing duplicates on another file.

All three types of parallelism usually operate combined in a single job.

An additional difficulty comes with making sure that the data being uploaded is relatively consistent. Because multiple source databases may have different update cycles (some may be updated every few minutes, while others may take days or weeks), an ETL system may be required to hold back certain data until all sources are synchronized. Likewise, where a warehouse may have to be reconciled to the contents in a source system or with the general ledger, establishing synchronization and reconciliation points becomes necessary.

Rerunnability, Recoverability

Data warehousing procedures usually subdivide a big ETL process into smaller pieces running sequentially or in parallel. To keep track of data flows, it makes sense to tag each data row with "row_id", and tag each piece of the process with "run_id". In case of a failure, having these IDs will help to roll back and rerun the failed piece.

Best practice also calls for "checkpoints", which are states when certain phases of the process are completed. Once at a checkpoint, it is a good idea to write everything to disk, clean out some temporary files, log the state, and so on.

Virtual ETL

As of 2010 data virtualization had begun to advance ETL processing. The application of data virtualization to ETL allowed solving the most common ETL tasks of data migration and application integration for multiple dispersed data sources. So-called Virtual ETL operates with the abstracted representation of the objects or entities gathered from the variety of relational, semi-structured and unstructured data sources. ETL tools can leverage object-oriented modelling and work with entities' representations persistently stored in a centrally located hub-and-spoke architecture. Such a collection that contains representations of the entities or objects gathered from the data sources for ETL processing is called a metadata repository and it can reside in memory or be made persistent. By using a persistent metadata repository, ETL tools can transition from one-time projects to persistent middleware, performing data harmonization and data profiling consistently and in near-real time.

ETL ALTERNATIVES

Data integration by design methods provide an alternative to ETL type data integrations. ETL methods are not required as the data in the source data system is integrated in place by recasting the master data of the database. The data integration by design method achieves data integration in days and weeks as opposed to the months and years normally required for ETL type data integrations. When dealing with existing legacy systems of various languages, databases and formats data federation or data virtualization tools are required.

Best Practices

Four-layered approach for ETL architecture design

- Functional layer: Core functional ETL processing (extract, transform, and load).
- Operational management layer: Job-stream definition and management, parameters, scheduling, monitoring, communication and alerting.
- Audit, balance and control (ABC) layer: Job-execution statistics, balancing and controls, rejects- and error-handling, codes management.
- Utility layer: Common components supporting all other layers.

Use file-based ETL processing where possible:

- Storage costs relatively little
- Intermediate files serve multiple purposes:
  (a) Used for testing and debugging
  (b) Used for restart and recover processing
  (c) Used to calculate control statistics
- Helps to reduce dependencies - enables modular programming.
- Allows flexibility for job execution and scheduling
- Better performance if coded properly, and can take advantage of parallel processing capabilities when the need arises.

Use data-driven methods and minimize custom ETL coding:

- Parameter-driven jobs, functions, and job-control
- Code definitions and mapping in database
- Consideration for data-driven tables to support more complex code-mappings and business-rule application.

Qualities of a good ETL architecture design:

- Performance
- Scalable
- Migratable
- Recoverable (run_id, ...)
- Operable (completion-codes for phases, re-running from checkpoints, *etc.*)
- Auditable (in two dimensions: business requirements and technical troubleshooting)

Handling of non-desirable values (NULL values, erroneous values, *etc.*)

- NULL DIMENSIONAL values
- NULL FACT values
- NULL PRIMARY and/or FOREIGN KEY values
- Erroneous or undesirable values.

DEALING WITH KEYS

Keys are some of the most important objects in all relational databases as they tie everything together. A primary key is a column which is the identifier for a given entity, where a foreign key is a column in another table which refers a primary key.

These keys can also be made up from several columns, in which case they are composite keys. In many cases the primary key is an auto generated integer which has no meaning for the business entity being represented, but solely exists for the purpose of the relational database - commonly referred to as a surrogate key.

As there will usually be more than one datasource being loaded into the warehouse the keys are an important concern to be addressed. Your customers might be represented in several data sources, and in one their SSN (Social Security Number) might be the primary key, their phone number in another and a surrogate in the third. All of the customers information needs to be consolidated into one dimension table.

A recommended way to deal with the concern is to add a warehouse surrogate key, which will be used as foreign key from the fact table.

Usually updates will occur to a dimension's source data, which obviously must be reflected in the data warehouse.

If the primary key of the source data is required for reporting, the dimension already contains that piece of information for each row. If the source data uses a surrogate key, the ware house must keep track of it even though it is never used in queries or reports.

That is done by creating a lookup table which contains the warehouse surrogate key and the originating key. This way the dimension is not polluted with surrogates from various source systems, while the ability to update is preserved.

The lookup table is used in different ways depending on the nature of the source data. There are 5 types to consider, where three selected ones are included here:

Type 1: The dimension row is simply updated to match the current state of the source system. The warehouse does not capture history. The lookup table is used to identify which dimension row to update/overwrite.

Type 2: A new dimension row is added with the new state of the source system. A new surrogate key is assigned. Source key is no longer unique in the lookup table.

Fully logged: A new dimension row is added with the new state of the source system, while the previous dimension row is updated to reflect it is no longer active and record time of deactivation.

Tools

Programmers can set up ETL processes using almost any programming language, but building such processes from scratch can become complex. Increasingly, companies are buying ETL tools to help in the creation of ETL processes.

By using an established ETL framework, one may increase one's chances of ending up with better connectivity and scalability. A good ETL tool must be able to communicate with the many different relational databases and read the various file formats used throughout an organization. ETL tools have started to migrate into Enterprise Application Integration, or even Enterprise Service Bus, systems that now cover much more than just the extraction, transformation, and loading of data. Many ETL vendors now have data profiling, data quality, and metadata capabilities. A common use case for ETL tools include converting CSV files to formats readable by relational databases. A typical translation of millions of records is facilitated by ETL tools that enable users to input csv-like data feeds/ files and import it into a database with as little code as possible.

ETL Tools are typically used by a broad range of professionals - from students in computer science looking to quickly import large data sets to database architects in charge of company account management, ETL Tools have become a convenient tool that can be relied on to get maximum performance. ETL tools in most cases contain a GUI that helps users conveniently transform data as opposed to writing large programs to parse files and modify data types - which ETL tools facilitate as much as possible.

SAMPLE WORKFLOW

As illustrated here, a typical ETL workflow will move the data through a few distinct phases. This allows each phase to be better defined and eases troubleshooting.

Source > Extract > Stage – this phase extracts all the appropriate data from each source system. The extract copies only data that has changed in the source system since its last run. The stage library contains all source information in a similar structure to how it appears in the source systems. All extracted information will remain in stage until it is successfully processed by the transform.

Stage > Transform > Warehouse – the data from stage is transformed into a warehouse. In this example this step includes some of the base transformations as well as the load of data into a single warehouse. In this phase, surrogate keys are added where needed, lookup value mappings are applied and related information from multiple source systems is combined into a single structure.

Any errors encountered here are reported and the problem data remains in stage until corrected. No information is removed from the warehouse and all data there is tagged with effective, update and end timestamps.

Warehouse > Load > Mart – the current effective date from the warehouse is loaded to the mart to support analysis. While this is the final load of the process, this step also includes a transform of the data to an optimized dimensional form for reporting and analysis.

Business intelligence in the enterprise is greatly enhanced by unified data. ETL can be an important tool when combining heterogeneous sources into one cohesive central repository.

ONLINE TRANSACTION PROCESSING (OLTP)

Online Transaction Processing (OLTP) is a class of program that supports, facilitates and manages high-transaction-oriented applications. The term may be ambiguous because some understand a "transaction" in the context of computer or database transactions, while others define it in terms of business or commercial transactions. OLTP may also refer to processing in which the system responds immediately to user requests, such as a bank's automatic teller machine (ATM). For our purposes, we use the first definition.

The primary features of OLTP are immediate client feedback and a high volume of individual transactions. For that reason it is typically used for data entry and retrieval transactions in industries that rely heavily on processing a large number of client transactions efficiently. These include banking, airlines, online retailers, supermarkets, and manufacturers.

Online Transaction Processing has two key benefits: simplicity and efficiency. Examples of how OLTP makes things simpler for businesses are reduced paper trails and faster, more accurate forecasts for revenues and expenses

OLTP frequently employs client/server processing and brokering software that allows transactions to run on different computer platforms in a computer network involving several companies. Database systems that support OLTP are usually decentralized to avoid single points of failure and to spread the volume among multiple servers.

Online Transaction Processing systems must provide atomicity—the A in ACID—which means being able to process an order fully or undo an order completely. In these transactions, partial processing is never an option. When a rental car is booked, atomicity combines the two system actions of reserving and paying for the car and both actions must happen together or not at all.

In large applications, efficient OLTP may depend on sophisticated transaction management software and/or database optimization tactics for processing a heavy volume of concurrent updates to an OLTP-oriented database. For even more demanding, decentralized database systems, OLTP brokering programs can distribute transaction processing among multiple computers on a network.

Online Transaction Processing systems can be adversely affected because web services and service-oriented architectures often have OLTP integrated into them. If an enterprise depends on OLTP, a system stoppage or breakdown can severely impact operations and revenues. This may happen due to failure of a server or communication channels, data corruption or maintenance downtime.

VoltDB supports the most demanding Online Transaction Processing needs with a blazingly fast NewSQL database system that is designed to run on modern scale-out architectures—fast, inexpensive servers connected via high-speed data networks. VoltDB addresses a new generation of database applications – real-time feeds, sensor-driven data streams, micro-transactions, low-latency trading systems – requiring database throughput that can reach millions of operations per second. What's more, the applications that use this data must scale on demand, provide flawless fault tolerance and enable real-time visibility into the data that drives business value. VoltDB products deliver the raw throughput needed to drive advanced, high-velocity OLTP applications.

OLTP VS. OLAP

We can divide IT systems into transactional (OLTP) and analytical (OLAP). In general we can assume that OLTP systems provide source data to data warehouses, whereas OLAP systems help to analyse it.

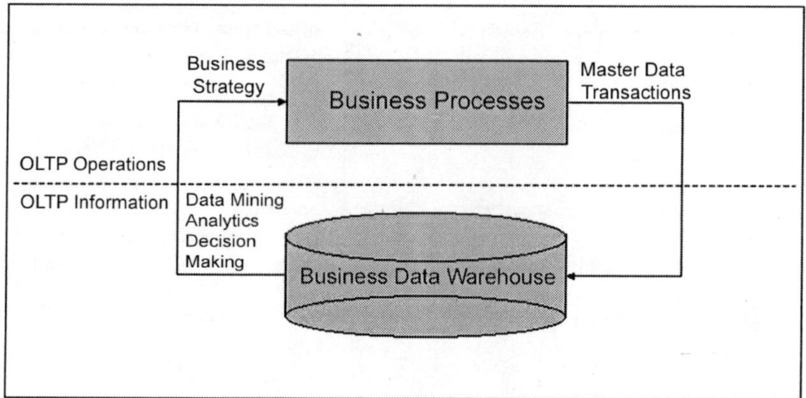

OLTP (On-line Transaction Processing) is characterized by a large number of short on-line transactions (INSERT, UPDATE, DELETE). The main emphasis for OLTP systems is put on very fast query processing, maintaining data integrity in multi-access environments and an effectiveness measured by number of transactions per second. In OLTP database there is detailed and current data, and schema used to store transactional databases is the entity model (usually 3NF).

OLAP (On-line Analytical Processing) is characterized by relatively low volume of transactions. Queries are often very complex and involve aggregations.

For OLAP systems a response time is an effectiveness measure. OLAP applications are widely used by Data Mining techniques. In OLAP database there is aggregated, historical data, stored in multi-dimensional schemas (usually star schema).

The following table summarizes the major differences between OLTP and OLAP system design.

	OLTP System Online Transaction Processing (Operational System)	***OLAP System Online Analytical Processing (Data Warehouse)***
Source of data	Operational data; OLTPs are the original source of the data.	Consolidation data; OLAP data comes from the various OLTP Databases
Purpose of data	To control and run fundamental business tasks	To help with planning, problem solving, and decision support
What the data	Reveals a snapshot of ongoing business processes	Multi-dimensional views of various kinds of business activities
Inserts and Updates	Short and fast inserts and updates initiated by end users	Periodic long-running batch jobs refresh the data
Queries	Relatively standardized and simple queries Returning relatively few records	Often complex queries involving aggregations
Processing Speed	Typically very fast	Depends on the amount of data involved; batch data refreshes and complex queries may take many hours; query speed can be improved by creating indexes
Space Requirements	Can be relatively small if historical data is archived	Larger due to the existence of aggregation structures and history data; requires more indexes than OLTP
Database Design	Highly normalized with many tables	Typically de-normalized with fewer tables; use of star and/or snowflake schemas
Backup and Recovery	Backup religiously; operational data is critical to run the business, data loss is likely to entail significant monetary loss and legal liability	Instead of regular backups, some environments may consider simply reloading the OLTP data as a recovery method

Bibliography

Adriaans, P., D. Zantinge: *Data Mining*, Addison - Wesley Publ. Co., New York, 1996.

Agosta, L. : *The Essential Guide to Data Warehousing*, Prentice Hall, Upper Saddle River, NJ, 2000.

Alpaydin, A. : *Introduction to Machine Learning*, The MIT Press, Cambridge, 2010.

Barquin, R., H. Edelstein : *Building, Using, and Managing the Data Warehouse* Prentice Hall, Upper Saddle River, NJ, 1997.

Berson, A., S. Smith, K. Thearling : *Building Data Mining Applications for CRM*, McGraw - Hill, New York, 2000.

Bezdek, J. C., & Pal, S. K.: *Fuzzy Models for Pattern Recognition: Methods that Search for Structures in Data*, New York, IEEE Press, 1992.

Bischoff, J., T. Alexander : *Data Warehouse: Practical Advice from the Experts*, Prentice Hall, Upper Saddle River, NJ, 1997.

Bow, S. : *Pattern Recognition and Image Preprocessing*, Marcel Dekker, New York, 1992.

Brandt, S. : *Data Analysis: Statistical and Computational Methods for Scientists and Engineers*, Springer, New York, 1999.

Cabena, Peter, Pablo Hadjnian, Rolf Stadler, Jaap Verhees and Alessandro Zanasi: *Discovering Data Mining: From Concept to Implementation*, Prentice Hall, London, 1997.

Callan, R. : *Essence of Neural Networks*, Prentice-Hall, Delhi, 1999.

Cherkassky, V., F. Mulier : *Learning from Data: Concepts, Theory and Methods*, John Wiley & Sons, New York, 1998.

Fayyad, U. M., G. Piatetsky - Shapiro : *Advances in Knowledge Discovery and Data Mining*, AAAI Press/MIT Press, Cambridge, 1996.

Feldman, Ronen and James Sanger: *The Text Mining Handbook*, Cambridge University Press, Cambridge, 1997.

Gray, P. & H.J. Watson: *Decision support in the Data Warehouse*, Prentice-Hall, Delhi, 1998.

Groth, R. : *Data Mining: A Hands - On Approach for Business Professionals*, Prentice Hall, Upper Saddle River, NJ, 1998.

Guo, Yike and Robert Grossman: *High Performance Data Mining: Scaling Algorithms, Applications and Systems*, Kluwer Academic Publishers, Delhi, 1999.

Han, J., & Kamber, M.: *Data Mining: Concepts and Techniques*, Morgan Kaufmann, Delhi, 2000.

Hand, D.J., Mannila, H. and Smyth, P.: *Principles of Data Mining*, MIT Press, Delhi, 1997.

Hastie, T., Tibshirani, R., & Friedman, J. H.: *The Elements of Statistical Learning: Data Mining, Inference, and Prediction:* New York: Springer, 2001.

Haykin, S.S. : *Neural Networks : A Comprehensive Foundation*, Prentice-Hall, Delhi, 1999.

Jain, A.K., & Dubes, R. C.: *Algorithms for Clustering Data*, New Jersey, Prentice Hall, 1988.

Jensen, F.V.: *An Introduction to Bayesian Networks*, London: University College London Press, 1996.

Kaudel, A., M. Last, H. Bunke : *Data Mining and Computational Intelligence*, Physica -Verlag, Heidelberg, 2001.

Kaufman, L., & Rousseeuw, P. J.: *Finding Groups in Data: An Introduction to Cluster Analysis*, New York: John Wiley, 1990.

Kil, D. H., F. B. Shin : *Pattern Recognition and Prediction with Applications to Signal Characterization,* AIP Press, Woodburg, NY, 1996.

Liu, H., H. Motoda : *Feature Extraction, Construction and Selection: A Data Mining Perspective,* Kluwer Academic Publishers, Boston, MA, 1998.

Michie, D., Spiegelhalter, D. J., & Taylor, C. C.: *Machine Learning, Neural and Statistical Classification*, Ellis Horwood, Delhi, 1994.

Nisbet, Robert, John Elder, Gary Miner: *Handbook of Statistical Analysis & Data Mining Applications*, Academic Press, Delhi, 2009.

Pendharkar, P. C. : *Managing Data Mining Technologies in Organizations:Techniques and Applications*, Idea Group Publishing, Delhi, 2003.

Poole, D., A. Mackworth, R. Goebel : *Computational Intelligence: A Logical Approach,* Oxford University Press, New York, 1998.

Pyle, D. : *Data Preparation for Data Mining,* Morgan Kaufmann Publ. Inc., New York, 1999.

Sergios Theodoridis, Konstantinos Koutroumbas: *Pattern Recognition*, Academic Press, Delhi, 2009.

Soukup, T., Davidson, I.: *Visual Data Mining: Techniques and Tools for Data Visualization and Mining*, Wiley, Delhi, 2002.

Thomsen, E. : *OLAP Solution: Building Multidimensional Information System*, John Wiley, New York, 1997.

Thuraisingham, B. : *Data Mining: Technologies, Techniques, Tools, and Trends*, CRC Press LLC, Boca Raton, 1999.

Weiss, S. M., N. Indurkhya : *Predictive Data Mining: A Practical Guide,* Morgan Kaufman Publishers, Inc., San Francisco, CA, 1998.

Index